10/2019

1

RISING

SHARON WOOD

RISING

BECOMING *the* FIRST CANADIAN WOMAN
to SUMMIT EVEREST, *A Memoir*

Douglas & McIntyre

1 2 3 4 5 — 23 22 21 20 19

First editions published simultaneously in 2019 in Canada by Douglas and McIntyre (2013) Ltd. and in the United States of America by Mountaineers Books.

Douglas and McIntyre (2013) Ltd.
P.O. Box 219, Madeira Park, BC, V0N 2H0
www.douglas-mcintyre.com

All Everest Light expedition photographs, with or without credits, were taken by expedition members with cameras provided by Leica.
Quote on page vi: From LETTERS TO A YOUNG POET by Rainer Maria Rilke, translated by M. D. Herter Norton. Copyright 1934, 1954 by W. W. Norton & Company, Inc., renewed © 1962, 1982 by M. D. Herter Norton. Used by permission of W. W. Norton & Company, Inc.
Part 1 quote on page 1: adapted from Barbara La Fontaine. "Scared of Bears and Scared of Being Scared," *Sports Illustrated*, July 18, 1966, 51.
Part 2 quote on page 173: Excerpt from KAFKA ON THE SHORE by Haruki Murakami, translated by Philip Gabriel, translation copyright © 2005 by Haruki Murakami. Used by permission of Alfred A. Knopf, an imprint of the Knopf Doubleday Publishing Group, a division of Penguin Random House LLC. All rights reserved. Copyright © 2005 by Haruki Murakami. Reprinted by permission of ICM Partners.

Edited by Lucy Kenward
Dust Jacket design by Anna Comfort O'Keeffe and Carleton Wilson
Text design by Carleton Wilson
Printed and bound in Canada
Printed on paper certified by the Forest Stewardship Council

Canada

Canada Council Conseil des Arts
for the Arts du Canada

BRITISH COLUMBIA
ARTS COUNCIL
An agency of the Province of British Columbia

Douglas and McIntyre (2013) Ltd. acknowledges the support of the Canada Council for the Arts, which last year invested $153 million to bring the arts to Canadians throughout the country.

Nous remercions le Conseil des arts du Canada de son soutien. L'an dernier, le Conseil a investi 153 millions de dollars pour mettre de l'art dans la vie des Canadiennes et des Canadiens de tout le pays.

We also gratefully acknowledge financial support from the Government of Canada and from the Province of British Columbia through the BC Arts Council and the Book Publishing Tax Credit.

LIBRARY AND ARCHIVES CANADA CATALOGUING IN PUBLICATION

Title: Rising : becoming the first Canadian woman to summit Everest : a memoir / Sharon Wood.
Names: Wood, Sharon A., 1957- author.
Identifiers: Canadiana (print) 20190114525 | Canadiana (ebook) 2019011455X | ISBN 9781771622257 (hardcover) | ISBN 9781771622264 (HTML)
Subjects: LCSH: Wood, Sharon A., 1957- | LCSH: Women mountaineers—Canada—Biography. | LCSH: Mountaineers—Canada—Biography. | LCSH: Mountaineering—Everest, Mount (China and Nepal) | LCSH: Everest, Mount (China and Nepal)
Classification: LCC GV199.92.W66 A3 2019 | DDC 796.522092—dc23

For my boys.

…I want to beg you, as much as I can, dear sir, to be patient toward all that is unsolved in your heart and to try to love the *questions themselves* like locked rooms and like books that are written in a very foreign tongue. Do not now seek the answers, which cannot be given you because you would not be able to live them. And the point is, to live everything. *Live* the questions now. Perhaps you will then gradually, without noticing it, live along some distant day into the answer.

—Rainer Maria Rilke, *Letters to a Young Poet*

Contents

Preface

THROUGHOUT THE PROCESS OF writing this book I have been asked, "Why now, after all this time?" Becoming the first North American woman to summit Mount Everest catapulted me into an accidental career as an inspirational speaker for three decades. Although my climbing has had an impact on who I am, I never expected this one climb to permeate my life to the extent it has. Not a day has gone by without some reference to Everest, whether from a friend or a stranger; from a journalist, a student or a speakers' bureau; or from an aspiring mountaineer or an autograph hound. I have been surprised and sometimes dismayed to discover Everest is *not* going away.

Everest has opened doors for me and expanded my world. But at times, Everest has felt like an overbearing friend. It has often preceded me, elbowed its way into rooms, sashayed across floors, cut swaths through conversations and embarrassed me. Outside of my work as an inspirational speaker, I have been quiet about this particular mountain. Some friends have accused me of being coy when I do not let Everest speak for me, but this is how it is: complicated.

When people in my audiences asked when I was going to write a book, I would tell them: "When I'm old and wise enough." And I would tell myself: *never*. However, much has changed. Access to Mount Everest has increased exponentially. Still, despite the mountain having been desecrated by commercialism, reality TV, garbage, and sometimes, questionable motives, a fascination with this icon of human achievement has endured. I've had more than thirty years to ponder why some folks can't hear enough about it. Climbing Everest reveals the best and the worst of the human condition. The story I have told to over a thousand audiences conveys the former: a story of exceptional teamwork and the impact it has had on my life.

My realization that Everest was going to remain both a part of my life and the public consciousness coincided with my children leaving home and resuming my original career as an alpine guide. Returning to my guiding work was a relief and a comfort. I realized how much I love to show others the elegance of moving over rock, snow and ice. More fulfilling than teaching specific skills, however, is helping people find themselves in the mountains. By showing others, I reminded myself that the mountains are a powerful teacher. All these factors inspired me to delve deeper into the story I usually tell audiences in less than an hour.

As overbearing friends can be, Everest wanted this book to be about it. But the mountain merely serves as a stage and a timeline for the real story. I did not know this until now. I had to write this story to "live the questions" and discover that the most important thing Everest has taught me is the value of relationships: my relationship with myself, with some remarkable people and with the world around me.

I have had to answer for my motives many times during this writing process. Who am I to talk about myself? I had considered this indulgence an unwholesome luxury until I realized one of the reasons I read memoir is to know I am not alone.

I have taken advantage of the liberal rules for non-fiction narrative to inhabit the young woman I was then, when the events were newborn, and I, less aware. I have recreated scenes and conversations to convey the events, the character of myself, my teammates and friends, and our relationships, to the best of my recollection. This story has been with me long enough to make me wonder whether I had it straight, especially after retelling it for so long. To this end, I asked a few teammates to read the manuscript to make sure events lined up with the facts.

My teammates have also helped me with several questions: How did we succeed on the seldom-climbed West Ridge of Everest when so many had failed? Eight men before us had died on this route out of a total of thirteen who had attempted it. And why was it that only two of us out of all the talented climbers on our team reached the summit? Then, why me? And perhaps the most vexing question: Why did I struggle with my Everest acclaim?

A buffer of three decades has given me the courage to expose both my frailties and my motivations, and allowed for admissions that I would not have had the insight or courage to disclose when I was younger. The years have seasoned my perspective and softened some edges. I squirmed with discomfort as I wrote into such self-centred focus and how seriously I took myself then. I passed the manuscript to more readers, this time to make sure I was accurately depicting myself. One friend told me he believes we could not have achieved what we did in our twenties without having taken ourselves so seriously. We were compelled to strive and put ourselves first when it came to realizing our capacities and who we were in this world. But to what end? This is another question I have wrestled with since my time on Everest, giving me both cause to cringe in shame, and fodder for growth and insight.

The questions, I realize now, are more important than the answers. After having raised two high-spirited boys I understand this. All I've ever wished for them, beyond good health and love, are challenges and questions that engage and compel them. As ambivalent as I may sound about Everest, I am grateful for how it has continued to challenge me even more so in writing this book.

So here we are. I had to rise to climb Everest, and rise to integrate that experience into my life. This need to engage in the questions is the irrepressible engine for writing my story.

PART 1

There is more in us than we know. If we can be made to see it, perhaps for the rest of our lives, we will be unwilling to settle for less.

—Outward Bound

CHAPTER 1

The Promise

March 17, 1986

WITH MOVEMENT COMES COMFORT. In the dark, between Laurie and Jim, mentor and leader, I doze as my head jounces and lolls between their shoulders. We are nestled in the cab of a five-ton diesel truck climbing via sixty or more switchbacks to reach Pang La, a 5,200-metre-high pass on the Tibetan Plateau.

While the rest of our entourage overnights in Shigatse, we are getting a head start with the slower-moving truck carrying our cargo. The truck heaves and sways over potholes and then races toward the next straightaway, pressing our spines into our seatbacks. At first we braced ourselves, our hands on the dashboard or the roof, careful to not touch one another in the jostle. But now we've surrendered to the movement and relax into each other. Rather than try to talk over the truck's throaty growls and sighs, I stare through the sandblasted windshield. It feels like no one else is awake in the world.

A scent—part feral, part mothballs—fills the cab. Rawhide and thongs wrap the driver's ankles, replacing the missing eyelets and laces in his boots. Bailing wire binds the rest of the boot to the sole. He wears a khaki green cap with turned-up fur-lined earflaps and a parka and pants with a time-worn sheen at the elbows and knees. I guess his clothing is Chinese People's Liberation Army cast-offs, and he, Tibetan. His face is all sharp angles. There is some fire in his eyes—a hint of hope that it's not over yet for his beleaguered country the Chinese now occupy. He has offered no name, nor answers to our questions, and I wonder if it's because he doesn't understand or if he's been ordered to remain silent. Soon, my eyes close and I feel myself being rocked and cradled as we rise.

I wake with a start when Jim slaps his palm on the dash. "Stop here!" he says. He raises his arm and slices the air. "Cut!" The driver pumps the brake and wrenches the emergency lever up and the truck comes to a stop. Then Jim points at us, the roof and the back of the truck. "We ride up on back."

Laurie yanks the door lever up and pushes his shoulder into the door. It creaks open and he steps down, then offers me his hand. In the dim of the pre-dawn light, the three of us stumble around to the back. We climb over our cargo and wedge ourselves so we can look out over the cab. Jim slams his hand on the roof and yells, "Okay, go!"

With the drawstrings of our hoods cinched tight around our faces, we huddle close to fend off a cold wind that bites through our clothing. Laurie pulls me into his side as he shouts over the din of the truck and the rush of the wind, "Any minute now!"

Jim reaches across my back and grips my shoulder. He points. "Here it comes, Woody!"

As we crest the top of the pass at sunrise, Laurie sweeps his arm over an ocean of brown hills crowned by the white wall of the Himalayas in the distance, and says, "Sharon Wood, welcome to Mount Everest!"

The driver pulls over to stop amidst rows of rock cairns festooned with string upon string of prayer flags streaming in the wind. Far off, the mountain that I've been planning for, thinking about, dreaming about, reigns above all else on the horizon, with a plume of snow tearing off its top. But what hits me harder than this first sight of Everest is how grateful I am to be sharing this experience with these men who have been so instrumental in bringing me to this magical moment. There's no one in the world I'd rather have beside me, and I sense I'll feel this way every day for the next two and a half months of my life.

We travel for several more hours before reuniting with our ten other team members, and our Chinese Mountaineering Association liaison, interpreter and their cook at the entrance of the Rongbuk Valley. Travelling in faster jeeps, they have caught up to us at this gateway to Everest, or Chomolungma, as it is known to the Tibetans.

Raging monsoon waters and extreme melt–freeze cycles obliterate the final stretch of the road to Basecamp every year. This year seems no exception and I am thinking we will have to walk the last three kilometres.

A straggle of Tibetans huddles in the lee of an abandoned stone hut. They are all sinew and tendon, with weather-beaten faces, and clad in a contrast of second-hand ski jackets, hide and homespun. We wait in the jeeps and watch our Chinese interpreter, Mr. Yu, inch open his door against the pressing wind to speak to them. His cap flies off his head and a Tibetan's arm darts out and snatches it mid-flight. Mr. Yu totters with arms out as he picks his way over the rubble toward the man. The Tibetan meets Mr. Yu with a bow and a thin smile as he returns his cap.

Mr. Yu and the men talk as they point upvalley. Then the Tibetans shoulder pry bars, shovels and pickaxes and make their way to the head of the cavalcade. As we start moving, some trot easily beside us while others ride the jeeps' bumpers like broncos, their bodies folding and rocking to the buck and jostle. When we roll to a stop at the edge of a torrent, they stride ahead through the hip-deep rushing water and leap up onto the ice-bound rock shelf on the other side. Some chop away at its edge while others pry boulders and shovel gravel. Soon, there is a ramp leading up the opposite bank. The labourers wade back toward us, their clothes wicking water up past their chests as they rearrange rocks they have rolled into the river for the vehicles to drive on.

It will take the dozen or so men a few hours to prepare the final stretch to Basecamp. While we sit warm and dry on soft, cushioned seats, their hardship, and our comfort, keeps my eyes from meeting theirs. *We are climbers here for good reason, not tourists*, I tell myself. But I recognize the Tibetan man's thin smile to Mr. Yu as one for us all.

* * *

By mid-afternoon, we unfold from jeeps and trucks, stiff from three days' travel on rough roads from Lhasa. Dazed and light-headed from the thin air, we take measure of our new home. I match landscape to images seen only on paper until now. Everest sits at the head of the valley, fifteen kilometres away. From where we stand the only sign that ice once filled this kilometre-wide valley are terminal moraines—piles of rocks and boulders thirty metres high that mark the end of the glacier's path and the beginning of ours.

It is a clear day, perhaps just above freezing, but I feel chilled. There is spite in this wind that rips at our clothing and pushes and shoves us. Gusts drive silt into our eyes and our layers. By day's end, that grit will have found its way right down to my underpants. Driven by instinct to make shelter before nightfall, we don more clothing and shift from pause to rush as we set to task.

Jim and Jane, our cook, trundle off to stake out a location for the mess tent. Their balance and reaction time, like mine, are off and they stumble like drunkards. The new altitude of approximately 5,200 metres above sea level is equivalent to a half atmosphere. Even though my heart bounds and my lungs fill and empty like a bellows to compensate, I can't get enough oxygen to fuel the simplest functions.

Barry and Kevin pass off loads from atop the trucks as the others grapple with the slippery boxes and plastic barrels. Shoulder to shoulder, Dwayne and I huddle over the records of inventory we packed six months ago. The wind snatches at the papers on our clipboard while I hold them down with both hands, and Dwayne checks off items as they hit the ground. We scramble to meet the volley of demands for tents, pots, food and tools. Dr. Bob, our team doctor, squints through dust-caked glasses as he points bearers to piles. If arranged end to end, the five tonnes of food and equipment—150 boxes, barrels and duffle bags—could span the length of a football field.

Jane's braids stream like windsocks as she directs the kitchen setup. James and Chris struggle to align the mess tent according to her instructions, their hoods slapping at their faces as they fight to peg down the billowing canvas. When the tent is ripped from their grip, Chris leaps after it and splays himself over top of it to keep it anchored. Dave is retrieving supplies from a fifty-gallon plastic barrel and shouts at Jane to remind him what she has asked for. Dan wrestles to hold a tent in place while Albi aims tent poles at the sleeves. Jim helps where he can, darting between one fray and another as if entering and exiting double-dutch skipping ropes.

A white suit sails past like a disembodied ghost. I look up to see Laurie, dressed in a one-piece painter's suit, trying to hand out the disposable garments so we can protect our clothing from the airborne silt. In these one-size-fits-all suits ballooning with wind, we look like astronauts—robotic and slow moving. And Everest may as well be the moon as I strain to imagine doing anything more difficult than this simple task of setting up camp. This seems more like a place where people might briefly step out of their vehicle, take a picture to prove they have been here and then drive off—not like a place that will be our home for the next two and a half months.

Our frenzied activity winds down as twilight approaches. Exhausted, we sit folded over our knees on the floor of the mess tent with our heads in our hands. I'm thinking we might just curl up right where we are for the night and go to sleep hungry. But Jane bustles. We follow her movements like dogs on the kitchen floor as she forages for food, pots, pans and utensils in the chaos of boxes and barrels and conjures a chowder from canned clams, milk, sweetened condensed milk, spices and potatoes. It seems a miracle. *This is one strong woman.*

After dinner I lead Jane to the tent staked out for us. She turns to me at the door and says, "God, that was hard. Everyone was done for the day. And then it was time for me to pull the rabbit out of the hat. So there I am, scrambling to throw something together for thirteen starving people, and I can't find the ovens I packed. I looked in every single box and barrel! How am I going to cook without them? This is what I've come to do, all I know how to do. What if I can't?"

"I'm sorry, Jane," I say, feeling like a block of wood for not noticing, not helping. "I think we're all asking ourselves that same question about now. We've all come to do what we know how to do here. What if we can't? You're not alone." I put my hand on her shoulder and tell her I'll help her look again in the morning. Then I hand her one of the water bottles I have filled with boiling water to keep us warm into the night. The hard lines on her face melt as Jane wraps her hands around the warmth. She closes her eyes, takes a deep breath and sighs—allowing a pause to absorb the single moment of luxury in that long day. *This woman has more feelings than I do, and shows them. Will it be a strength or a weakness here?*

* * *

The next morning I stand beside the piles of boxes and duffle bags, watching the trucks drive away. As the sound of engines fades, the whistle of wind amplifies the emptiness of this barren land. The only hint of life here is a few sprigs of dead grass poking up through rubble and patches of snow. Seven two-person dome tents now stand on this lonely patch of ground, surrounding the larger white canvas mess tent and the smaller addition attached to it that will be used to cook in. Another small group of tents, belonging to our Chinese officials, sits about a hundred metres away from ours. And a short walk leads to a latrine that looks like a sentry box set among boulders.

We pick at the piles through the day, but mostly we lie around listless. And it's no wonder; it will take us days more to adapt. And even then, we can't hope to ever function at full capacity at this altitude or higher.

By the third day in this new world, our appetites and our sleep have improved and our headaches abated. Another team is due to arrive any day now, and Jim asks for volunteers to hike up the valley and stake our claim for Camp One. This camp will be the first of six on the mountain. We will have to share our Basecamp and Camp One with one other team, and Jim is eager to get first dibs on the best spot. My hand shoots up along with Dave's.

The two of us set off late that morning to hike about nine kilometres up the valley and three hundred metres higher. We lose sight of Everest as we gain the lateral moraines running parallel to the Rongbuk Glacier. We won't see the mountain again until we round the bend of Changtse, the peak immediately north of Everest. Dave is ahead at first as we pick our way along faint trails, and the way his lanky frame flows in a languid dip and bob as he walks is familiar. Including Dave, I have worked and climbed with five of the eleven men on our team. I know them all well enough to recognize their stride from afar. To amuse ourselves on the endless stretches homeward bound, my friend and co-instructor Marni and I used to imitate each of them walking and bust our guts laughing. James splays his hands and feet, and positions his palms face down as if he is pressing on air. Except on the steepest ground, Albi turns one foot or the other sideways, in an ever-switching side step, to always get one foot flat on terra firma. Laurie walks with a jaunty swagger, and Dwayne, as if he's stalking prey. Their gaits are as indelible as a signature, and my knowing them is an intimacy I feel grateful for but don't dare utter aloud. It is a private comfort.

Although I worked with Dave for years, I had never climbed with him until a year ago when we agreed, as one of the conditions of getting on this expedition, to climb with every Everest team member in advance of the Everest climb. We met up in the Peruvian Andes and spent a week on steep ground learning whether we would wait, retreat or lean in under threat, which are all the right calls at particular times.

Dave is no stranger to difficult decisions. On an expedition to the south side of Everest four years ago, he along with Jim, James, Dwayne and Laurie and the rest of their team had to make a hard choice, and a shadow crosses him when I ask about it now.

"The decisions we had to make then still haunt me," he says. "And, well, let's just say I've come back to try doing it right this time and put that trip behind me."

I know "doing it right this time" is what drives the five of them, especially Jim. Where some consider Canada's first ascent of Everest a success, Jim considers it a debacle. The twenty-six-member team was rife with politics and conflict. Three Sherpa and one Canadian died in two separate accidents in the notoriously crevassed and avalanche-prone Khumbu Icefall. Each man struggled to come to terms with the deaths and with the decision of whether to leave the mountain or stay on. They had to choose between their loyalty to fellow teammates, the pull of the summit and their principles. Regardless of who remained and who left, I admired their integrity and couldn't help but wonder how I would respond if I were in their position.

Dave, Jim, James, Dwayne and Laurie are the nucleus of our new team and have picked their teammates, strategy and the route carefully this time. I feel the weight of their hopes and losses. And I reel with thoughts of how we have all arrived with our own histories, motives and expectations. "Well," I say to Dave, "it feels like a privilege to be with you guys here, now."

The beauty of talking while walking on uneven ground is how we must keep our eyes on our feet and sometimes reveal more than we would when looking one another in the eye. Our conversation drifts between what may happen here in the next two months and what we have left behind. Dave has left a new career as a teacher and his wife and their young son. Most of the men have put their lives on hold for this trip. For some, who have spent years training and preparing for expeditions at the expense of loved ones and careers, their future is uncertain. I have left a single duffle bag of possessions, stunned parents and a budding romance with a new man. What will change in our time away, and who will wait for us?

The afternoon sun penetrates the cold mid-March air and begins to thaw the surface of the moraine. A patch of glacial silt, wet clay-like sand, sucks at my boot soles. The sight of the perfect impressions left behind by my footsteps brings to mind a child pressing her hand into freshly poured cement and imagining someone discovering the record of her existence years later. I think about those who have trod over this hallowed ground before me. Did they brim with wonder as I do? What will this place make of us, or take from us? Will we all come home?

Five hours of slow walking brings us to the bend of Changtse and the location for our Camp One. Everest, hidden by the ridge of

Changtse since we began this morning, is now visible, rearing up at the head of the valley, about six kilometres away. We catch glimpses of its North Face through scudding clouds: chrome shields of ice, ribbons of snow woven through striated black rock, and horizontal slices of yellow sandstone. A distant roar, the sound of the jet stream colliding with the summit pyramid, is constant—and so powerful it reverberates in my bones.

We shuck our packs and sit atop them to graze on nuts and chocolate bars and guzzle water. From our viewpoint on the moraine above the valley floor, we see the full extent of the glacier stretching from Everest to Basecamp. The section between here and Basecamp is mostly concealed by rubble, but here the glacier transitions to a kilometre-wide swath of ice pinnacles that lies between us and the 6,700-metre-high Lingtren on the other side of the valley. These strange formations jut upward like shark teeth, some as high as ten-storey buildings. We puzzle over how we will navigate through that seemingly impenetrable maze of ice to reach Everest in the days to come.

Our pack animals are due to arrive any day now, and we picture shuttling loads of gear on their backs and ours so there will be enough supplies to support our advance another day up the valley to the base of Everest. But right now, my head aches and I gasp for air just sitting still. Somewhere below, ice blocks crack, topple and grumble to rest. Their impact should be imperceptible but I feel the earth tremble. Or is it me?

CHAPTER 2

Neighbours

WEATHER PRESENTS LIKE MOODS on this mountain—powerful and pervasive. The bluster that met us on the day we arrived had me wondering whether I could bear this place. Now, just a few days later, it is as calm as a benign smile. I feel the warmth of the sun on my back as we stand outside our tents at Basecamp sorting supplies into loads to carry up to the higher camps. But any sense of peace I feel this morning vaporizes when someone shouts, "Incoming!"

I sink in despair as I see the string of vehicles rolling up the valley. It has to be the American team. They opted to stay a few extra days in Shigatse to acclimatize while we pushed on to get to Basecamp first and claim the best site. Part of me had begun to believe they might never come—it would be a miracle—but hope has served me better than dread in the short term. Another part of me bristles, ready to defend my territory. The road leads right past our camp, so of course they will stop and say hello. As the whining of engines grows nearer, I move farther away and keep my head down and on my work.

Gravel crunches under tires, doors creak open and slam shut, and shouts of greetings and laughter between our teams ring out. Diesel fumes cut through the pure air. Instinct forces my head up when I hear his voice. My eye finds the curve of his broad swimmer's shoulders amidst the group of ball-capped Americans. Just then, Carlos raises his gaze as if he's caught my scent. I drop my head. But, still, I steal glances. Annie Whitehouse, the only woman on their team, stands among them.

I had met Annie the week before at the crowded arrivals baggage carousel in the Chengdu airport. The Chinese Mountaineering Association arranged for our teams to arrive at the same time—eleven of them and thirteen of us. I was behind Annie when I overheard her ask a teammate about the Canadian woman climber. I was tempted to shrink back, but why delay the inevitable?

I had stepped forward and introduced myself. When I offered my hand, I noticed that I was much taller than her. I'd felt like a cat with its tail standing straight up and all fluffed out, sizing up its opponent.

My small-minded smugness was short-lived as Carlos burst in. "Hey, Sharon! So I guess you two have already met, huh?" Before I could withdraw, he hugged me. Then he stepped back and draped his arm across Annie's shoulders.

I'd looked on, paralyzed, until Jane's voice broke the spell. "Come on," she'd said. "They're loading our bags."

I can't stop myself from looking at them now as they chat idly by the jeeps. I snatch up a bag and carry it into the mess tent. I cover my ears to shut out their voices and pace out the minutes until they leave. Jim comes over when I step outside, and we stand together watching their vehicles crawl up the valley, straining and bumping over braided streambeds and rock piles.

Jim puts voice to our thoughts. "So what do you want me to do here?"

"Carlos is my problem," I say.

"No, you're wrong there. Carlos is *our* problem if he is going to affect your performance."

I pull my elbows in tight and drop my face into my hands. Carlos and I had been lovers, and a strong climbing team on mountains all over the world for years. But personal ambitions grew to eclipse devotion to our relationship. We had both been responsible for embarrassing displays of volatility: jealousies, betrayals, holes kicked through doors, shame and in the end, a broken heart—mine.

Everyone on the team knows about us but respects my privacy. My reaction to Carlos's arrival exposes me. Humiliates me. And it opens a door. Jim reaches through and puts his arm around me.

"They're not going to go away, Woody. I suggest you harness some of that rage to get yourself to the top—first."

There is an ongoing, highly publicized race to be the first American woman to reach the top of Everest. Annie is among the few who have already tried once. This time she is with a much smaller team that includes Carlos, who summited Everest in 1983, and another well-known and accomplished climber, Todd Bibler.

The Americans stop about four hundred metres up the valley and get out to inspect their campsite. With my eyes still fixed on them, I say, "This isn't going to be a race, Jim."

"Don't worry. Once we're on the mountain, you won't see them anymore."

"Well then," I say, "get me climbing, but no race—of any kind. And not a word to the media about my personal life. They'll turn this climb into a circus."

"You have my word on the press, but—" Jim points up the valley, where wisps of cloud stream like silk prayer scarves from the summit of Everest. He puts his other hand on my shoulder and looks at me. "Becoming the first North American woman to reach the top of that mountain is another matter."

The Americans start unloading their truck and Jim moves to block my view of them. He grips my shoulders. "Are you listening? Carlos is history and this is the present! Don't let him get to you. Remember what you've come for. You're with the boys and we're going climbing. You're more than ready for this, but I can't do it for you. What I can do is let Carlos know he isn't welcome in our camp."

We stand quietly for a while, Jim's arm draped over my shoulder and mine around his waist. I hadn't expected him to care about my private and embarrassing little drama. And he doesn't. But it heartens me to discover that he does care about something much larger—and about inspiring me to want that goal. I have a friend and a definite leader in this titan of a man.

I feel myself rising to Jim's resolve. Our team is among the 3 per cent of expeditions that will attempt one of the more technical of a dozen other routes on the mountain. Our objective is the West Ridge Direct. The Americans' approach is as bold as ours: a lean team and budget, no Sherpa and a difficult route—the Great Couloir on the North Face of Everest. Our strategies are similar but for two exceptions: we have an on-site leader, and our route has never been climbed from the Tibetan side. Having Jim, by far, is our most significant difference.

* * *

Within the same week, a Spanish team attempting the Northeast Ridge arrives to complete the neighbourhood. This time I line up with Jane and Jim to welcome the caballeros. Some ride in on the back bumpers of their one-ton pickup trucks; the rest sit atop the loads, all of them laughing and shouting back and forth. They roll to a stop and doff their hats as we exchange introductions while their Chinese Mountaineering Association liaison officer and their translator remain in the vehicle looking straight ahead, seemingly resigned to their sentence in this godforsaken place.

One of the Spaniards flashes a smile, nodding at Jane and me as he speaks in rapid-fire Spanish to his friends. The group laughs and elbows one another before Mariano, their team physician, translates. "Jerónimo says"—he looks skyward for the English words—"it is a delightful surprise to discover a sparkle of women among dull and uncivilized men. I think he speaks for all of us, as we are all delighted to see, ah, I mean, meet you." I eye this Jerónimo, and he smiles back.

"Bueno!" one of them shouts, eager to get going, and drums his hands against the side of the truck. Chickens startle and squawk in their crate as the vintage trucks cough and roar to a start. The Spaniards shout, "Vámonos, vámonos!" and resume their cavorting as they roll away.

Hardly dull and uncivilized, I think. I lean into Jane and say, "I think we've just received an invitation."

"We should at least go and check out how those chickens fare," she replies.

Jim adds, "Well, well, isn't the presence of such lively and charming Europeans a contrast to us cretins. A pleasant surprise for you girls, eh?"

"Indeed," says Jane.

* * *

With climbers, Chinese Mountaineering Association liaison officers, translators and helpers included, all told about forty of us occupy the Rongbuk Valley in the spring and pre-monsoon season of 1986. Over the next two and a half months, our three teams will share resources. We'll exchange food for rope with the Americans, and share the cost of the Spaniards' telex machine, which will become one of our two forms of communication with the outside world. Once a week, Jim will exchange telex messages with our media and expedition liaison, Jane Sharpe, who works for our major sponsor, the Continental Bank, in its Toronto head office. She will relay our progress to our friends and loved ones, the media and bank employees, who are on their own climb in the finance world.

Loomis Express has donated four deliveries of mail from Canada, which will arrive by way of an employee who bags the letters and packages from a central depot in Vancouver and hops a jet to Nepal. After three days of travel overland to Tibet, he will stagger into Basecamp with a splitting headache from gaining altitude too rapidly. We will pounce on the poor guy for the care packages, letters and news he bears—our lifeline. Our team will count on the shared support from the American and Spanish teams, as Jane and I will on the charms of those Spaniards.

CHAPTER 3

Friends, Nomads and Spirits

FEATHERY COLUMNS OF FROST sparkle in the morning light and crunch underfoot as I make my way to the cook tent. I push back the door flaps to find Jane with her toque on, a white apron tied over top of her expedition-issue blue-and-yellow one-piece suit, cracking eggs into a pot.

She holds a thin, oblong brown egg between her forefinger and thumb in triumph and says, "See, they made it. So far not a single broken one!" She cracks it against the edge of the pot. "Check out the colours of these yolks." A dozen orbs, ranging in size from large marbles to ping-pong balls, and ascending from pale yellow to burgundy red, bob in the pot. She cups a small white egg with brown specks in her hand and strokes it with her finger. "What do you think this came from—a sparrow?"

I imagine those eggs have been plucked from every nest within walking distance of Lhasa.

Jane had haggled for the eggs at a market stall on a noisy street the week before. The vendor's eyes had flared wide when Mr. Yu translated her request to order a thousand eggs from him. Then the egg man shouted something in Tibetan, shook his head and waved his arms in dismissal.

Mr. Yu turned to Jane, and said, "No, not possible! He doesn't have that many, and no way to pack them."

Jane put her hands on her hips. "We must have protein," she declared in her Irish lilt. "Let's just start with the first egg, shall we?"

Jane snatched up a handful of straw. "This," she said, picking up the egg, "is how I want them wrapped, one by one." She deftly enveloped an egg in the straw and placed it gently down on the table, all the while smiling at the vendor. "There now, just 999 more, please. And we'll pack them in"—she scanned the other stalls and pointed at an empty washing machine box—"in that!" She turned to Mr. Yu. "Please ask him whether he can fill the order if we give him a day. We'll pay him for a thousand, whether he counts them or not, as long as the box is full—of eggs."

I liked this woman more by the day. The next morning that washing machine box full of eggs was delivered to our hotel.

* * *

The yaks, hired to ferry our supplies up to Camp One, arrive at Basecamp that afternoon. We watch the procession of Tibetan nomads and their long-horned beasts amble past our camp. The yaks' hair, dense and nearly dragging on the ground, is braided with brightly coloured cord, tassels and dingle balls. Bells dangle from embroidered and beaded collars, each one clanking a distinctive pitch. The shaggy, sloe-eyed bovines look to weigh over a tonne each, and some exceed the height of their owners. They are known to work at elevations of up to seven thousand metres, travelling easily over mountainous terrain, which makes them the best high-altitude pack animal in the world.

The four yak drivers, dressed in crude yak-hide jackets and chaps with discarded down-filled expedition parkas overtop, urge their charges on with airy whistles and guttural growls. A coin the size of a silver dollar with a hole through it glints in the lead man's hair, which is trussed on top of his head with crimson twine. A pungent scent of oils and yak dung smoke wafts as they pass. The herdsmen take little notice of us as they parade by. They set up a yurt just beyond our camp to live in over the next ten days.

After dinner that same day, Jane tugs at my arm. "Come on, let's go for a stroll to check out the yaks."

One of the yak drivers is standing outside smoking a cigarette when he spots us on our way and shouts to the others. The other three come out of the yurt and line up to watch us as we approach. Jane gives them a tentative wave and they motion us on.

However, any romantic view of the nomadic Tibetans, and sympathies for their plight as a people whose country is occupied by the Chinese, is shattered when we get close enough to see their gapped-tooth smiles. One of them cups and jiggles imaginary breasts, and thrusts and undulates his pelvis, then the rest laugh and join in. Jane and I both swing an arm out like a gate to stop one another.

"Oh dear," I say. "I think they have something else in mind."

"Gross!" Jane says. "I guess we're not going near those boys alone."

We cut short our visit to the yak herders and return to the mess tent where our teammates are lounging in collapsed boxes as if they are recliners. They sit around a table fashioned from a four-by-eight sheet of plywood balanced atop upended plastic barrels. A picture of the Dalai Lama duct-taped to a centre pole presides over the tent's inner chambers. A Canadian flag hangs from a rafter; from another, a teddy bear in a miniature white t-shirt imprinted with our red Everest Light dragon logo dangles in a hangman's noose. A sponsor has given each of us a bear with the confounding request to hold a teddy bear picnic on the summit. The teddies won't get higher than Camp Two, where one will meet an ignominious end skewered through its bottom on a broken ski pole stuck into the snow.

Dan's long body spills out of his box and his feet rest on the end of the table. At the other end of the table, Jim is writing a letter. Kevin and Barry parry with Albi over the effectiveness of the Canadian political system. Although Dan's eyes remain fixed on the magazine in his lap, he thrusts a jab into the debate: "The Opposition is just a bunch of left-wing idiots who get in the way of getting the job done."

Albi pounds his fist on the table. "That's what a parliamentary system is for—to make sure the job gets done right!"

The table springs up, and Jim startles and shouts, "Jesus, man. Settle down!"

From a corner of the tent, James glances up from strumming

Jane's guitar to grin and shake his head at the ruckus. Dave, Chris, and Dr. Bob, most likely engaged in a conversation about Tibetan Buddhism, don't even bother to look up. Chris is responsible for the picture of the Dalai Lama. He has brought hundreds of these portraits into the country to give Tibetans a forbidden comfort and hope for their leader in exile.

We stand at the door for several minutes before Jane says, "You guys won't believe what just happened."

Dan lolls his head upward from his magazine. "Do tell."

When Jane finishes telling the story, Barry smiles, sucks a breath in through his teeth and says, "What do you expect any red-blooded male to do when he sees two flaxen-haired wenches walking toward his camp?"

Albi adds, "Say, I believe that alpha male with the coin in his hair dags has a shine for Woody." He chortles like a maniac.

Kevin says, "How about the cowboy with the yak-hide chaps for Jane? You can bet he's into some kinky bondage."

The boys laugh and spiral into yak and sheep jokes, and Jane and I leave them to it. We have established a bedtime routine of heating water to fill bottles that will warm the cold spots in our sleeping bags throughout our restless nights.

As we dip through the flaps of the cook tent, Jane pulls her hood up against the chill and says, "Such nice boys one on one."

I laugh. "Such dogs in a pack."

As we wait for the pot of water to boil, we hold our palms in front of the burner as if it were a campfire. The soft glow of the flame lights Jane's face in the dimming light of the tent. Minutes pass before she asks if it is always like this. "I feel like a completely different species from those guys over there," she says. "I thought I was used to working with men over the years up at the heli-ski lodges, and I liked it. But it's different here. They all seem to be reduced to some kind of primal existence in terms of the way they relate to one another—some of them, anyway." She asks if I get lonely as the only woman on these trips.

"I do get incredibly lonely, but I don't know any different. Some of these guys feel like brothers and strangers to me at the same time." I tell her I try not to over-analyze. "*Doing* is my salve," I add. "I aspire to become free of existential angst." I sigh. "I'm not there yet."

"Do women just think about this kind of stuff more?" she asks as steam escapes from under the lid of the pot. "It's like we interrupted some kind of male bonding thing. You know? They're like dogs sniffing one another's bums and blustering to see who will cower, who will stand their ground and who doesn't care."

As I hold out a water bottle for Jane to fill, I say, "You know, though, I'd rather be with these men than a gaggle of women who dance around to bolster or avoid hurting one another's feelings. Terrible thing to say, I know, but I feel even more like a stranger then. Men just come straight out and say what they want to say. At least you know where you stand with these guys. I think some of them aren't sure what to make of us at some kind of unconscious level and I guess I'm not either, for that matter. I can tell you now that before we met I was more worried about what to make of *you* than of any of them."

"Ditto on that, sister!" she says, and we laugh. As we retire to our tent, Jane lowers her voice. "Can you imagine what they'd say if they could hear us now?"

* * *

In this short time, I have felt strangely more substantial when Jane is around. It's not as if I ever saw myself as inferior, but her presence validates something in myself that I can't quite identify and hadn't known I was missing. I start thinking about this one night after dinner while we are lounging around watching Jane give Chris a haircut. She moves from side to side, turning Chris's head this way and that. As she snips away, I realize it isn't that I am uncomfortable with these men, but I am more animated and interested when she is around. I wouldn't have thought of it this way until she retires early that night to our tent. Without her, the rest of us revert to our normal: the boys start telling stories, which seems like a contest, and I often grow quiet and tune out. It is my cue to exit.

It isn't as if the boys don't draw me in. I am working my way toward the door when they start talking about Makalu. I was on that mountain with Albi, Dwayne and Carlos two years earlier. Dan asks me how high we had gotten and I nod at Dwayne to give the answer. He too is standing by the door, as lean and still as a mannequin with his team jacket hanging off his shoulders, weighing the best time for his exit.

Dwayne shrugs. "Oh, maybe 8,400 metres or so and about a hundred metres from the top." But he doesn't venture into the story like others might. You have to bleed him for every word.

"Pretty close then, eh?" Dan says. "Why didn't you go for the summit?"

"Too late in the day," Dwayne answers. There is something about Dwayne that causes others not to press him. I admire that.

I leave the tent in Dwayne's wake. A brilliant golden thread traces Everest's summit skyline. Now that I am alone with a half hour of daylight left, it is time to pay homage to this mountain and the climbers who have come before us.

Marty Hoey—the only woman on an ill-fated sixteen-member American team—fell to her death from high on the North Face of Everest in 1982. She was a mountain guide and strong climber and the first American woman to attempt Everest. I didn't know Marty, but I've learned enough of her story to recognize that she, like me, was a woman in the male bastion of mountain guiding and Himalayan climbing. Her memorial cairn rests atop the moraine just beyond Basecamp, among those of others who haven't come home from this place. As I head toward the cairns, following rock markers and weaving my way up through the boulders, I glimpse the Chinese officers sitting around a table playing cards. The wind swallows the sound from the tents and meets me as I crest the hill. As if it is taking my hand, I lean into this force.

I first felt the alpine take my hand when I was eleven years old, hiking in the Coast Range of British Columbia with my dad. More a companion and mentor than a father, he was a pilot, amateur philosopher, avid hiker and skier, as well as a student of yoga and other Eastern disciplines long before it was *de rigueur*. Best defined as a seeker, Dad measured the value of a person by his or her quality of character rather than their status or education. His views shaped the way I would be in the world.

At the time I was a tomboy who climbed trees and loved playing soccer with the boys during school breaks. Yet the girl in me came out at parties in boys' rec rooms where we would turn out the lights and kiss our faces off with the Beatles crooning "Lucy in the Sky with Diamonds." But then for the longest time I teetered on the brink of adolescence with a single bud of a nipple, which had me worried I might only grow one breast. Worse was that all my previous friends had blossomed into bras, which excluded me from the coquetry and trolling for boys and made me a target for teasing. And just like that, I fell hard from champion kisser to outcast.

By then we had moved from a backyard of wilderness in Dartmouth, Nova Scotia, to the paved suburbs of Burnaby, BC. My older brothers, Randy and Larry, and sister, Barbara, had lost interest in outdoor pursuits. So whenever Dad could get away, he and I would escape together to the mountains, hiking in summer and skiing in winter. He kept a constant eye on the forecast for the perfect powder day at our local hill, Grouse Mountain, especially on weekdays when he knew there would be fewer skiers. But before we went anywhere, he'd always ask if I had anything important going on at school. Doing anything with him was more important to me than sitting in a classroom for most of the day, and soon we'd be charging down chutes steep enough to see the bottom of the run through the tips of our skis. On those days, he urged me to follow my instincts. "Be an individual," he'd say. "Don't be afraid to stand out." Dad showed me freedom and passion, which promised infinite possibility. School confined me, threatened to domesticate me, and promised nothing more than a banal future, especially for a girl. It left me wanting something more.

I felt like something more in the alpine from my first day and I particularly feel that now, at the sight of Everest's silhouette against a deepening sapphire sky. Before me are a half-dozen or so carefully stacked piles of rocks, each the size of a person and faced with a flat stone with words etched on it. "In memory of Marty Hoey, 1951–1982" reads one, and "In memory of Peter Boardman and Joe Tasker, lost on the Northeast Ridge, 1982" another.

The sense of these lost climbers' spirits in these stones sets me back on my haunches. Marty's climbing partner, Jim Wickwire, was with her the day she died. In his memoir, he writes that he and Marty were waiting at an anchor, watching their teammates climbing above them. Like me, Marty had modified her gear to make it easier to pee. But unlike me, she had cut the leg loops off her climbing harness. When tied into a rope, these two bits of webbing not only distribute the climber's weight, they also prevent her from slipping out of the waist belt in the event of a fall. It isn't hard to imagine the scenario that unfolded: Jim hearing crampons scrape and a cry from Marty, and then seeing her empty harness dangling from the rope as she tumbles like a rag doll down the North Face of the mountain until she disappears from sight.

Less is known about how Peter Boardman and Joe Tasker, two of the best climbers in the world, perished on the unclimbed North Ridge, but again, I can imagine them above 7,900 metres where exhaustion and hypoxia dull vigilance, and the human body can no longer acclimatize. The window of opportunity to get to the top and back is limited to how long one can keep upright and think straight. If they could die up there, it could happen to anyone. I hug my knees and turtle my head deeper into my parka.

Ever since that first meeting with the alpine, I have looked for a benign essence every time I arrive at a new mountain. The ancient Romans called it *genius loci*, the distinctive atmosphere or pervading spirit of place. And my dozen years climbing in some of the great ranges of the world have taught me that it is *not* geographical significance or the beauty of a mountain that dictates that essence. There have been times when I've sensed a malign presence and used this reason to turn tail on climbs. Not feeling right can easily be misread as fear, especially by ambitious partners, and I loathe using this seemingly flimsy excuse. But I believe in deferring to the most conservative person, and I trust any climber on our Everest Light team to have experienced this uneasy state and to know and respect this unspoken rule. On Everest, will we be able to discern such an insubstantial sense? How will we fare?

The light is fading. Everest melds into the sky and the wind eases to a gentle breath as if putting itself to rest. Down valley, clusters of dimly lit tents push up out of the darkened earth like phosphorescent mushrooms. I give a passing glance to the American camp on my way back and wonder which tent Carlos and Annie are sharing, and then let it go for a newfound comfort I find with Jane in unpacking our day's thoughts and events.

Jane is bundled in her insulated parka and sleeping bag, still reading, when I get back to our tent. The beam of her headlamp blinds me when she tilts her head up to greet me. "I was just about to give up on you and turn out my light," she says. "I filled our bottles. Yours is in your sleeping bag." But she hasn't given up on me, and by now I know she won't. I know I have a friend in Jane.

CHAPTER 4

Rescue

DURING OUR FIRST SIX weeks on Everest, we plan to fix over eight kilometres of rope and carry nearly two tonnes of supplies and equipment to establish and stock the six camps between Basecamp and the summit. Each camp will be a day's climb apart and several hundred metres higher than the last. With fewer climbers and no Sherpa support, the work normally done by much bigger teams will mean a greater number of repeat trips for us. We estimate that each of us will climb the height of Everest an equivalent of seven or eight times by the time we complete our set-up to position ourselves for the summit bid.

In the past days, the yaks have been helping us ferry equipment up to Camp One. We've passed them often on trips there and back. Jane and I have steered clear to avoid the yak herders making a sport of us. But the boys have laughed and joked with them and traded gear and mementos.

Now as we prepare to move higher, Jim divides us into three sub-teams to work in a rotation of multi-day shifts. While one team is leading and fixing ropes, another team will carry equipment and supplies in support and the third team will be resting and recovering. If someone falls out due to illness or fatigue, a member from another group will fill their place.

Albi, Dwayne, Dave and Chris make up Team A and have started out in the lead to find a route up the next six kilometres to the base of the mountain and establish Camp Two. Jim, Kevin, Barry and James on Team B will carry loads in support. And Dan, Laurie, Dr. Bob and I are on Team C on rest in the rotation. Dr. Bob and Jane remain in Basecamp with Laurie and Dan, who are recovering from colds, stalling our Team C on the rest rotation before we've even stepped out of the gates.

I am eager to start acclimatizing to the higher altitudes, so I move up to Camp One. Already, in this short time, a tentative spring has us shedding layers like armour as we settle into a peaceful treaty with our new world. We are down to shirtsleeves through the warmth of the day, snow patches have withered in the high desert air and more ground has appeared. Our tents are pitched on the edge of a raised carpet of dense, cropped, dead grass, which we call our putting green because it defies the lifeless surroundings of rubble and rock. Only later, when we see the yaks pawing and mowing this grass one day, do we realize their dung must provide the fertilizer for it to grow. Teams A and B are here, and we all gather for meals, which we cobble together in a six-person tent just big enough for nine of us to cram into if we keep our backs tight against the walls.

While the others work toward establishing Camp Two, I make daily trips to Basecamp to retrieve loads, and Dan, Dr. Bob and Jane often join me in carrying them up to Camp One. While I wait for my team's turn to start work, my mind, like my feet, grows restless as I shuffle between the lower camps. I can't understand why I have to wait to start working higher. So I corner Jim one morning to ask him why I am being held back.

"You're sticking with Laurie because you're his closest friend," he says and looks around to make sure no one else is listening. He leans in. "Laurie hasn't made a single trip up to Camp One yet. I don't know what's wrong but something more than a cold is keeping him down. We need him. We need every back we can get to carry loads. The sooner you get him on his feet, the sooner you'll be climbing with him. And if anyone can do it, you can." He tells me to be patient and that my turn will come soon enough.

Jim's rationale has me trotting down the trail that morning with a mission. Laurie is a large part of how I came to be on this expedition and it is my turn to rescue him. Nearly twelve years ago, I was a disenchanted seventeen-year-old student on a standard twenty-four-day Outward Bound course. I was not getting the climbing and adventure the program had promised. After walking in circles, lost, with my group for several days in British Columbia's North Cascades, I mutinied and hitchhiked back to camp headquarters. The director had threatened to expel me, but for reasons unknown he gave me another chance. A few days later, I met Laurie.

It was a warm day in June, and Laurie stood out among the other instructors assigned to the three-day rock-climbing segment of the course. While his co-workers chatted idly as they waited for the students to assemble, he stood quietly to one side of the group with his hands clasped and his legs like tree trunks, rooting him to the ground. He tossed his head to flick a generous sweep of sun-bleached hair out of his eyes. It wasn't physical attraction that made me watch him; it was the way he watched us, as if he was looking for someone he recognized. His gaze stopped when it reached me—and he flashed me a conspiratorial grin. When the instructors started sorting students into groups, he shouted, "Who's rock climbed before?" My hand shot up and he said, "You! You're coming with me."

Over those few short days we spent together, Laurie ushered me into a world of possibilities on vertical rock: edges the thickness of silver dollars on sheer walls that I could stand on, raised pimples on blank slabs my feet could stick on and fingertip-deep fissures I could grip just enough to rise a few more inches. Every new thirty- to fifty-metre section of a climb—every pitch—presented a new puzzle to solve. I channelled any fear I had of the expanding space beneath my feet into the focus and strength I needed to keep climbing higher. When I reached the top of a pitch, Laurie would hoist me onto a ledge the depth of a bookshelf. The anchors that secured him there—the complex web of ropes and knots connecting metal hardware like pitons and nuts that he'd driven and slotted into cracks—were, to me, an art form. Laurie embodied the Outward Bound instructors' credo of showing students they could be and do more than they knew. He gave me a glimpse of my potential and a likeable self. I wanted more of that.

By the end of the course, buoyed with confidence and a vision of myself as a future Outward Bound instructor, I had the audacity to ask the school director for a job. He let me down gently, telling me all the instructors had expedition experience abroad, and once I had gained that, I should apply. I was hired as an assistant cook later that summer and climbed with the instructors on their days off. I recognized my kind in those wild, free spirits who altered students' lives. And I would return a few years later as an instructor.

Since then, Laurie had become a lifelong friend and mentor. He'd coached me up frozen waterfalls and rock climbs, and instilled in me a discipline to focus and save my emotions for safer times—when I wasn't climbing. As my skill and confidence grew over the next few years, he recommended me for a spot on an all-women's expedition to Canada's highest mountain, Mount Logan, where I celebrated my twentieth birthday.

* * *

I stand at the door of Laurie's tent an hour and a half later. Steam billows from beneath the quaking lid of a pot on the stove in his vestibule. I say, "Laurie, open up! You've got a boil, and a friend at your door."

"Is that you, Sharon?" he asks in a gravelly, sleep-laden voice. I watch the zipper rip around the half-moon flap door; it falls open to reveal Laurie propped up on one elbow, half out of his sleeping bag. He rolls his eyes rather than his head and squints up at me. "Sharon, what are you doing here"—he glances at his watch—"so early?" His unshaven face and listless tone are shockingly uncharacteristic for my compulsively fastidious friend.

I say, "I've come to get you."

"Oh, yeah? Well, I'm not going anywhere today."

Laurie had been in good form ten days before on our first morning in Lhasa. Late for breakfast and late for everything, he strode across the empty hall, which had once been a ballroom, toward our table like a man with a purpose. Fresh from the shower, his hair was slicked back and the rest of him neatly packaged in a clean white t-shirt tucked into high-waisted bell-bottom jeans with a press line down the front and red suspenders to hold them up.

Beside me, Jane uttered under her breath, "What's with that swagger and the suspenders?"

"Jesus, Skreslet!" Kevin said. "How'd you get that perfect crease in your jeans? Got your own personal drycleaner?"

Dan mumbled, "On Skreslet time again, eh, Laurie?"

I sat mute in my chair as the others teased my friend in a way that felt dangerously close to insult. Did they resent his cachet as the first Canadian to climb Everest? Ironically, Laurie's renown had given us the credibility we needed to gain our sponsors' confidence, which had got us all here.

Laurie proffered a cursory nod to everyone, then pulled up a chair beside me and whispered, "What do you say to a hike after breakfast to round the edges off our headaches?" We had flown from sea level to Lhasa at 3,650 metres the day before, which made our condition predictable.

After breakfast, we set out up the mountain behind our hotel. The hillside was bald but for patches of scruffy, low-lying shrubs. I fell into a steady measured step behind Laurie as his feet padded like cat paws up the hardpan slope. The two of us had walked up the approach slopes back home on Mount Yamnuska many times like this and always beneath circling ravens. And now we walked together as equals and close friends, while a flock of similar black birds spiralled lazily above us.

Laurie stopped for breath and pointed up at the birds riding the thermals. "Look at those guys. You can tell the intelligence of an animal by the amount it plays. Ever wonder why they like to hang around humans and mountains?"

"Nope, but tell me instead why the hell Carlos has chosen to hang around *us* in *these* mountains at *this* particular time." Laurie and Carlos are friends, and seeing them greet each other so warmly the few times our teams have met so far rankled me. How could he forgive Carlos for doing this to me?

He laughed. "Oh, Sharon, you're an old soul with karmic work to fulfill in this cycle. Carlos is still clumsy and unconscious in his methods. I bet he doesn't even know why he's here. But he's meant to be. And it's up to you to see how you can serve one another now."

I sighed. "Old soul and work, you say. I say, tortured soul and problems."

"Look at that guy!" he said, pointing at a bird that had landed on a string of prayer flags strung between two rocks at the edge of an overlook. The string bowed under the weight and the bird spun upside down. It dangled there for a few seconds before it released its grip and plummeted like a rock, then opened its wings and caught an updraft, shooting straight upward. Laurie laughed and said, "What a clown! They're here to teach us to not take ourselves so seriously, and some mastery too. Did you see how he pulled out of that drop? Do you think he doubted he could? That's what you need to learn: don't dally in the fall and never doubt your ability to spread your wings and rise out of it."

As much as Laurie annoys me with his esoteric slants on life, I love him for it. He draws from a deeper well, altering my prosaic view of problems like an oyster takes grains of sand and turns them into pearls. His view has rescued me many times over by instilling in me a faith that this life is a mystery to unfold rather than a problem to solve.

* * *

But now Laurie lies in his tent at Basecamp, his eyes fixed in a dull stare. Not used to being the one to buoy *his* spirits, I say, "How about we take an easy stroll up to Camp One, no weight, nice and slow, and see how we go? You can always turn around."

He draws a breath through clenched teeth and turns his head away. "I'd like that—but not today. Trust me, I know what I need to do right now. We've gained altitude too fast and I need more time to acclimatize. I'll be up there with you soon." I bend down and give him a hug, realizing there's no more I can say.

34

I walk over to where Dr. Bob and Dan are sorting loads for the yaks to carry to Camp One today. "What time are you planning on heading up?" I ask.

"We're not," Dr. Bob says. "It's our rest day. You should try it sometime—resting, I mean."

I go in search of Jane and find her in the mess tent kneading dough. She wipes her hands on her apron, then whips it off, lays it over the loaves, and sprinkles it with water. We never found the ovens we had packed, so Jane shows me her experiment in progress. She has laid forks inside the bottom of a stewing pot and will set a smaller pot with the loaves inside on top. Then she'll place a lid over the works. "And voilà: freshly baked bread, I hope!" she says.

* * *

I arrive at Camp One by mid-afternoon and find it deserted. The sky has turned pewter. The wind teases at tent flaps, nudges half-empty boxes and barrels and pins errant bits of litter against the rocks. As I go to fetch a pot lid that clatters and rolls toward the edge of the moraine, I catch sight of the boys returning. In their yellow suits, they bob in and out of sight like beacons in the sea of broken ice below. I'm struck just now, near the end of this bleak day, by my view of us as insignificant specks amidst this Himalayan tableau. *Yet here we are*, I think, *believing ourselves large with self-proclaimed purpose to climb this mountain*. Our importance seems fragile in this moment.

The thought has me recalling what a Sherpa once said: his people were confounded over the hunger of Westerners who came clanking with ironmongery to conquer these mountains. His forefathers had never felt the need to climb them, as they felt the power of the Himalayas already within them. The Sherpa said his people felt full while those climbers seemed empty. *We are those climbers.*

I question this delusional grand plan of ours: all this stuff, our fancy suits and armour. I wish I didn't feel the need to question, but I can't stop looking for more meaning when I'm caught in these moments of stillness and doubt.

CHAPTER 5

Weight

THE ZING OF A zipper opening a tent door nearby jolts me awake. Soft light filters through the frost-lined walls of my tent. The bottle I filled with hot water last night lies cold in the bottom of my sleeping bag. Frozen turf crunches underfoot as someone passes by, and a few minutes later I hear Jim's faint murmurs and the crackle of radio static in the distance. Pots and dishes clatter in the mess tent, signalling the start of the day.

James and Jim are planning to spend their first night at Camp Two and I hope to join them for part of the walk. I fish the water bottle out of my bag and have forced down the full litre by the time I am dressed and out the door.

"Morning, Woody," James says as I push back the flaps and enter the wall tent. He and Dan sit across from one another with the stove between them in the centre of the tent.

"Morning, boys," I say. "You sound chipper, James. How was your night?"

"Better," James says as he scoops snow into the pot to melt for our drinking water. "I found another sleeping pad for my nest and slept warmer for it."

Dan shoots me a weak smile, then drops his head back onto his knees. I know that look. On Makalu, I was devastated by a cold that scoured my throat raw in the first stage of our expedition. When the others moved up to Camp One, I had to stay behind, alone. The illness crushed my fragile psyche and mired me in those few angst-ridden days that felt like an eternity. All I could think about was, *Would I ever climb out of it? Would I ever catch up?*

Dan has always struck me as the antithesis of fragile. I moved to his town of Field, BC, a waterfall ice climbing mecca, for the winter of '77. He was already a mountain guide by then, and I was climbing by day and sewing custom alpine clothing by night to support myself. A few years later he served as a generous mentor, preparing me and some other aspiring guides for our ski and alpine exams. Where most people use both hands and feet over scrambling terrain, Dan looks like he's walking on a sidewalk, and he floats through wind-crusted snow as if he has a tray of drinks balanced atop his head. So, of course, despite the chest cold he can't seem to shake, Dan keeps plodding.

The lid of the pot begins to tremble and a ring of steam streams out from under the lid. James rocks onto his knees to turn the stove down and snatches up the bag of hot chocolate crystals. As he's mixing our drinks, the door flaps fly open and Jim bursts into the tent holding the walkie-talkie.

"The lads are starting up the headwall today!" he tells us, tossing the radio to James before blowing into his hands to warm them. "They're all up and eating breakfast," he says. "Dwayne's pretty sure Barry and Kevin will stick to their plan of digging out Camp Two a little more then come back down to Camp One today."

Jim looks for a place to sit among the bags and food, and I pat the place beside me. He nestles in close. "See," he says, "I knew there was an advantage to having some women on this trip. You can sit closer to them than a guy." I roll my eyes and give him a shove. "Just joking, Woody—we know you're our secret weapon." It takes so little for the big man to pull me in.

I'm lost in my own thoughts, not hearing another word until James says, "Hey, Woody, you still up for coming with us today, in let's say half an hour?"

"I'm in. That should give me enough time to get my face on." Dan tips his face up to catch my eye for a second. I love being with these boys—so much gets said without being spoken.

"Good thing, Woody," Jim tells me. "I want you looking your best for the photos."

* * *

Camp One is still in shadow when we start out at 9 a.m., and our breath comes out as white puffs. Until now I've been wearing light-weight high-top trekking shoes, but today I switch them out for my plastic double boots. I've bought mine a size too large to provide more room for insulation and they feel like I have shoeboxes on my feet. The extra heft to lift my foot makes me think of the adage I often say to my students: "One pound on your foot equals five pounds on your back." But the heavier rigid boots are justified as soon as we step off the top of the moraine and dig our edges into the rubble and silt that has set up like cement on the sidehill leading down to the glacier.

Some sources claim the Rongbuk Glacier is retreating more than twenty metres a year. The arid, high-altitude air and solar radiation have sculpted its surface into pointy monoliths called penitentes. What had looked like an impassable maze to Dave and me on our reconnaissance yields to passageways. As James and I wend our way through, I peer up at these formations, some leaning perilously. Others have toppled and lie in fragments like fallen ancient Roman statues, white and porous from oxidation with edges rounded by time. The more recently sheared ice surfaces refract vivid hues of turquoise. Compressed by its own weight over centuries of time, the ice mass is nearer the density of water than snow. More plastic than rigid, the glacier flows and bulldozes around or through obstacles and when forced beyond the point of flexion it cracks into crevasses. It is hard to imagine that this ice is over a hundred metres thick until we step across a crevasse. Its bottom disappears into darkness, and faint drips and trickles echo its depth far below.

I gasp for breath and my heart drums hard and fast against my rib cage. A piercing ache strums like guitar strings in my temples to the rhythm of my heartbeat. I look out through a slight haze of stars and my thoughts linger in a dreamlike state seconds behind what I see or feel. All are usual side effects of acclimatization, but they can quickly progress to more serious and even fatal symptoms if a person gains altitude too fast for the body to adjust. Climbing at altitude for years is the best training. Work high, sleep low, gain no more than three hundred metres over three days is part of the formula. Pacing is another, adjusting to the angle of the slope and the ever-thinning air with the minimum of exertion.

I follow James, as we have followed each other many times since we met seven years ago on a sun-dappled morning beneath a canopy of giant conifers in Camp Four in Yosemite Valley, California. He was looking for climbing partners that day and he found us, a group of instructors from Yamnuska Mountain School that included my friend Marni and me, as well as and Dwayne, Albi and Dave. Pale-faced and freckled with a shiny and prominent sun-scorched beak, James looked more Canadian than native Californian. A thick crop of curly brindled blond hair sprang out from under his cap and flowed past his shoulders. Soft-spoken with a refreshing propensity to inquire rather than disclose all he knew and had done, he assimilated into our tribe of climbers as if he had always belonged. We liked him so much that we invited him to join our crew the next summer. He remained in Canada, growing with us through guides' certification courses and exams, climbing higher and harder routes, and becoming Marni's partner and co-owner with her of Yamnuska Mountain School.

I find myself looking at the familiar ragged line of old sweat stains that encircle the threadbare band of his cap. I rarely see James without a cap. Underneath it is a mind that works outside of the lines of conventional thinking—a kind of genius. He could have been a world-changer, but he has changed ours by choosing this profession instead.

I'm testing my balance stepping from rock to rock when I'm suddenly nine years old again, trailing my brothers on a railroad trestle bridge behind my grandparents' house in West Vancouver. We scaled rock cuts and leapt gaps from one barricade to another. I tell James about the day Randy, my oldest brother and the master diviner of unconventional fun, brought a tractor tire inner tube home.

Larry, three years older than me and my sibling-rival, and I stood by while Randy inflated it and turned it into a giant doughnut. Then he stood it on end and said, "Here, see if you can fit inside this." I'd wedged myself into the hole, with my back against one wall and my feet pressed hard against the other, and Randy had rolled me around the yard until I got so dizzy that I fell out. Soon Larry and I were competing to see who could stay inside the longest. Larry and our neighbourhood pack took the inner tube to the huge hill at the school grounds. They did a test run, and the thing made it all the way down, clear onto the soccer field. The next time they put me in it and gave it a mighty shove. Larry enjoyed that.

James chuckles his throaty croak of a laugh. "Yep, it's a wonder we survived those early years." He was a loner, having spent much of his time as a kid dodging bullies and exploring the canyons in his back-yard in San Diego. Then he skipped two grades in school and found himself in university by the age of sixteen, and less than a four-hour hitchhike from Yosemite. "Climbing," he says, "was my kind of fun."

By late morning we are peeling off layers of clothing on this unusually calm day. We waste little energy on movement or emo-tion, stopping only to top up with calories and drink frequently—aiming for six to eight litres of water a day to stay hydrated in this moisture-sucking atmosphere. After a few more hours, we gain the final rise to arrive at the snowline and a cache, roughly six thou-sand metres above sea level and thirteen kilometres from Basecamp. We've been stashing supplies at this site on a pile of rubble atop the ice until the lead team can determine the location of our Camp Two.

From here a smooth carpet of snow stretches a kilometre and a half farther, to where Everest thrusts upward out of the glacier into a cobalt sky. Crevasses, which have been visible to this point and easy to avoid on the bare ice, are now concealed under the snow the rest of the way to Camp Two, making it too dangerous to travel unroped. James and I shrug out of our packs, sit atop them and wait for Jim and Dan to arrive. A few empty fuel canisters are lodged in the cracks of the rock wall I lean against, probably left by the New Zealanders who used this area as their camp last year.

In Canada, we studied pictures of our route and knew it from bottom to top in theory. But at close range Everest takes on a new appearance. A bergschrund, a gaping crack in the glacier, runs jagged for several kilometres across the base of the face like a defensive moat. Above it, shields of ice buckle and bulge over rock bands. Where it is too steep for the ice to cling, it has fractured into seracs, ice columns the size of semi-trailers. Some of the seracs have calved off onto the glacier below, exposing cleanly cut aqua-blue walls.

The first 1,300 metres of our route up the mountain follows a spur of mixed rock, snow and ice that protrudes from the face like the edge of a pyramid. The angle eases near the top, where it intersects with the far end of the shoulder of the West Ridge at 7,300 metres. I search for our lead team on what looks to be a 150-metre-high headwall that leads to the spur.

"I can't see them. Can you?" I ask James.

"Nope, but what I want to know is, where's Camp Two? We should be able to see it somewhere between here and the base of the spur. You'd think those guys would have set it far enough away to avoid the run-out zone if that face ever slid."

Two figures appear on the glacier walking toward us, dwarfed against the backdrop of the North Face. "That must be Barry and Kevin," I say.

Just then, a pack lands with a thud behind us, followed by a greeting from Dan: "I feel like shit."

Jim arrives soon after him, ragged and puffing, and asks, "Can you see them yet?" He pulls out the radio, his eyes fixed on the mountain, and calls the lead team.

He reaches Dwayne, who says breathlessly, "We're maybe sixty metres up the headwall. Probably can't see us yet. We're tucked behind some rocks here. Albi is in the lead right now. We're hurting a little. Moving pretty slow. Got a late start."

"What's the climbing like?" asks Jim.

"No 'schrund to deal with where we got onto the headwall. But it's steep—in your face right off the deck. Not hard really. Just awkward.

More rock than we thought. The ice is pretty bulletproof. Should get easier with more traffic."

We watch Kevin and Barry walk toward us across the glacier, joined by a good length of rope between them in case one of them falls into a crevasse. A few minutes later they step off the snow onto the rocks.

Kevin yanks his hat off. "Phew, it's like an oven on that glacier!" His face glows pink from sunburn, and Barry's, mahogany—looking even better for the baking.

"Good party at Camp Two last night?" I ask.

"Oh, yeah, tons of fun," Kevin says as he unclips from the rope and tosses it aside. "We've got the splitting headaches to prove it."

It's this affability that's made Kevin and Barry ringers for the team. That and their impressive list of ascents since starting to climb together as teenagers: on our local 350-metre wall, Yamnuska, then onto bold alpine routes in the Rockies, the Cassin Ridge on Denali, multiple routes in Chamonix, France, and their alpine-style ascent of 7,800-metre-high Rakaposhi in Pakistan.

While they settle in, I wander off to pee, which I can manage with a fair degree of discretion thanks to the design of our one-piece suits. Laurie and I worked with our sponsors to customize a base layer, mid-layer, wind suit and an insulated layer. A continuous zipper runs down the front between the legs, and clear around to the small of the back on each of them, so we can unzip—even with a harness on. I unzip just enough to expose my crotch while the rest of me stays warm. The image of Marty Hoey's empty harness dangles in my memory.

As I rejoin the group Dan is musing. "That's big country up there." He is sprawled full-length with the back of his head cradled in his hands, looking up at the mountain. As a veteran ski guide, he has evaluated plenty of terrain and is good at judging angle and avalanche hazard. "It looks like that slope on the upper third above the spur kicks back more than I thought. In the perfect storm that slope could cut loose and produce one mother of a big fucking avalanche."

Barry and Kevin claim that Camp Two is in a better location than it looks from here, because any avalanches from above will split to either side of the spur. "No doubt you could command the parting of the avalanches, Dan," quips Barry, "just as Moses commanded the parting of the Red Sea."

Dan gives Barry a sideways glance.

Kevin adds, "But it sure would be a good show if that slope above decided to go when you were on that spur."

They tell us the camp is a flat area with room for several tents, a few minutes away from where the technical climbing starts. We all agree that once we pack out a good trough and mark the route and crevasses with wands, we'll be able to travel to Camp Two without a rope and eliminate the need for the cache.

Jim looks up at the spur and says, "Bet we could dig a tent platform into the base of that rock band, probably around 6,700 metres. Looks like as good a place as any for Camp Three, eh?"

"Yeah, I figure," Dan says.

While they carry on discussing the details, I scope out the rest of our route. From where we plan to place Camp Four on the far west end of the shoulder, we will follow a hogback that tapers to a spine, which stretches two kilometres and gains another three hundred metres to where it abuts the summit pyramid at Camp Five. I imagine trying to walk that ridge, straddling what looks like the sharp peak of a rooftop that plunges over 1,400 metres to the glacier below. From Camp Five, the ridge tilts steeply upward. Our route will continue up its edge, winding through a series of rocky ramparts riddled with snow and ice another 1,200 vertical metres to the summit. Snow scoured from the upper southwest flanks of Everest roils into a plume and I shudder as I imagine myself inside that maelstrom. It isn't so much the climbing that worries me, but all the factors combined: the altitude, the sub-zero temperatures, the gale-force winds, exhaustion, hypoxia and the flagging psychological stamina—all make for a daunting scenario.

A loud crack followed by a rumble reverberates through the amphitheatre of the valley as a serac peels off. It shatters and billows into a white cloud as it bowls down the face. When it nears the bottom, the yawning bergschrund swallows it whole.

Barry lurches to his feet and says, "Guess the mountain gets the last word, eh? If we're headed for Basecamp, we better get moving. You coming, Woody?"

"Yep. But why all the way to Basecamp today?"

"Cuz that's where the good food and the best sleep is," Kevin replies. Motivated by fantasies of Jane's cooking, Kevin takes off like a Formula 1 race car weaving around spillway zones from the afternoon melt-out. Jim and James rope up to cross the glacier to Camp Two.

I revel at the thought of having Barry to myself on the way down. Although we both instruct at the Yamnuska Mountain School and Barry is voluble in a crowd, he is quiet around me. It is the first time we have been alone together since we left Canada, since pretty much ever, except for one rock climb—a notoriously bold rock route called *Thor* that is typical Barry: bold for the lack of protection on technically difficult ground. While Barry fed out rope to me as I climbed above him through the crux, he shouted encouraging words. "Wow, you've sure got a talent for spanning those long legs of yours wide and making it look easy!" I guess you could call that flirting, but he was funny too.

He's known for choosing the hardest, steepest lines and attacking. "It is about war, not beauty," he'd say. Lacking Barry's muscle and brawn, I think of elegance when it comes to climbing hard ground.

The two of us suffered through our Association of Canadian Mountain Guides Assistant Ski Guide's course along with Dwayne. Course was a misnomer; endurance test was more like it. Fortunately for us, the examiners were looking more for mountain sense than good ski technique. It was their job to sniff out weakness and stalk us to exhaustion during those twenty-one days. We saw one another in some thin times where Barry was the epitome of grace and loyalty.

The inimitable Barry Blanchard is an enigma to me—warm and playful, and as guarded and masculine as they come. If there is a best time and place to get to know this man, or anyone for that matter, it is here where time and hardship bind us and expose us. As we trot down the trail together I try to draw him out, but I get little in reply and begin to feel like I am prying. I know by now that I push some people away and draw others closer to me with my questions.

When Barry and I crest the top of the moraine at Camp One, we see Kevin, Jane and Dr. Bob chatting beside the stockpile of supplies. Once we're within earshot, Dr. Bob says, "Jane and I heard there were some empty bunks up here so we thought we'd see what sleeping at 5,500 metres feels like." He smiles and his blue eyes sparkle an ever-vital intelligence.

Barry slumps, puts his arm around Jane and sighs as his visions of her cooking evaporate.

"Come on, Bubba." Kevin motions to Barry. "No time for crying. Let's head down for a good sleep for a change and rustle Skres into action." They give Jane and me a hug.

The two of us stand and watch Kevin and Barry trot off. We listen to their fading patter for a bit before Jane says, "What's their story anyway? Those guys are so cozy and friendly to me when they're together, but do you think I can get to know either one of them if he's alone with me?"

"Yeah," I sigh. "I hear you. They both seem like a man's man with an impenetrable protocol of friendship reserved for their own kind. If banter is their invitation, it's as good as a foreign language to me. I don't mean that I don't adore them. Most women can't resist them. That, in part, is my problem. I've always had a crush on Kevin."

Jane laughs. "Has it ever occurred to you that they probably think the same thing about us? But I don't feel that separation from the rest of the guys, other than Dan. You gotta wonder what their story is."

CHAPTER 6

The Power of Story

AFTER DINNER THAT NIGHT, Dr. Bob, Jane, Dan and I huddle in the mess tent waiting for a pot of water to boil. When Jane asks if she can join us on a carry to Camp Two, Dan scoffs.

"The next thing we know you'll be gunning for the summit," he says.

"Why not?" she replies.

"Cuz you're the cook, *not* a climber."

"But I can walk, can't I? We've got two tonnes of stuff to get from here to there. I may as well be useful, and it's too depressing staying down at Basecamp with just the Chinese and Laurie, who seem to keep to themselves." I tell her I'd love it if she came with us tomorrow.

Dr. Bob changes the subject. "It's getting close to seven. Think I'll wander out and see if I can raise anyone on the radio."

We follow him to the high point on the moraine. He has transformed from clean-cut, white-collar department head of clinical neurosciences at the University of Calgary to mountain man. His perfect teeth flash white against a tanned face with a week's worth of salt-and-pepper stubble as he speaks into the radio. A conversation is already underway between Barry at Basecamp and James and Jim at Camp Two.

Barry asks, "Where do you propose we move Camp Two?"

James's voice crackles out of the radio, "Out of fucking harm's way! That's where. What were you guys thinking? At the first sign of a snowflake, I'm outta here!"

CHAPTER 6

Jim comes on the radio. "We're thinking of moving Camp Two back to where the Kiwis put theirs—at the cache, where we've been dropping our loads."

Barry says, "That doesn't make any sense. It'll make extra work to move it back, and make the stretch from Camp Two to Three at least another hour longer."

Dan motions to Dr. Bob to hand over the radio. He speaks plainly. "If it starts snowing hard, we're fucked no matter whether we're at that cache, a mile away or right under the face. James is right: look at the size of that face. I say we clear out of Camp Two at the first sign of a storm, like he suggested."

Jim adds, "At least until you all get a good look at the camp location and vote on what to do about it." He reports that the lead team has made a good dent in fixing lines on the headwall and, if the weather holds, he and James will push the ropes up to the spur tomorrow. With Kevin and Barry out of the rotation for a couple of days, Dwayne, Dave, Chris and Albi are going to stay to help carry some spools to the high point.

When we sign off, I put my hand on Dan's arm. "Nice work, Dan. I've never heard James sound so chafed about something." The jabs he made at Jane were disturbing—but now I think he has done a good job of defusing a volatile clash of opinions by being the voice of reason.

"Yeah, well, he has something to worry about and we should all be listening," he says.

I *am* listening and I dread the first storm.

* * *

The next morning after breakfast, Jane tries on the spare plastic double boots that Dwayne has loaned her. She clomps around and dances splay-footed, then collapses over her ski poles laughing between gasps. "Lordy," she says, "my feet are big enough already, but with these things on it looks like I've got clown feet. How do you walk in these?" I show her how to turn her foot sideways on the

48

uphill and keep her heel on the ground to avoid levering off her toes and straining her calves. Jane trekked the Annapurna circuit in Nepal as one of the conditions for joining this team. Although that trip was much tamer than this one, she's no stranger to skiing and trekking and she soon catches on. It was the same a week ago when I coached her on how to pee into a two-litre wide-mouthed bottle so she could stay hydrated without having to venture out into the cold at night. She's taken that on as she does all the complexities of thriving at altitude, all in.

Jane and I start out together ahead of the other two. "Look at that rock on top of that ice pedestal! Is it going to stay there or fall over, and when—now?" she says. Then moments later: "I can't believe this place. It's beautiful! Do you know how lucky we are to be here?" Her fresh eyes make me look around in a way I haven't before. Rather than the long plod getting in the way of the climbing, the approach walk becomes an event in itself.

We reach the cache and catch sight of our boys on the headwall, they look to be the size of ants. Jane gasps as she registers the immensity of the North Face. "Okay," she says, "I can see where the fun ends for me. I'm quite happy down here, thank you very much."

Dr. Bob arrives and takes it in too. He tells us he doesn't feel half bad for his first time this high. He is conducting a study of the neuropsychological effects of prolonged exposure to high altitude. Back in Calgary he gave us all a test to write and plans to administer the same one as we reach each higher camp. He says, "I expect some pretty interesting results, given how slow-witted I feel at this altitude."

I'm dull-witted at the best of times when it comes to tests, I think. I plan to dodge them to avoid further humiliation.

Dr. Bob is not a climber but is keen to get on the mountain to experience what it is like to ascend the ropes. His primary role on the team is as our physician. He provided us all with individual pharmaceutical kits containing remedies for digestive ailments, painkillers, sleeping pills called Halcion, which are short-lasting with a minimal hangover affect, and a high-altitude drug, Diamox. He will also record most of our radio transmissions.

After a long break, the three of us unload oxygen bottles, tents and food bags marked for higher camps, putting them under a tarp weighed down by rocks. Soon after we start back down we meet Dan, who is still on his way up.

"Hey, big guy, how's it going?" Jane asks.

Dan keeps his eyes on the ground and says, "I'm headed for Base-camp tomorrow for a decent night's sleep. See ya."

As he trudges onward, Jane says under her breath, "Whoa. Do you get the impression that Dan is a dour sort of fellow?"

"I haven't known him to be effusive at the best of times," I reply. "But I know how he feels. I imagine he's just really disappointed that he's feeling so shitty."

* * *

We all go in different directions the following day. Jim's plan of three teams moving through lead, support and rest rotations has eroded because everyone's rate of acclimatization is different and Dan and Laurie are still not well enough to move to a higher camp. Jim has to return to Basecamp to deal with an extra charge of thirty thousand dollars the Chinese want to add to our tab. And as Barry puts it, "They only want to deal with the big man." He and Kevin stay low as well to arrange and accompany the final yak loads to Camp One. For the next three days, Jane, Dr. Bob and I carry much-needed supplies from Camp One to the cache.

We start out with our loads the next morning. Where Jane and Bob are relaxed, and chat and stop to take pictures, I am antsy and ready to push harder in preparation for the next jump in altitude in a few days' time. I load my cassette player, slip on my headphones and begin charging up the trail matching my cadence and breathing to the rhythm of rock and roll. Sometime later, huffing and with my eyes on the ground, I am brought to an abrupt halt by the sight of feet right in front of me. I look up to see Jim and Chris grinning down at me and I whip my headphones off.

Jim says, "Good tunes, eh? What are you playing? We could use some of that to get us moving faster on these carries too. We've been watching you barrel up the trail toward us for the last few minutes."

Chris smiles carefully, a trickle of blood oozing from his sun-ravaged lips. He brings a hand up to stop the smile from cracking them any farther. He is a slight man to begin with and looks even thinner after his first shift up high. He brightens when I tell him Jane and Dr. Bob are behind me. So far, they seem to know this quiet and gentle wildlife biologist the best. Given Chris's propensity to burn, Jane will call him Crisp, and it sticks.

Chris, like the rest of us, has previous experience in the Himalayas having climbed Pumori, a beautiful peak near Everest, where he gained a reputation as a solid team player. Even though I knew the least about him, knowing that Jim chose us all based on our ability to work with others I trusted Chris from the beginning. When Bob and Jane catch up and linger to talk, I bolt ahead again only stopping when I arrive at the cache.

A couple of days later while Jane and I are waiting for Dr. Bob to catch up, Jane says, "I've been thinking. Stewing is more like it. Why do you think Dan has a problem with me?"

"He's just grumpy. Don't take it personally," I say and bend to pick up my poles. *Let's not go there,* is what I want to say.

"Wait." Jane lays a hand over my poles. "You're defending him, aren't you?"

A moment of stillness comes between us as she waits for my eyes to meet hers. I say, "Here's the thing. You invent ovens to bake bread, feed and nurture us, carry heavy loads—all in a day's work—and you're cheerful about it. This is not a happy place for him right now. We'll all feel like that at some point on this expedition, and by the time it's all over we'll all have taken a turn at misbehaving."

Jane thrusts her hands into the air, punctuating each word she says. "He's not making this a happy place for *me* right now. I'm as fucking miserable as he is! My ovens don't show up, so yes, I invent some; there's stuff to carry, so I carry it. I'm trying to make the best of it, so I'm cheerful." She adds, "I just want him to stop being so mean to me! Surely others see what's happening. Why is no one saying anything?"

I blurt, "Because you're expendable; you're not a climber. He won't have to depend on you. So you're his whipping post."

"What?" she exclaims. "I don't get you climbers. I'm on my own here, aren't I?"

We walk the rest of the way back to Camp One together, but alone in our own thoughts. I wish I could take back what I've said. It seems I am more faithful to climbing than to any one person; climbing has become the only thing I have always been able to count on.

That night the two of us lie awake as we have many nights, listening to one another unwrap our life stories. The dark makes it easy to feel transported without interruption. Tonight Jane takes me to Ireland, where she was raised, and tells me how she ended up being on her own since she was fifteen. "I didn't feel like I belonged, and I've always wanted that."

I tell her she's the first friend I've had who has gone it alone since she was fifteen—like me.

"What's your story, then?"

I tell Jane about my siblings, Barbara and Randy, born nine years earlier than me, and my second brother, Larry, three years older than me. Randy was athletic and taught me how to ride a bike, run atop spinning logs in the water, fling my body around on the high bars and do flips. I dogged my future fashion model sister's heels, watching her put on make-up and try one dress on after another before a date. And when no one better was around for Larry, we were either playmates or enemies. My siblings, however, were less interested in me than I was in them. They would have to sneak out of the house with my dad to enjoy an outing unencumbered by their baby sister. My mom wasn't outdoorsy so I'd get left behind with her until I was old enough not to slow them down.

My concession prize was having Mom to myself for the day. We had always gotten along. My mom and the queen looked identical in my eyes—still do, actually. My grandparents had pictures throughout their house of the monarch posing regal, sashed in satin, with her hair perfectly coiffed in short curls and "not too much lips," as my mom would say about her lipstick. I was convinced for the longest time that she and the queen were the same person and couldn't understand how Mom could rule the kingdom, run our household and have time for me all at the same time. As I got older, I saw another side of my mom—frazzled. I pictured her prying Larry and me apart when we fought, clashing with Barb, arguing with Dad and slamming doors. Who wouldn't with the likes of us, and a job like hers? She seemed trapped. Chores and all things domestic were her life. Adventure was my dad's life.

I think of us as a pretty average dysfunctional family, which dissolved by the time I was thirteen. Barb and Randy had moved out of the house and Larry, no longer fond of the outdoors, was doing his own thing with his friends.

I had known my parents were growing apart. Their solution for a crumbling marriage was for Mom to take an office job and my dad to spend less time around home. I had had him to myself for years of mountain excursions, but that joyful life vaporized when he started taking off for entire summers to fly crop dusters and firebombers. I missed him.

I probably would have been fine if I hadn't been idle and confined to the suburbs. Despite my mom's efforts to set boundaries, I left the house whenever I wanted and strode out of stores wearing two pairs of jeans under my own. Boldness made me feel smart, my heart pound and my senses flare. I was drawn to the kids who bought drugs and my loot on street corners, the kind who were wild, inside and out. It wasn't as if I was trying to be a bad kid. It was more about a fierce need for adventure seared into my DNA. By fourteen, I was doing acid, and was fascinated with the altered state of consciousness it revealed and highly engaged in riding the wave.

I tell Jane the story about the night I took too much and the wave got too big for me. It sucked me down under. There was no end to the nightmarish visions and sounds, which had me believing myself permanently condemned to the closest thing to hell I would ever experience. Although I couldn't tell Mom what was wrong when I called her at work, she must have heard the terror in my voice because she got home *fast*.

"Wasn't she mad?" Jane interrupted.

"No, she wasn't mad, bless her. My mom knew I was out of control. I think she really wanted to help me but was at a loss for how."

"So, what did she do?"

"Nothing. That was what scared me most. What could she do?" I never felt more alone than when Mom and I sat across from one another that morning at our kitchen table. "I can see it now," I say. "We both stared at the Formica tabletop, black with gold specks, me at the swirling galaxies and she at the black holes, lost in space—lost to one another. And I suddenly realized then that she couldn't save me. And just that brought me down from my high."

My mom was brimful with problems. A few weeks before, she had received a call from a stranger telling her to ask my dad to leave his wife alone. Then she got another call from a police officer telling her I had just been arrested for shoplifting.

I describe to Jane my probation officer. "He was the one who finally got through. So, on our last meeting he said"—and I imitate his voice, which was like the actor John Wayne's, slow and with rounded syllables—"'You're the writer, director and actor of this one big play called *My Life*. Now get on outta here and make it the best one that ever was.' Maybe he told every kid the same thing. But the way I heard it blew the gates off the hinges, and I left that office with a dream of heading for the mountains!"

I remember the day before my sixteenth birthday when Mom drove my boyfriend and me down to the highway. Before I got out of the car into the slashing rain, she asked me, "You sure you don't want to wait for a better day?"

"Nope. Ma, this is *the* day."

"Nothing stopping my girl, is there?"

I always kept my head down when I defied her in the past. This time I looked into her eyes welling with tears. Never had I seen tears. I took Mom's face in my hands and kissed her on both cheeks and was off.

A few days later, I walked into the employment office in Jasper, Alberta, and left with a job as a tour boat guide at Maligne Lake, fifty kilometres out of town. To get my boat-operating license, I had to be eighteen so I told the manager I'd been robbed and the thief had taken my ID. That one lie catapulted me into the world of adults and handed me a ticket to the life I wanted.

Jane laughs. "How'd you manage pulling that off? I thought you were a skinny, flat-chested teenager, for God's sake!"

"I was! But I was learning that boldness was like putting on a magic cape that made me appear more than I was. If I wanted what I was after, I could make it happen." I tell Jane about living with university students that summer, driving boats, going to bars—and channelling my fear of being discovered into a fierce vigilance to protect this amazing new life. "I read voraciously to educate myself, kept a dictionary at my bedside, carried it everywhere and listened carefully. The cost of that lie, however, was how alone and on guard I always felt, despite how most of them assumed I was one of their own. I have spent the last ten years making sure no one ever learned the truth."

"Well," she says, "that explains why you came across as cagey when I first met you."

"What do you mean by cagey?"

"Unavailable, wary. You didn't give anything away."

"Oh, you mean like a block of wood?"

"That too," she laughs. "You come by your last name honestly."

* * *

The next morning, we pick up where we left off. "Jane," I say, "I'm sorry I told you that you were expendable yesterday. Please know you're not. I don't know what I'd do here without you, and everyone else here loves who you are—other than perhaps Dan, for now—and what you bring to this expedition as well."

"Thank you," she says. "Most of the time I know that, but it helps to hear it now and then." I notice a transparency and tenderness about Jane that I hadn't been able to identify until now.

"I hear you. I'll work on reminding you more often, less wood, more soft. That's what I can do."

After breakfast the two of us head down to Basecamp together, each of us quiet and lost in our own thoughts. Jane is the first person I have told this whole story to. It strikes me now how this austere way of life on Everest exposes our character, and being here feels like a chance to renew and fortify who I am now.

CHAPTER 7

Redemption

JANE HAS SLIPPED OUT of the tent before I wake. After several days up high, I have slept soundly in the relatively thick air of Basecamp. I take my resting pulse as I do most mornings, as a means of monitoring my acclimatization. Fifty-two beats per minute; it is down from seventy-two since the last time I was here. At home it is thirty-nine.

It is eerily still, and the light is different—soft, yet bright—making it hard to guess the time. When I unzip the door, a wafer of snow slides off the roof of the tent onto my head. In a rare absence of the wind, Basecamp lies under a blanket of undisturbed new snow, which muffles sound and light.

I find Jane in the cook tent with Mr. Leo, who is the Chinese cook and her helper. The slight man, a head shorter than her, stands with his arms crossed and a blank look on his face.

"I'm getting sick and tired of trying to get this guy to help out around here," she says. "I just asked him to get some water and he won't. This morning, his excuse is he doesn't have the right shoes for the snow. I don't speak Chinese but that's the gist of it. There's only a dusting of snow on the ground, for God's sake!"

The spring where we fetch our water is just a couple of minutes away, and the chore seems a minor one. I glance down at his flimsy canvas running shoes. Then his eyes briefly meet mine and he turns to leave. I touch his arm and he spins away as if I've hit him with an electric cattle prod. "Here." I smile as I thrust two buckets into his hands and give him a little shove toward the door.

Mr. Leo accepts the buckets, then drops them and shouts for help. Mr. Yu arrives and a rapid exchange passes between them, which ends with Mr. Leo thrusting a pointed finger down at his feet. All eyes drop to his shoes. "Forget it," Jane says, sighing, and reaches for the pails.

"Please wait!" I say to Mr. Leo. "I've got something you may like." I run to our tent and return with a pair of winter boots that a sponsor has donated to each of us. I offer him the boots and say, "Here's a present for you."

Mr. Yu says, "They have no laces."

"Well." I mime the action of pulling the laces out of my shoes and threading them into the new boots, and speak very slowly. "Take the laces from your shoes and put them in these."

Jane stirs a pot of porridge, bearing down hard on the wooden spoon. "I was told Mr. Leo was paid to help us. How has that changed?"

Mr. Yu speaks as if reciting an old Chinese proverb. "The laces," he says, "there are none. You see, then he will not have laces for his shoes."

I huff, "Oh, come on, he's done fuck all since we've been here!"

They both stagger backwards. Mr. Yu says, "Mr. Leo says he won't take orders from womans."

"That's it, I've had enough!" Jane stomps to the door, throws back the flaps and yells for Jim. Moments later, he dips deep to clear the threshold of the cook tent door and I stand back to watch everyone talk at once: Mr. Yu in English, Mr. Leo in Chinese and Jane in an escalating pitch.

Jim asks us all to step outside and we all wait to see what he will do next.

"Well," he says, "it sounds to me like Jane needs a little help." Jim bends down, picks up the buckets and hands them to Mr. Leo.

Mr. Leo spans his fingers wide open, palms down, in refusal. Then he picks up a rock, the size of volleyball, and hefts it above his head. Red-faced and with arms trembling, he looks straight at us. While Jane and I back away, Jim stands firm, snatches the rock from Mr. Leo and turns to Jane. A sly smile ripples and he rasps in his best

Clint Eastwood imitation, "Jane. I'm going to go ahead and make your day." In one smooth motion, Jim drops the rock, grasps Mr. Leo's waist between his big hands, picks him up and holds him with his toes just skimming the ground. Mr. Leo kicks and squirms. Jim sets him back down gently. As we watch Mr. Leo scoot off, Jim says to Jane, "I think it's time for us all to move to Camp Two."

Jim can't know how much his defending Jane means to her. Their relationship will shift to a better place as of today.

The next morning the wind pats and tugs at our tent, waking me before my watch alarm goes off for the 7 a.m. radio call. I bundle up and go fetch the radio from Jim's tent. Keeping my head tucked deep inside my hood as I talk into the radio, I say, "Hello, anyone awake?"

Albi responds, "Ah, it's so nice to hear a melodious feminine voice through this noise box. I'm the only one up so far, but once Chris, Dave and Dan rise from their beauty sleep, we'll be heading your way today. Any gossip to report from down there?"

I tell him about the showdown with the Chinese yesterday and Kevin and Barry eating an eighteen-egg omelette between them. They plan to head up to Camp One today, and Kevin claims they might feel good enough to make it all the way to Camp Two.

"Dwayne here at Camp Two. Good to know someone's sticking up for Jane. There's been no new snow since yesterday, so Dave, James and I decided it hasn't amounted to enough to worry about. We're going to try to make it to Camp Three today. Then I'll probably head to Camp One for a couple of days of rest."

* * *

It is too cold and windy to relax in the tent that day so I go for a walk up to the memorial cairns. On my way back I see someone in the distance, bundled in a down parka, striding toward me. As we draw closer to one another, I realize it is Annie. What to do? Before I can decide on a course of action, she looks up and beams me a warm smile.

"Hi," she says. "Sharon, right?"

"Yes, that's right," I say. "Hi, Annie." Her soft and placid expression puts me at ease.

"You and Jane look alike. I wasn't sure."

"Lucky me," I reply. "I'll take that as a compliment."

"How's it going?" she asks. "You guys on the route yet?"

"Yep," I say. "The boys are hoping to make Camp Three today. How about you?"

Annie says, "We're heading up tomorrow, and the next day we'll wander up to the base of our route to see where to put our Camp Two. Pretty big face to get much sleep below, huh?"

We turn to face the mountain, standing side by side with our insulated parkas zipped to our noses and our hands jammed into our pockets. "What route did you try when you were here before?" I ask.

"The West Ridge from Nepal. Longer story, but we got up high into the Hornbein Couloir and then my teammates made a route-finding mistake in the Yellow Band and lost too much time. Doesn't take much. Turned around and that was it. I frostbit my fingers and we were too wasted to go back up for another try."

I am reading *Everest: The West Ridge*, a book by American climber Tom Hornbein, who was part of the first American expedition to summit Mount Everest in 1963. Tom and his teammate Willi Unsoeld were the first climbers to find a line up through the North Face. I tell her the Hornbein will be our Plan B if we run out of time or steam to climb the ridge direct.

Annie says, "The problem with the West Ridge is it's like climbing two separate mountains, with that mile-long ridge between the summit pyramid and the top of the spur where you first gain the west shoulder. Crossing that ridge isn't hard, but it takes an extra camp and a whole lot of extra pain and time to go from twenty-four to twenty-five thousand feet." She offers to tell us what she knows about the Hornbein, if we need to go there.

We talk a little about our teams. Theirs has ten members, plus the expedition leader who has raised the money, got them to Basecamp and has gone home already. Annie prefers her team's lean and laissez-faire approach compared to the large-scale Everest expedition she was on three years ago.

Annie surprises me when she asks casually, "How do you and Carlos know one another? You climb together?"

Carlos hasn't told her anything about us. Strange. I say, "We were on Makalu a couple of years back and then on the South Face of Aconcagua and in the Peruvian Andes more recently."

I don't give away much, and I am even more impressed when she doesn't press me for details. She listens with innocent interest as I talk, and speaks with ease, with no rush to fill in the spaces. She is as easy to talk to as any other climber I might happen upon, but I hold fast in that neutral space of simple exchange. We will see each other in passing a few times more. And now, I want to.

"Good luck," she says as she turns to leave. "Dig in. It's a bit breezy up there."

"Thanks," I say. "You too."

* * *

On my third and last day of rest at Basecamp I spend the afternoon reading in the tent and basking in the warmth of the sun. I am stripped down to my base-layer and lying semi-reclined on two bunched-up sleeping bags like a chaise longue when Jane comes by.

"Hey, Woody, I found us a little treat." Her use of my nickname hints of something new. She flips open one side of her jacket, like a hawker, to reveal a shiny gold-and-red package of Dunham cigarettes. "I found these in the stash that Jim bought for the Chinese liaison officer in Chengdu. I didn't think they would notice one pack was missing."

I bolt upright. "Whoa!" I flash back two months to Canmore. Jim chose Jane as our cook over Colleen, who is Dwayne's partner and a good friend of mine. Colleen played a major role in food planning and packing for Everest, and had supported and accompanied us on the last part of our Makalu expedition. But Jim was adamant about leaving romantic partners behind to protect and build the solidarity of our team. Jane had experience cooking for large groups but she had never been on an expedition, nor did she have any high-altitude experience. I couldn't understand why she was recruited onto our team at the last minute, in part, perhaps, because of how hard I had to fight to win the confidence of some team members before I was invited to join. While the rest of my teammates voted Jane in, I held out.

Jim told Jane that I was her only obstacle to getting on the team, which is why she came to my house one cold February day a month before we were to leave for Everest. She sat across from me at my kitchen table, running her hands over its surface as if she was smoothing out the wrinkles. "Let's get right to it," she said. "What's your issue with me?"

I pushed my chair back and leaned forward, laying my hands on the table's edge. I asked, "What's in it for you to serve a group of self-absorbed prima donnas while they try to climb a mountain?"

She sat tall, pressed her palms into the table, leaned forward and looked straight at me. "I'm serving something much bigger than just you and the boys, and I want to play a part in making that something happen. Helping people is what I do, and I'm good at it. That's enough for me. What's in it for you?"

I pulled my shoulders back and said, "I want to be a part of this team, run with the best and get to the top. And I'm good at it."

"Well, then, I guess we'll make a good team," she said. "I can help you do that. So let's get it out. Anything else?"

"What about the men?" I said. "They'll be after you. Married or not, three months is a long time." I knew this factor had made some of my teammates reluctant to invite me. I was hurt when I discovered that. As if I was a temptress. But there had been romances on American expeditions that had caused conflict.

"Come on, if you don't think I've fought off my share of lonely randy mountain guides. You too, I imagine! So, where are we at?"

It was then that she reached into one of the two identical team-issue briefcases beside her. She'd reached into mine and soon realized her mistake, but not before she discovered a package of rolling tobacco. "Is this yours?" she asked, perplexed. "You mean to tell me that a hard-ass woman like you smokes?"

"Yes, I love the occasional puff—especially at times like this."

"Does anyone else smoke on this team?" she asked.

"Of course not!"

Jane drew in a breath and then laughed. "I have a package of the very same tobacco in *my* briefcase, for times like this. Let's have one, shall we?" she said, and we settled.

Now, Jane stands at the door of our tent. "What do you think?"

I whisper, "You're a star, Jane."

Her face lights up. "Well, get dressed and let's go for a stroll!"

* * *

With the bulk of our high-altitude supplies now at Camp One, and Camp Three nearly in place, it is time to move up. We will only return to Basecamp on our rest cycles, which will work out to be about every ten days. With most of the climbers working at Camp One and above, Jane will move to Camp Two to help out. I relish the idea of her company as we start working our way up the mountain.

Jane and I pay our first visit to the Spaniards on our way out of Basecamp. The five climbers who are down on a day off all stand up to welcome us into their small wall tent, which is furnished with a real table and chairs. A map and some pictures of their route lie on the table, which give us a better starting point than just gawking at the handsome men. The chickens scratch and dive for crumbs as we nibble on European pâté, hard bread and strong cheeses. At first sight, their expedition appears the most spartan of those in Basecamp, yet it is the most richly supplied with the comforts that matter here. They speak little English, and we, little Spanish, leaving us to laugh more and say less, but we luxuriate in the velvety texture of their voices and their attentions. They all stand up again when we push back our chairs to leave. When we go to shake their hands, they gently touch our shoulders and air-kiss us goodbye.

Once out of earshot, Jane says, "Well, doesn't that little visit make you think about what we're missing?"

"Yeah, and then some."

"So tell me something about your new guy, *not* the old one. I've had enough of him already." She laughs. "Do you miss him?" she asks.

"Yes and no," I say. "I can't afford to miss him; it would drain me. I'm pretty focused on the here and now—on the climbing. It's a better bet than men."

Jane asks slyly, "Okay, but which Spaniard would you go for, if he was the last man on earth?"

"Jerónimo," I say.

"Ha, you didn't even hesitate!"

"You?"

"Tote," she sighs. "Right, then! From now on, whenever you bring up Carlos, we're going to talk about our fantasy guys. Deal?"

Our walk back up to Camp One that day takes just three and a half hours instead of the original five. This, and the fact that we chat non-stop is a sure sign we are acclimatizing well.

As we arrive, I recognize Dan's tall form silhouetted on the edge of the moraine. He must have heard our laughter and caught sight of us because he gives us a wave.

Jane holds her arms up high. "We can still dream, can't we? It's good to feel alive!"

Indeed!

CHAPTER 8

One Hundred Trips

JANE REMAINS AT CAMP ONE to organize loads while Dan, Dr. Bob and I move up to Camp Two for our first rotation in support. I am encouraged by the ease with which we are all moving and we reach the cache by late morning on this cloudless, calm day. Well rested and eager to see new ground, we take less than an hour to reach the camp. We stand looking at the four tents pitched in a shallow dip beneath a massive rock buttress at the tip of the spur. A circle of stamped-down snow surrounds the camp, marking a perimeter where the boys have probed for crevasses. Shovelfuls of snow shoot out from a hole at the edge of the circle. We can just see the back of Dwayne's head, and a leash that trails up out of the hole to a stake driven into the snow.

Dan shouts, "Hey, Dwayne, you trying to make that crevasse bigger?"

Dwayne hasn't seen us yet, and anyone else would have been startled, but not him. "Sort of," he says in a muffled voice. "I'm digging a shitter. Just thought I'd make myself useful until the guys get back down today."

I edge toward the lip of the crevasse where he has been digging. Dwayne stands a metre and a half lower on a sunken snow bridge that blocks the section of the hole he is standing in like a cork. When I peer down, I feel the rope come tight on my harness as Dan backs up to keep it taut between us. The vertical walls on either side of the snow bridge disappear into a deep black cavern big enough to swallow our camp whole. An involuntary shiver ripples through me

65

as I look into that icy maw. It takes an instant to replay the first and only time I'd fallen into a crevasse. I was nineteen years old when Marni and I and three of our six clients slid down a mountain face into a bergshrund. We were lucky on two counts: the bergshrund didn't pinch closed and compress us between the walls, and we landed on a stopper much like what Dwayne is standing on now; and our otherwise hard landing was slowed by the drag of my own team who remained above. We were ten metres down inside the hole. We did not have crampons. Sheer smooth ice walls flanked us on either side. The dripping melt water soaked us within minutes. Trapped in that hole with no one above knowing how to rescue us, we would soon be hypothermic. Left with no choice but to act fast, I fashioned foot stirrups and attached them to the only two old, dull and bent ice screws we had, and proceeded to aid climb my way out. Splayed against the ice and the cold seeping into my chest, I remember best the intense infusion of purpose and that came over me. Strangely, this experience was one of the most formative in my climbing career in terms of the confidence I gained in knowing I could perform when a situation went sideways. The near miss was a hard lesson learned, and a mistake I wouldn't make again.

Why Dwayne is so comfortable working inside that hole *alone* today, I can't understand. I say to him, "Good thing you've got a leash on there, boy scout, but really—."

Dwayne climbs up the steps he has carved, pulls the surgical mask he wears to protect his lips from sunburn off his face and snaps it on his forehead. He ambles over to where we stand by the tents and unclips his leash, which was tethered to a snow stake. He's got a new beard since I've last seen him as well as the usual high-altitude hack from working in the thin, dry air. I spin him around for examination, keeping a gentle grip on his arm. "I see you're on that high-altitude weight-loss program again, eh?" I say, noting his stick-like legs. On Makalu, our expedition doctor ran some tests to measure our fat-to-muscle ratio. Dwayne started at 9 per cent fat, and after three months of living between 5,800 and 7,900 metres, he was down to 4 per cent.

He taps his sunburned lips and says, "I'm looking forward to getting out of this tanning booth and low enough to get a few good sleeps."

I realize that I still have my hand on his arm. I treasure my freedom to be tender and admire in a way men aren't allowed to with their own kind.

Dwayne was one of the first of the crew I met when I started work at the Yamnuska Mountain School in the summer of 1976, but it takes time for two quiet and reserved people to get to know one another. In 1979, we lived together in the mountains for five weeks while teaching a climbing course, and still, after all this time, I don't know him as well as some of the other men on our trip. But I feel comfort in his presence where others might feel unsettled by his silence. He observes more than he speaks, and when he does say something, people listen.

* * *

Our original work teams are permanently scrambled, and it's difficult to keep track of who's coming and who's going from what camp. Kevin, Barry, James, Dave and Chris spend the day pushing to set up Camp Three for the next team to move into. Tomorrow, I will join Albi, Dave and Chris in carrying loads to Camp Three. In preparation, I file the ten downward-pointing and the two frontward-pointing spikes on my crampons, which I'll need on my feet any time I'm above this camp. I remember that Dwayne said the ice was bulletproof, and I always sleep better when I am as prepared as I can be for the next day.

For my first trip, I pack a couple of sleeping bags, a water bottle, food and extra layers of clothing. Once we've loaded our packs, Albi hefts and holds one in each hand like an old-fashioned scale. "Good boys and girls," he says. "Not too heavy. We're here for a long time, not a good time. Just a hundred more loads like this and we'll be ready to take a crack at the summit, eh?"

We set off together and it takes us less than five minutes to walk to the headwall, which starts around the corner of the rock buttress above our camp. The first rope runs up a steep ice slope to a rock outcrop about thirty metres above us. Then, ropes continue upward, weaving through patches of ice and fractured rock. To give myself a chance to find my breath and my feet on my first time up, I hang back to let the boys get ahead. I clip an ascender to my harness. Once the last man clears the first rope, I clamp my ascender onto it, slide it up the rope and fall into line. Whenever possible, I flex my ankles to weight all my downward-pointing spikes and sidestep up the ice. On higher-angle snow and ice, I will kick my two frontward-pointing spikes into the ice, which is faster but more strenuous because all my weight is levered off my toes. I will alternate one foot sideways and one toe in to climb most of the headwall. On each step upward, I push one hand against the face of the mountain for balance. With my other hand, I grip my ascender and tug just enough to unweight my lower foot and place it above the other foot.

Although Dwayne has told us we will want two ascenders on this section, I am determined to use only one to ensure I count on balance more than strength to make the thousands of steps to Camp Three. But after a couple of rope lengths of scraping, wobbling and yanking on my single ascender, I clamp the other one onto the rope. An hour later I pull over the headwall onto a small balcony on the spur where Dave, Albi and Chris sit with their backs to the wind.

"How's it going, Woody?" Dave asks. He holds out the hood of his jacket to keep it from flapping over his face.

I lurch forward to counter a gust and say, "Like a kite in this wind, and without feet yet."

"I felt like that too at first," he says, "but that headwall got easier by the day as I became better acclimatized."

I shuck my pack and join them to look at the new view. The glacier below tapers into a tongue of ice whose tip laps at our Basecamp. Three kilometres beyond, the Himalayas end abruptly, turning to brown hills on the Tibetan Plateau. Across from us are the two mountains that towered above us when we were in the valley carrying between Camp One and the cache. "Looks like we're a good ways up Lingtren already," I say. "What is it, 7,000 metres or so? Hopefully we'll be looking down on it from Camp Four within a week's time."

"Yep, we should be looking almost straight across at the summit of Changtse by then," says Chris through a surgical mask. "It's about 7,500 metres, I think."

Albi points up at the face above us. "So Woody, see where the spur we're on runs into that rock band? Camp Three is at the base of it."

I notice a bank of clouds billowing on the western horizon. "It looks like some weather is coming in," I say.

"Nay, lass," Albi says, "that's far enough away to be in India. It won't be here anytime soon. Days away, if it reaches us at all."

We get up to continue our ascent. "Come on, Woody," says Dave, "file in. We're not going any faster than you."

Albi rocks up to a stand. He slides one ascender and then the other up the rope and slips into a rhythm. When a gust of wind catches him mid-step, he regains his balance with ease. The climbing is by no means exciting or difficult for experienced alpinists—we have spent years on ground like this where we mastered the practice of minimal output for maximum gain. All we need in order to endure all the trips ahead of us is to acclimatize.

Now that I am above the headwall, I can relax my focus. And for the first time, it seems, I realize I am climbing on the spur of Everest, which inspires a new sense of the terrain. Now I witness rather than measure the results of this miracle where tectonic plates have shifted, collided, buckled, folded and thrust upward to make the Himalayas. My mind wanders from the miraculous creation of the Himalayas to the abstract geology lessons I suffered in high school, and then to how liberated I felt when that school door closed behind me for the final time. At the time, I was righteous about my decision to leave school, hell-bent on a better life beyond its doors. Yet despite no one knowing, in my own mind I lived with the stigma attached to "high school dropout" as if I was lazy, dimwitted, a loser. That branding drove me to prove myself to myself and in part, that shame has put me here on higher ground than most humans will ever reach.

In the last hour that day, the wind's strength increases and mine flags. I wait at an anchor to let Dave pass me. If I want to make it to

Camp Three, my only chance is to think smarter rather than fight harder. The crosswind blows the ropes sideways in sweeping arcs between spans. After Dave goes by, I switch to the windward side of the rope and discover that the wind presses my body into the rope and up toward the next anchor, harnessing the force like a sailboat to the midpoint of the span.

I see the boys disappear inside a crevasse a short distance above me. Soon after, I watch shovelfuls of snow spurt from that hole and disperse into spray. As I draw closer, Albi appears on a ledge cut into the slope and the downhill side of the crevasse they have been tunnelling into. He stands, legs spread wide to brace himself against the buffeting wind, and shouts, "Welcome to your future palace, Woody!"

When I climb up onto the ledge, Dave reaches out from where he and Chris are sitting in the cave and takes my pack so I can crawl in beside them. I look around in amazement at the extent of the work they have done. There is room for all four of us, as well as a tent. It is so quiet and calm compared to outside.

"The only problem with this place," Dave says, "is that it keeps filling up with spindrift and we have to dig it out every time."

"Seems a small price to pay for a bombproof shelter over our heads," Albi says.

Dave and Chris have a pot on the stove. After a few sips of tea and a short rest, my pounding head urges me to descend. "We'll see you down there," Albi says as I am leaving. "We're going to dig out a little more to make it fit for a princess."

Back out in the wind on the ledge, I thread the rope through my figure-eight device, which will help brake the speed of my descent, and clip it into my harness. I lean back and out over seven hundred metres of space to fully weight my harness, and then with one hand above the brake and one hand below, I turn sideways and run down the ice. As I reach each anchor, I remain clipped in with a backup leash while I transfer my brake device from the upper rope to the lower one, and then transfer the backup leash to it as well. I reach the bottom of the lines in a fraction of the four hours it took to climb up.

* * *

I carry another load up to Camp Three the next day, and when Dave and Chris rotate into a rest the following day, Albi and I move up for our first night at Camp Three.

Halfway up, the temperature plunges and Albi's storm from India blows in. Even though it is so cold that bare skin will freeze in seconds, I stay warm. I generate heat as long as I keep moving. Blessed with good circulation, I rarely need more than boiled-wool gloves on my hands and a few layers on my body to keep me comfortable. A balaclava covers my face, but I have forgotten my goggles and my sunglasses soon become useless. Ice cakes my eyelashes and all but freezes my eyes shut. I climb the rest of the way up the ropes more by feel than by sight.

The only way I can tell we have arrived at Camp Three is that the rope ends here. Just as Dave said, snow has drifted into the opening of the cave, and it takes us hours to reclaim it and re-pitch the tent, which we find collapsed inside. When we finish, I shuck my outer boots and crawl inside the tent to join Albi. He hands me a steaming brew, and I lean back and smile at this old friend of mine.

I met Albi for the first time nine years ago on a bitter minus-thirty-degree day. He was meant to be leading me up one of my first waterfall ice climbs, Louise Falls, though my initial impression of him didn't inspire confidence. His craggy face was flaked with sleep and frost, and he looked as though he'd slept in his clothes. Feathers puffed out of the holes of his duct tape–patched down jacket. His dented helmet barely fit over a boiled-wool balaclava that partially covered one eye, which forced him to tilt his head back and sideways to see. And when he upturned the contents of his pack onto the ground, a frozen clump of rope, ice screws, slings and a harness dropped out, which he untangled while cursing and muttering like a madman. Yet tied around his neck, just so, as if he were a proper English gentleman, was a silk cravat—a nod to his British roots. This man was the epitome of dishevelment, but as soon as he ticked his first tool into the ice he underwent a transformation. Where I had seen others bludgeon their way up, he picked his way upward with elegance and light, precise taps.

Now, propped up on one elbow, Albi looks across the tent at me and says, "There's the happy woman I've come to know and love."

"I'm happy to be climbing—finally. "

"The harder and the nastier it gets, the more you like it." He sighs. "You're a strange bird, Woody."

"I know." Despite the storm that is raging just a few metres away, I feel secure in the little sanctuary we have worked hard and long for. "This way of life is so refreshingly simple, you know?"

"I do, I suppose," he says. "But I'm not sure simplicity is an issue for me." Albi bats his eyelashes. "You need to learn how to be shallow and vacuous like me." He unzips the door and reaches out to scoop up some more snow to top up the pot on the stove. "You see, Woody, you think too much. You're plagued with existential angst and your only respite is when you're up to your eyeballs in some life-and-death tussle. That's why you love it, and hence you're good at it."

"Thank you, Doctor. I bet you don't talk this way to all your friends."

"No," he says, "they'd probably hit me. But this is what you like to talk about."

"That's why I love you."

Albi looks at his watch, "My my, how time flies with oxygen-deprived brains and muscles engaged in little tasks. It's time for our 7 p.m. chat." He pulls the radio out of his jacket. "Hello to all you campers out there! This is Albi and Woody at Camp Three, checking in."

The radio crackles to life. "This is Jim at Basecamp. Anyone on yet?"

"Hi Jim, this is Albi and Woody at Camp Three," Albi answers.

"What are you still doing there?" Jim says. "I thought we had decided to abandon the mountain at the first sign of a storm."

Albi replies, "It was hard to tell how hard it was snowing. Seems like this storm has more blow than snow."

"It doesn't matter how much it's snowed!" Jim says. "What matters is we all decided to clear out when the first storm hit—like right now! Hello Camp Two, are you on?" All we can hear is radio static for a minute or so and then Jim saying, "Good to hear you made it up there today, Laurie. Can you tell how hard it's snowing?"

We can only pick up the words, "Hard to—wind."

Albi says, "Camp Two, Camp Three here. We're reading you one by five. How much snow did you get at Camp Two? Jim, will you please relay for us?"

"Sounds like reception depends on line of sight tonight. Standby, Camp Two, while I relay your message to Camp Three," says Jim. "Laurie said there's a lot of drifting snow and they can't really tell how hard it's snowing. Nevertheless, I repeat, it's a storm so what the fuck are you doing there?"

I take the radio from Albi. "Hi, Jim. We didn't realize how bad it is. We pretty much just climbed into the tent to have a cup of tea after spending all this time digging it out. We didn't know how much time it had taken until just a few minutes ago. What would you do if you were us?"

"Well," Jim says, "at this stage, it's probably safer to sit tight than to try getting back down."

We agree that if it is still storming in the morning, we'll get out of here.

"Nice one, Woody," Albi says after the call. "You hit that one back into his court."

The flame on the stove has been slowly turning from blue to green and now starts to flicker. "Seems we're competing for the same oxygen," says Albi. "Better shut down for the night after we fill our bottles."

Albi begins to snore soon after we turn the stove off. I envy the way he can sleep anywhere and through anything. The wind keeps me awake; protected as we are in the cave, it still reaches us, drawing back and sucking in the tent walls. Sometimes the wind exhales with a deep sigh right away and other times it pauses at the top of the intake, as if holding its breath. The longer the pause, the more thunderous the return.

I toss in my sleeping bag, cycling my hot water bottle from my feet to the small of my back to my stomach, recalling a time when

Albi and I were in a similar situation two years ago. We were less than fifty kilometres away, perched on a small platform we had cut out at 7,300 metres on the West Ridge of Makalu. Within a few steps to either side, the ridge plunged 1,500 metres to the valley floor. We had just set the tent up and were enjoying an intimate view of the Himalayas on that calm afternoon.

Albi had nodded his head toward Everest and said, "You should think about coming with us in '86. Look what we just pulled off here. Three days of hard labour, climbing and fixing through mixed ground above seven thousand metres. After this, you'll have more experience than most of the members already on the team. You were as strong as me if not stronger. You'll pass muster. You must know that by now."

Oh, I knew I had the ability to dig deep, work hard and endure. I'd turned twenty-one with him on the Nose Route, wide-eyed by the nine-hundred-metre-high airy sweep of vertical granite on El Capitan in Yosemite. I fell leading on the first day of that three-day climb and grabbed a fixed rope with my bare hands, which I didn't let go of until I smelled burning flesh. Instead of giving up, I slathered my burnt hands with ointment and gloved them with tape for the duration of the climb. I turned twenty-five on the Cassin Ridge on Denali, where my partner and I were stuck cowering from a storm under a boulder at 5,800 metres for thirty-six hours before we could top out. And I would turn twenty-seven there on Makalu. Despite that experience and the years of climbing and guiding in the Rockies, I knew it wasn't enough. Nor was I enough for the Everest Light team to invite me to join them.

As if Albi knew what I was thinking, he said, "Two years, Woody. You've got two years to get the experience you need for a ticket to Everest."

At that moment, I had glanced over at Everest. Tendrils of cloud curled around the summit like sinister fingers where none had been moments before, and a breeze rustled the tent. I leapt up to drive in the tent stakes and tighten the guy lines. Minutes later, we were both in the tent, our backs pressed hard against the windward wall as the poles splintered, the stakes popped and the floor ripped under our heels. The wind died nearly as fast as it came that day, and the next morning we sped back down the ropes, rattled by the power of Himalayan storms.

Now I lie awake, rattled by the force of another storm as Albi snores beside me inside a hole on the side of Everest. But I'm here, thanks in part to him. The tempest outside diminishes in sound only as it buries our tent. Finally I take a sleeping pill—to put my thoughts to bed.

* * *

When I wake, Albi is crammed against me and I can feel the roof of the tent just centimetres from my face.

"Albi, wake up!" He snorts and bolts upright, hitting his head against the ceiling. He then starts punching at the walls of the tent to get more space, but just the frost lining of condensation from our breath sprinkles down on us.

"Bloody hell," he says. "How hard can this snow be packed in here?" He draws his arm back and punches the wall closest to the cave opening. A crack of light appears. "Ah! And then there was light!" And he lies back down. "Your turn, Woody."

I wriggle around to unzip the door of the tent, which opens to a solid wall of snow. My gut lurches and my throat constricts. "Oh, God. Have I ever told you how much I hate snow caves?"

Albi rests a hand on my shoulder. "This isn't the first time this cave has filled in overnight. The only difference is we're in it this time," he says. He points to the crack of light on the side of the tent. "Air isn't far away. There's a hole. In fact, do you remember what a palace this was yesterday? It can be that way again, and soon."

I start scraping at the wall of snow with the pot. With nowhere to put the snow but inside the tent, Albi scoops it into a pile that fills most of what little space remains. I never imagined I'd feel such relief when a blast of spindrift hits my face. We zip the door back up and pull on our insulated suits. Then I worm out of the tunnel and into the raging storm, and start digging out our tent. Every few minutes I fold myself over the shovel and gasp for breath.

"Enough," Albi yells. "I've got enough room to get the stove going now." While we wait for the snow to turn to water, we call Jim. He says it is pretty windy at Camp Two and the boys have a lot of digging out to do as well. They are pretty antsy to get out of there—as are we.

A short time later we step out onto the ledge to begin our descent toward Laurie and Dan at Camp Two. I can see little beyond my feet in the storm. When we start down, we find the ice blown clean except for a few sections where we have to stop and wrench the ropes free from densely packed snowdrifts. The snow-loaded slopes looming six hundred metres above our heads worry us, and we quicken our pace. I breathe easier when we drop off the spur into the lee of the headwall.

At the bottom of the fixed ropes, Laurie gives me a rib-crushing hug and Dan hands Albi and me each a loop from their rope to clip into. He says, "We've told Jim you're down. Let's get outta here!"

Although Dr. Bob and Chris walked out just a few hours earlier, there is no sign of their tracks. Dan takes the lead, breaking trail through drifts of knee-deep snow. As I hurdle from step to step to keep pace, I feel a part of it now—a part of the team and the one hundred trips we'll make.

CHAPTER 9

Proving Grounds

MOST OF US STAY at Camp One and carry loads to the cache over the next three days while waiting out the storm. By now we have passed over that ground enough times to start naming the features. There is a round frozen lake amidst the jumbled penitentes, which we call the Montreal Forum after the boys skate around on their boots there one day pretending to be famous hockey players. We name the five-storey-high ice tower that leans precariously over our route the Leaning Tower of Pisa, and place bets on when it will fall over. The Bowling Alley is a hundred-metre-long icy gauntlet lined with boulders marooned atop rows of melting-out ice pinnacles. We always quicken our pace when we walk past those last two features.

The storm that forced us off the mountain allows us to regroup into our original teams. Laurie, Dan and I cycle into another rest. The first courier is due any day, which inspires me to make a trip to Basecamp for the mail.

Liberated from my heavy boots, I wear my light trekking shoes, which have me flying down the trail. Before I have time to recognize the red-and-blue fleece jacket and pants that a sponsor provided for the Makalu expedition, I run into Carlos. I slow to a walk to discourage conversation. But he waits. I've been dreading this encounter, the first time we will be alone together since he showed up at my house without notice and told me he was coming to Everest.

That night I was determined to get out of my car and walk right past him and into my house. I hadn't seen him since he'd left me four months earlier, after not coming home one night. I'd then discovered that the woman he'd been with that night wasn't the first over the four-year span of our relationship. "Outta my way," I said, but he barred my way to the door.

"I need to talk to you," he said.

I pushed past him to open the door. "Not happening."

In a reedy voice, he pleaded, "Just give me five minutes."

"For what?"

"For your permission."

He craned his head to catch my eye, which I refused to meet. I felt his hand on my arm and twisted away. "Get on with it, Carlos."

"I want to go back to Everest." He had climbed a new route on Everest, the East Face, in '83.

"Go ahead. I don't care what you do now."

I watched his foot push and arrange the snow in ridges and mounds. "The trip is this spring, on the north side. We'll be at the same Basecamp."

"No!" My head dropped to my chest. I heard myself whine, "Why? You were supposed to go to K2 next spring."

"Well, I'm not now. I want to climb Everest without oxygen instead. An American team is going and this is my chance."

I turned for the door. "Well, do it any other time but when I'm there."

"It would be better for both of us if I had your permission."

My fingers gripped the doorknob. "No, Carlos. You mean it will be better for you. Not for me."

"I'm afraid I'm going to have to go anyway."

"Why doesn't that surprise me?" It was all I could do not to slam the door in his face. Instead I pressed it shut behind me and listened to the snow crunching underfoot as he walked away. I hadn't realized I was holding my breath until I let out a gasp and slid down the wall to the floor.

A few days later I found out that Carlos had rekindled an old romance with Annie over the winter. Annie was his introduction to that team.

Now Carlos stands on the trail between me and Basecamp. He looks gaunt; his pack, jacket and pants hang limply from his shoulders. He shoots me a smile as I approach. "Hi, want to walk down to Basecamp together?"

"Why would we do that?" I say.

He coos, "Come on, I'd like to be friends."

"Friends?" I keep my voice steady. "You betrayed me, lied to me and then you show up here. Why now?"

"Because I want to climb Everest without oxygen."

"That's not what I heard," I say. A few weeks back, when Laurie ran into Carlos in Lhasa and asked him why he was in China, Carlos answered, "To put the first American woman on top of Everest." But I want to hear those words from Carlos, not Laurie. "There are plenty of expeditions every year, and with your resumé, you could join most any of them. So, I ask again, why now, when I'm here?"

He looks older than his thirty-three years. More than anyone I know, Carlos wears his strain on the outside. Dark hammocks hang below his bloodshot eyes and a crease cleaves his brow. Anxiety gripped him at the start of every trip we shared. Sometimes he couldn't touch or talk to me for days. Now, another woman's problem—not mine.

He stops, turns and reaches out to touch my arm. I recoil. He replies, "I didn't know when I'd get another chance if I didn't come now."

"No, that's my story because, unlike you, this *is* my only chance and it looks to me as though you're doing your best to spoil it."

"I've been honest with you," he says. "And I respected you enough to ask your permission, didn't I?"

The skin on my arms prickles and an ache throbs at the back of my throat. *No*, I think, *don't lose it, not here.* I say, "I hate you for doing this to me. I'd rather not hate you, but apparently you've got nothing to say to change that. So, fuck off." I break into a hard run, not so much to get away from Carlos but to give rein to my fury.

Why is he here now? My footfalls landing hard on the *now*. I don't want to be the same woman I was when I was with Carlos, but still he has a hold on me.

In late summer of 1982, all the senior Yamnuska mountain instructors except for me left to climb Everest. Without warning, our boss hired Carlos, who had never worked with us before, to co-lead a five-week mountaineering course with me. I was furious. We had opposing approaches to teaching and argued daily. Even so, and to the puzzlement of many, including me, we fell in love and went on our first climbing trip together that fall, to Yosemite Valley in California. It would be the first of many.

In April 1985, we had set off for two months in the Peruvian Andes. Carlos and I had loved and fought in equal measures. He was my best friend, my lover, my climbing partner and my captor. By then, I was sure we would spend the rest of our lives together. It would be an adventure and it would be hell—and I couldn't imagine life without him. Carlos had climbed here several times, and it felt like home to him. We spent our first week hiking out of Huaraz, starting on potholed streets that narrowed to cobbled roads and trailed off through open hills to the mountains. I brimmed with love for this companion-cum–tour guide at my side.

But over breakfast one morning, at the end of that first week, and just after Carlos had been musing about us getting married, he caught himself. "Why did I have to fall in love with a climber? Why can't you just be a normal girlfriend? Right now, I'd be looking forward to some simple time together, some nice hikes and a bit of sightseeing. But instead I'm stressing over how we'll climb together and dreading it." My eyes stung and my heart plummeted. It wasn't the first time I had heard this lament from him. Yet still, I rose and fell every time.

Over the next month we made a few multi-day trips up side valleys into the Cordillera Blanca with burros and camp guard in tow. But due to an unseasonable amount of snow that rendered the avalanche hazard high and the mountains out of condition, we didn't get up anything, which left us lost for who we were when we weren't climbing. This problem resolved itself for me in the second month. While Carlos was busy leading a trek, I climbed with my future Everest teammates: with Dave on Cerro Artesonraju and with Albi on Cerro Huandoy.

Carlos asked me to come with him the second month while he guided a client in the mountains above the Ishinca Valley; more than he wanted me to come with him, he didn't want me to climb without him. So, I found myself plodding up the trail behind Carlos and his client, three burros, a burro driver–cum-cook and two chickens. When we rounded the final bend at the head of the valley, I saw the six-thousand-metre-high Cerro Tocllaraju leaning into the sky. There and then, my plan to be a submissive girlfriend unwound as fast as an anchor rope off a ship's deck.

I took in the glasslike polished ice face in measures: six hundred metres high and an average angle of fifty degrees. I scoped the crux: halfway up, the route narrowed into a vertical section like the waist of an hourglass to pass through rock bands. The ice on the crux was shades darker than the ice above and below it, indicating that it might be too thin for crampons to bite. I heard myself say, "I can retreat if I can't climb it." The final hundred metres tapered into a steep pyramid, with its third side a lower-angled ridge and an easy way off.

The valley we had been following ended abruptly half a kilometre ahead at a terminal moraine. The glacier had receded over the centuries to where it now lay, three hundred metres above the valley floor. Traces of footpaths led up through spine-backed lateral moraines to a ramp that led onto a glacier. A fresh snowfall draped the gaping crevasses and seracs I would wend my way through to get to the West Face of Tocllaraju. Compelled by an urge to respond, I would go—*now*. I bolted for where our group was unloading our gear to set up Basecamp, packed up, and was on my way. I was not sure what Carlos thought of my sudden change of plans. It wasn't that I didn't care. More telling was the strength of the draw.

Late that afternoon, I encountered a straggle of climbers unroping at the glacier's edge. Behind them, their track, like an erratic graph line, jagged, spiked and paralleled the crevasses in search of snow bridges to cross them. The team was Czech and spoke little English. In a patchy exchange, they pointed at the low-angled ridge leading to the summit of Tocllaraju and told me they had climbed it. Or was that just what I wanted to hear? I could climb the face but not descend it. Their track would be mine, and the only route off the mountain.

I followed their trough, ploughed knee-deep through heavy, wet snow, until I came to a hard stop where one of their feet had broken through a snow bridge spanning a cavern below. Crossing the glacier in the peak of the day's heat when the snow strength was weakest was a poor decision—unnecessary. I could turn around now and camp on the edge of the moraine to wait out the night and cross the glacier in the morning once the snow had frozen and strengthened. But even a single step back could break the spell. I might lose my resolve and return to Basecamp. I asked myself, *Am I motivated by Everest and the identity of an alpinist it promises?* Or was it absolute passion, the irresistible pull, the delight at the sight of every new puzzle to solve?

Yes, I wanted to be here now—pure and simple.

I put on my harness and crampons. Then I tied a long leash to my pack and heaved it onto the middle of the snow bridge where it landed with a soft thud and stayed put. Then I got down on all fours, splaying my body across as wide a surface area as possible and wallowed across.

An hour later, I veered off the Czechs' track, dropped my pack and climbed a short way up the face to mark the best bridge over the bergschrund for the next morning, when it would be dark. I was back down on the glacier by sunset, where I stomped out a platform to settle in for the night. I lay in my bivouac sack, propped up against my pack, watching the mountain disintegrate into darkness, with the hiss of my stove the only sound beneath the star-studded ceiling.

By 2 a.m. my mind was on its feet: would I cave and turn back, or rise to an all-consuming focus that I yearned for? *Just begin. Believe and begin.*

I was walking by 3:30 a.m., carrying a light pack with a litre of water, some granola bars, a bag of nuts, an extra jacket, a short length of rope and a couple of ice screws and pitons. The light of my headlamp confined my world to a ten-metre radius. On each out breath, to calm my trepidation, I chanted in cadence with my step: *just begin, just begin.* The hard freeze overnight made the snow firm enough to walk atop. Within a few minutes my world tipped steeply upward. The beam of my headlamp now spotlighted a metre-wide circle on the face in front of me.

I felt the transition from snow to ice underfoot. My crampon points and picks of my axes sank in as easily as darts into a corkboard. I settled into a new cadence of *axe, axe, foot, foot,* rest, *perfect balance, axe, axe, foot, foot,* rest, *perfect balance,* where all hesitation was consumed by will—simple.

I felt entranced—as if I was floating. More space opened beneath my feet, demanding a precision in balance and economy of effort. My senses flared for the slightest change in feel, look and the sound of my points penetrating the ice. I had sought this place of certainty before—a state of mind that channelled adrenaline into focus. Once elevated to this state, it was harder to go back than to move forward— toward more. The only fear became failure, which threatened a backward slide to what I was, rather than to what I could be.

First light revealed a dim view of the crux just above me. The day before I had scoped this narrow vertical passage from below and planned to turn around here if I couldn't find enough rock to drive a piton or ice to thread an ice screw into. But turning back was not an option. I could see veins of ice thick enough for my front points and axes, and features to stand on. After a few body lengths of delicate climbing where no more than a centimetre of my picks pricked the thin ice, I found myself above the crux.

The sky was awash in lavender and pink by the time I reached the steep and bulbous snow formations capping the top of the face. The vertical snow bulges defied gravity and me. I attempted to burrow up through the hip-deep unconsolidated snow by gouging a trench and pressing my feet and body against the sidewalls, but they collapsed and it felt too insecure. I backed down and tentatively traversed below the obstacles in search of higher-density snow and an easier route to the top. When I reached the edge of the West Face, I was relieved to find a lower-angle ramp that led to the top. When I punched my right foot into the new slope, it felt denser.

All it took was one kick to disturb that layer of new snow, which clung to the ramp just beyond the angle of repose. A crack appeared, and in the time it took me to jerk back onto my left foot, it ripped across the slope. I heard a swishing sound as the snowfield disintegrated into fragments then vanished over the edge. It was over in an instant. *Was I delirious, was I seeing things?* Then as if in answer, a rumbling cloud roiled up from below.

My heart pounded in my ears. The near miss sent me scuttling back across the West Face to my abandoned trench, where I bolted upward, gasping on fumes of adrenaline. In order to gain any traction I had to spread my weight over the largest surface area possible. I swam with my arms and legs to propel my body upward until I reached the top.

I stepped out of the shadow of the face and into a fiery orange wash of alpenglow. Dread doused my relief when I couldn't see any footprints *anywhere*. I raced across the top for a look over the other side in hope of finding the Czechs' track back down, but saw nothing. Hope kept me plunging down the knee-deep snow slope—looking, praying—until I reached the breakover, where the slope dropped away so steeply I couldn't see the ground below it.

I thumbed through the pages of my memory for everything I had learned about snow stability and stopped at the winter of 1979. I was with a group of ski industry professionals, enduring a lecture on slope configuration from snow hazards expert Chris Stethem, the best in the business. I had rolled my eyes as he stood at the front of the meeting room, pointing at a giant image of a woman's breast he was using to illustrate weaker and stronger terrain features. He slowly traced his pointer from the upper swell, drawing it down to the nipple and then horizontally across the curve, where he let it rest. "Right here at the breakover," he explained, "where angle tips, is where the tension is greatest." I was one of two women in the room, and he shot me a sly smile. *Asshole.*

But he was effective. As I shot back up my tracks, I puzzled over something that the Czechs had tried to convey the day before. Had they said "avalancha"? Did they stop before the summit because of an avalanche hazard?

Back on the summit, I ran across to look over one side and then the other. "Shit, shit, shit, shit! What am I going to do?" I howled. "Stop it! Calm down. Sit! Eat something. Think." And I plopped down on my pack. I felt the faint warmth of the sunrise on my back. I watched the shadow line of this peak creep down the mountainside across the valley. A light breeze came up as if caused by the movement of the earth turning toward the sun. I was a part of the ride that morning and viewing it from the top of the planet.

I looked down at our Basecamp and thought, *I could still be asleep or just rousing, sipping a cup of tea and later seeing Carlos and his client off on an acclimatization hike.* Then I'd wander off somewhere just to kill time. I could be safe. Either way, killing time or killing myself, I'd be dead. Instead, I was here, inside this body vibrating to

nore alive.

descending the way
Axe, axe, foot, foot,
ne ice. Unlike climb-
ace, every step down
far below.
the next five metres
urned from fatigue.
at trickled down my
see my feet past the
I shrugged one arm
ough the pack strap,
eased my jacket out
go. I envied the ease
a stop on my track

I slotted my front-
he thin veneer of ice
tion. I poured all of
nward and each axe

med for respite and

I stopped and chopped out a ledge to get my feet sideways and my weight on my heels. I looked back up at the section I had just climbed down and shook my head in wonder. A few hours ago, I hadn't thought it possible to reverse the moves I'd made to climb up this section. Where was the line between what I could and couldn't do? This question would bring me back to the edge again and again.

It was noon by the time the slope's angle eased and there was snow instead of ice beneath my feet. Knowing that a fall wouldn't kill me now, I ran down the rest of the slope whooping and hollering, "I'm down. I'm down! Thank the gods!" I snatched up my jacket and an hour later, I stepped off the glacier onto the moraine and kissed the ground.

A few hours before, at the top of the mountain, I had said my vows and prayers: *If I make it off this mountain, I will be satisfied and never need to do this again. I will appreciate everything and every day of life I have from this day on.* Once I was safely down, I thought of what Laurie once said in a presentation I attended: "Climbing shows us that we are more than we know. We purposely climb ourselves into trouble—to a place where the only way out is through. It's then, in the fight, that we discover more in ourselves."

I now felt like I was more than I knew. But how long would that last before I needed to remind myself again? Not long, I discovered: I would solo the North Face of Ranrapalca two days later and then Carlos and I would do our last climb together and a new route on the Northeast Face of Huascarán Sur. I arrived home to a formal invitation to join the Everest Light team.

CHAPTER 10

Mentors and Muses

BLESSEDLY, JANE IS IN the mess tent when I burst in panting from my sprint to escape Carlos.

"Whoa, girl!" she says, looking up from sorting a heaping pile of mail. She hands me my share of packages and letters. It feels like Christmas.

The first package I open is an early birthday present from Marni, who has sent me seven pairs of underwear, each one labelled with a different day of the week—the perfect gift. More than anyone else, she is the girlfriend who would know that laundry in a place like this gets done at best once every couple of weeks, and then only my underwear and socks in a bowl of warm water. I miss her as soon as I start reading her letter: "I hope, no matter how hard it may feel up there at times, that you remember how far you've come since you first told me you wanted to go to Everest with the guys."

Marni was the first person I dared tell that I wanted to join the Everest Light team. "So, why don't you ask?" she'd said.

"They might say no."

"It sounds like you're already prepared for the worst. So what have you got to lose by asking?"

Marni has been pushing me out of my comfort zone since we met in 1976 as co-instructors for a three-week mountaineering program. Marni, with her social work background, was good at talking, and I, with my climbing background, had stronger technical skills, so we stuck with our strengths for the first session we taught together. But then during the second three weeks she insisted we switch roles, and we coached each other through, becoming fast friends.

Another package contains a couple of cassette tapes with recorded letters and playlists from my boyfriend, Chris. We'd first met on that avalanche safety course in 1979. He was a wicked womanizer and full of himself, and I didn't like him much then.

But late last fall, we'd met again by chance in an airport waiting for the same flight. Carlos and I had just broken up, and I was on my way to Vancouver to visit my folks. Chris had recently spent three weeks in the hospital learning about insulin use and getting stabilized after being diagnosed with late-onset juvenile diabetes. We found seats together on the plane and, by the time we stepped off, we'd planned the first of many romantic dates. Over the past winter, I've fallen for this now humbler man, and I store away these cassettes for the long carries up high when I will most need them. I will listen to them again and again.

In addition to personal letters and parcels, the courier has also brought a bunch of press clippings that Jane Sharpe of the Continental Bank has bundled together for us. After dinner that evening, we lounge around the mess tent table reading the articles about ourselves on Everest. It's fascinating, but I'm not sure I like it. Over the past years, I've tried to escape all expectations except my own.

On the radio that evening, Laurie reports the day's activity from Camp Two. It took Barry and Dwayne all day to reclaim the fixed ropes from beneath drifted snow and reach Camp Three. Then, after several hours of digging, they found our tent, buried behind two and a half metres of densely packed snow, destroyed. Exhausted by the effort, they retreated to Camp Two in darkness.

I am relieved to hear Laurie's voice so strong and present on the radio that evening. He tells us he'll put in another day with James carrying up to Camp Three, then take his rest at Camp Two and wait for my return. The boys have finished building the kitchen at Camp Two and claim it is ready for Jane to move up and turn it into our Advance Basecamp. From all the news, I assume I won't be making another trip down to Basecamp until near the end of our time on the mountain.

Two days later, I head up to join Laurie and Dan at Camp Two. As I start out for the long day ahead, I insert the first of Chris's cassette tapes into my player. His warm, gravelly voice greets me with, "Good morning, it's a beautiful bluebird day here at Worlebury Lodge," and I am transported to his log cabin above Alta Lake in Whistler. He describes his world after an overnight snowfall, the snow-laden peaks above, the rippling waters below. I can hear the crackling fire in his wood stove as he opens it to put in another log. I feel as though I am waking up with him. I can see the nameless resident cat lying in the sunbeam streaming through the window, smell the woodsmoke, feel Chris's breath on the back of my neck. I had tried to expect nothing, steeled myself for him to move on, but I am relieved by the way he has come through for me. Chris gives me a life to look forward to once I return home.

He announces the playlist of the day: Dire Straits, *Brothers in Arms*. The first song up is "So Far Away." This playlist and the one on his next tape, the Rolling Stones' *Tattoo You*, will help me more than I can know on many hard days ahead.

By the time I reach the cache I'm engulfed in Everest's shadow. The upper mountain glows in a golden wash and the wind has eased to a light breath. I head up the glacier in the now well-beaten trough. Halfway along, I look toward Camp Two and see a lone figure standing on the rise above it. Laurie knows I am coming and has promised to watch to make sure I cross the glacier safely.

As I draw closer, Laurie announces in a commentator's baritone voice, "Here she comes, ladies and gentlemen, the first woman from the western hemisphere to climb Mount Everest!" He takes my pack and drops it, exclaiming, "Jesus, what have you got in here, your cosmetics bag? I guess when you're famous you never know when you'll have to put your face on for those photo ops, eh?" He pulls me hard into his chest for a hug. And as the air expels from my lungs, I tell him that I've picked up another spool of rope at the cache on my way by.

We walk toward the cook shelter and I see half a dozen tents where there were just two on my last stay. The kitchen is now a pit hollowed out of the glacier and covered by a large orange tarp strung over a ridgepole, guyed out taut and anchored down with snow stakes and blocks of snow. A Canadian flag, waving lazily from two avalanche probes bound together, marks one side of the entrance. The other side is marked with the teddy bear skewered on a ski pole jabbed into the snow. I follow Laurie down five carved-out steps into the hole in the glacier.

Dan is sitting on one of the snow benches that line three sides of the pit. He looks up from the stoves he is tending and says, "Welcome to our humble abode. Pull up a seat and stay a while." I smile when I notice for the first time that the motif of frolicking reindeer on his toque has them humping each another in a merry ring around his head. Two stoves that we had adapted to hang from the ceiling of our tents extend down from the rafters. Dan scoops a cup of snow from a nylon stuff bag he's filled and dumps it into a steaming pot. "Nice place, eh? What do you think?"

I look up at the network of rafters and ridgepole rigged from skis lashed together with wire, rope and duct tape, and say, "Ingenious. Nice work, guys." I add, "Jane will be delighted when she moves up for the long haul."

Dan holds a foil package. "That's good cuz all we've got to eat up here right now is 'silver surprise.'" Whenever he speaks, his overgrown moustache wriggles as if he has a furry animal on his lip. "I don't know what you guys were thinking when you stripped all the packaging off these things. You can't tell what you're going to get until it's too late."

I smile to myself, pick up an unlabelled package and dangle it between us. "You see, Dan, seven months ago Dwayne and I imagined that we might all be getting a little bored with prepackaged meals about now. So, by removing the labels, every one we opened would be a surprise. Good idea, don't you think?"

Laurie grins. I'm not usually so quick on the return, but Dan's complaint seems trifling, given how Dwayne and I had scrambled to meet the Chinese authorities' requirement to send our supplies for inspection six months ahead of the date we were to arrive. The two of us were in charge of packing and shipping, while other expedition members were responsible for ensuring various parts of those supplies were accounted for and sent to us at a warehouse in Calgary by the shipping deadline. However, the goods hadn't been arriving fast enough—or at all.

One night, during a daily progress update by phone with Jim, who is in Toronto, I finally had to tell him that some of the guys were dragging their feet thinking the expedition wouldn't happen because we didn't have the money to get to China yet. They couldn't see the point in getting the goods because they didn't think we'd ever see our stuff again. I too had been considering other plans for the spring but hadn't dared tell him.

"What?" Jim said. "You can't be serious! I've been working my ass off and you say the guys are making other plans. Who are these guys?" He told me he would fly out the next day and directed me to get everyone together for a meeting the next evening. He said to tell anyone who couldn't make it that they were off the team.

The next night Jim stood before us at James's house and said he'd "been pounding the streets" looking for one more key sponsor to give us enough money to get to Everest. One sponsor! That it could happen any day now, but only if we believed it would. "I have promised anyone who will listen that we will climb Everest by a new route and in a style that will make them proud to be Canadians. So tell me now. *Right now!* Are you in or are you out? Those who're in, get with the program because we're going to Everest in the spring!"

The room fell quiet enough to hear a cat jump off the bed upstairs. If I'd ever had any doubts about Jim, I knew then we had the leader we needed.

After that meeting, everyone got on the phone to follow up with sponsors on their designated items. In the course of a few days the remaining supplies poured into that warehouse, along with volunteers to help sort, label, pack and ship five tonnes of supplies in the few days we had left to meet the deadline. We'd been in such a hurry then, ripping those silver packages out of their excess packaging and stuffing them into barrels.

"Yeah," Dan says. "Well, so far we've figured out the smaller ones here are the desserts. Tonight, mine was peaches and Laurie's was pears. They're pretty good warmed up. These bigger ones are dinners. Laurie got the Hawaiian pineapple chicken and I got beef stew. What else have we got to choose from, do you know?"

I squish each of the four dinner packets he has handed me, trying to guess the contents. I recall selecting our menu very carefully. "We ordered twelve dinners, each some international dish. We also picked some blander ones for Camp Four and above. But we sealed those in a clearly marked bag. Don't worry, though—they'll still be a surprise."

I drop one of the foil packages into a pot of boiling water and stretch out on a snow bench with my feet up while I wait for the meal to heat. And as Laurie resumes his explanation to Dan about firearm suppressors, I feel as content as that cat in the sunbeam at Chris's Worlebury Lodge.

A few minutes later, I fish out my dinner, rip off the top and say, "Ah, what a *surprise*, it's Szechuan for me tonight. See, isn't this fun?" I squeeze out the ginger beef and noodles into a measuring cup and scoop a spoonful into my mouth. "Thank you so much, gentlemen, for toiling over a hot stove all day to prepare this for me."

"Ha," Laurie says. "Jim was right about the civilizing effect women have on a group of louts like us. Did you see how Sharon plated that meal instead of eating it out of the package? And did you hear what she called us—gentlemen? Dan, you'd never even think of thanking me, let alone call me anything other than dumb-ass." He sits kitty-corner to Dan on the bench and looks at me. "All we do when you or Jane aren't around is complain. You women notice things differently. Stick around and keep doing what you're doing."

When I finish, I scrape my plastic cup with my spoon and rinse it with a bit of hot water to clean it out. When I look around to dump the wash water, Dan points to the waste hole behind a bench.

Laurie passes me a bag of smaller silver packets. I pull one out and guess by feel that it's cherries, and plop it into the pot.

Dan tells me, "Camp Three is a lot bigger than when you last saw it. I don't know how long Laurie and James spent fixing it up, but they rigged a tarp over the cave to lie flush with the incline of the slope. You can seal it completely from inside or out."

"See what I mean? I would never have heard Dan speak so nicely about the work James and I did if a woman wasn't here." Laurie nods at my cup, spoons the packet out of the boiling water and flops it into my cup like a fish into a boat.

Dan lets out a sniff of a laugh. "Yeah, and Laurie would never serve me like that."

They watch me rip open the packet and squeeze the contents into my cup. "Well, what do you know, it's a bowl of cherries."

"Wait," says Dan, rummaging through the mess of cans and food packets on the bench. He produces a can of sweetened condensed milk. "Try this on those cherries. You could stand to pack some more calories on that skinny ass of yours." I dip the can into the hot water, empty the contents into my cup and dig in.

I drift off to sleep that night with a full belly and gratitude for my teammates. In anticipation of my arrival, Laurie tidied a tent up for me, airing out a sleeping bag and laying it on top of *two* sleeping pads. When I thanked him for the second pad, he joked, "I tried to find a third, you know, so I could put a pea underneath to see if you're really the princess they say you are." Dan may be imposing and gruff, but now and then he passes out a little veiled tenderness, as he did with the thick sweet cream for my cherries.

We know that our bodies, minds and spirits will dwindle with each day we spend at high altitude—that our ability to perform is finite—and we estimate that we are limited to another month, at best. By then we will have burned through any fat reserves and muscle, and the tedium of shouldering another load, day after day, will wear our resolve to nil. Although no one might admit it in such a way, we serve ourselves when we nurture each other. Our success depends on the good health and welfare of every one of our teammates, and our lives depend on each of us being alert enough to notice a fraying rope or fortify a weakening anchor. I sleep deeply that night, well cared for and fuelled with sugar and spice.

* * *

For the first time since we arrived, Team C is set to lead in the rotation. Dan, however, makes the difficult decision to descend to Basecamp in the hope of ridding himself of his persistent cough. So Laurie and I set out for Camp Three on our own. I move with more ease and balance that day, and we pull into Camp Three together a half hour ahead our previous best time.

We establish a routine, where each morning Laurie gets up first and passes me a loaf of Christmas fruitcake and a length of sausage to put in my sleeping bag to start thawing. While I remain snug in my sleeping bag, Laurie piles everything from his side of the tent on top of me. Then with a whisk broom he sweeps the frozen layer of condensation off the walls and ceiling onto the floor on the empty side of the tent and out the door. I then roll over to the cleared area, and he does the same on my side of the tent. Once the tent is clear of frost, he'll lie back while I start the stoves and prepare breakfast.

I start one stove outside in the vestibule, and another one that hangs from the roof of the tent. Both stoves melt snow for the first hour. As soon as the pot inside the tent starts steaming, I transfer its contents to the one outside and shovel more snow into the one inside the tent. It will take over three hours, repeating this process, to melt enough snow to hydrate us. Once the sausage and fruitcake have thawed a little in my bag, I pass them out to Laurie to slice. In between rounds of boiling water, we place the slices in another pot that I've heated with a few sizzling dollops of butter. We eat as much fruitcake and fried sausage as we can stomach, and drink perhaps four cups of tea and a full litre of warm water, and then fill our water bottles for the day. All the while we move carefully around each other and the stoves, as if in a choreographed routine.

During the day, we work together fixing ropes ever upward. The sky is cloudless and calm, and our crampons bite easily into wind-blasted snow on the thirty-five-degree slope. I lead out as far as sixty metres, where I build an anchor by driving in snow stakes or threading screws into the ice to secure the rope to. Then Laurie packs up what remains of the spool of rope he has been paying out and ascends the rope I've just set to the top anchor where I wait. When he arrives, we switch positions, and I belay him while he leads the next span. We continue to leapfrog one another through the day and return to the routine of melting snow and boiling water into the night to get hydrated and refuel.

Near the end of the third day, we have strung out more than a thousand metres of rope over six hundred vertical metres of ground to reach the top of the spur, and the location of our Camp Four. Here, we sit on the shoulder of Everest, 7,300 metres above sea level, taking in the view. Row upon row of peaks, girded with white corrugated faces, shimmer in the sunlight. Nearest to us, and due west, I look down on the 7,160-metre-high summit of Pumori. The north-facing side of the ridge we sit on drops away 1,300 metres to the Rongbuk Valley and the bleak brown Tibetan Plateau beyond. The other side of the ridge plunges over 1,500 metres into the glaciated valley on the Nepalese side of Everest—the Western Cwm. This is the gateway to Everest's south side and the Khumbu Icefall, an ever-shifting four-kilometre-long jumble of seracs the size of apartment buildings. Directly across the Cwm, the North Face of Nuptse towers to a height just shy of 8,000 metres. And at the head of the Cwm stands Lhotse, the fourth-highest mountain in the world, at 8,500 metres.

"Hmm, I guess I'll have to wait till I stand on the summit to see Makalu, eh?" I draw in deep yet empty breaths, and my voice sounds high and squeaky as if I have breathed in a lungful of helium. "It seems unreal to be here sitting on the shoulder of the highest mountain in the world. I feel so lucky to be here with you, and on a day like this."

Laurie laughs deeply. "We're blessed. I won't forget these days we've had together. We got a hell of a lot done in three days. And

Sharon, you're going strong; you should be proud of what we've accomplished."

I follow his gaze to where the summit pyramid of Everest rises above the end of the ridge two kilometres away. Ethereal wisps of spindrift trail off the summit against an indigo sky. He muses, "Hopefully we'll have many more beautiful days like this, and you'll be standing atop that summit in another, what? A couple of weeks or so if we can keep going like this. It shouldn't take more than a few days to fix to Camp Five."

I think, *Only 1,500 more metres to reach the summit of Everest, just a long day's climb—if it wasn't above 8,000 metres.* "I really want a chance to climb that, Laurie. That is—if my turn comes around."

"Yeah?" He turns to look me in the eye. "Here's two questions you better start asking yourself then, Sharon. How bad do you want that turn? And how will you recognize it when it comes along? If you don't know that, you'll end up doing what Dwayne did in '82 when he gave his turn up to someone who wanted the summit more than he did. I made sure to tell him the same thing at the start of this trip. As noble as everyone is on this team, no one is going to hand the summit to you on a platter."

"How did you know it was your turn, Laurie, when so many others wanted to go for the summit as well?"

"Jesus, it was a faint glimmer of a message," he said. "The only way I knew it was mine to take was that I'd committed to giving my best. After teaching seven years and forty-nine courses at Outward Bound and telling every one of my students to give more than their best, it was time for me to do the same. I figured Everest was my test—the ultimate Outward Bound course. You remember the school motto: 'To serve, to strive and not to yield?' That's what I did. I served my team and something much bigger than any one of us alone. That's where you earn the right to take your turn, and recognize it when it comes."

CHAPTER 11

Shit, Grit and Yin

CAMP TWO HAS BECOME our Advance Basecamp and the cook shelter is bustling when Laurie and I arrive, less than an hour after leaving Camp Four. Jane has moved up, and half a dozen of us gather on snow benches chatting while she prepares dinner. Pots and pans hang from rafters. Cans of food, bags of drinks, noodles, soups and cups fill shelves that have been carved into the snow walls. With what Jane has brought up from Basecamp and dug out of the food stores beneath the tarp, she makes a spectacular dinner.

"Linguine alla lobster is the entree for tonight," she says as she drains the pot and dishes out the noodles. We hold out our plastic measuring cups in a web of outstretched arms while she spoons over the sauce. Cozied up together, savouring the concoction as if it is a four-star meal, we look like a large happy family. It's a sight I couldn't have imagined before this trip, and it feels like home. I love that the boys have started calling Jane "Fearless," not just as a play on her last name, Fearing, but aptly for her spunk and mostly as a signal that she belongs to this family.

I am also grateful to be sitting upright with my feet on terra firma and with nothing more to do than indulge a hearty appetite. It is a relief not to be in that crevasse at Camp Three where, folded up in the dim light of the cramped space, Laurie and I fought for the same oxygen as the stoves. And where anytime we were outside, we had to stay alert to avoid a fatal mistake by failing to clip just one carabiner or taking one misstep untethered.

Now that Jane has moved up from Basecamp, we share a tent again and I can't wait to debrief our time apart. As we chat she gives me a back massage, working the knots out of sore muscles earned from carrying heavy loads. She says, "You should see what happens to these guys when they come down for a rest; they get all scrubbed up and then strut around all fluffed up and frisky!" She grinds her elbow into a tender spot just below my shoulder blades. "I did this for Jim one night down in Basecamp, and whoa, it started to get a little too cozy. I shot out of there!"

"All these guys are the same. Well, not quite all of them," I say. "Get them far away enough from home and they start behaving like you're the last woman on earth. It's perfectly natural, of course, and it's why our species is still around. Nothing wrong with that, I suppose, just as long as you don't believe the story. That's the problem, though: What woman doesn't want to feel special?"

"Yeah, well, it sure puts me in an awkward position," she says. "Crikey! I can't believe what a tiny little back you've got." She grabs the points of my shoulder blades and pinches them. "Would you look at these little things!" I feel her probe my back for the muscle between my shoulder blades. "This scrawny chicken's back should belong to the cook."

"Ouch! Have you ever got strong fingers!"

"That's my point: my broad shoulders and strong fingers should belong to the climber."

"Hey!" Kevin shouts from an adjacent tent. "Jane, Woody! It sounds like you've got a party going on over there. Can Bubba and I come over?"

"No," we sing out.

"Well, then," Barry says, "keep it down. Some of us are trying to sleep."

Jane lowers her voice. "I didn't realize they were that close. I hope they didn't hear us earlier."

"Every word," Kevin says.

"Haven't you guys got anything better to do than eavesdrop?"

"Not when the gossip is that juicy," Barry replies.

* * *

I had intended to take a couple of days of rest at Camp Two. But after lying around, reading and eating for a day, I grow restless. That night Jim relays news from Barry and Kevin, now at Camp Four, saying they need more rope and supplies to start fixing toward Camp Five. He urges anyone who feels well enough rested to work while the weather is good, which is a good reason to cut my rest short.

The next morning we are just waking up when Jane says, "What time is it?" Her sleeping bag is cinched tight, exposing half her face and one eye.

I pull my watch string out from around my neck. "Eight," I yawn.

Jane unzips her bag. "God, I'm hot." She sits up, rips off her hat and runs her fingers through her hair. She strikes a mock pose. "How do I look?"

Her shoulder-length straight blond hair is plastered flat from sleeping in her hat, and when she tries to fluff it, it sticks up like straw. I laugh. "As good as me, no doubt."

"Oh God, how long has it been since we've had a shower?" she sighs.

"Going on five weeks, I think."

"Hurry up and get to the top of this damned mountain, will you? We're about due for a shower." She hugs herself and reaches for a thought. "No, a nice hot bubble bath would be better."

"Holy shit!" we hear Albi shout, then the sound of snow crunching under boots, which stops beside our tent.

Dan asks, "You girls been out to the shitter this morning?"

"No. Why?"

"Because it isn't there anymore," Albi laughs. "Didn't you hear that big crash in the night and feel our tents move?"

We look at one another, and say, "No."

99

"No kidding?" Dan says. "I'm amazed you slept through. There's a big crevasse where the shitter was. If you happen to be looking for it this morning, you'll have a long climb down." He adds, "Guess I know what I'll be doing on my day off."

Jane holds up her near-full pee bottle and says, "Thank God for this. That would have been a rude surprise to be sitting on the pot when it crashed into the abyss in the middle of the night. I wonder if the Nalgene bottle sponsors ever imagined they'd be saving lives?"

We clamber out of our tent to join Albi, Dan and Chris at the edge of a hole big enough to swallow a bus. A jumble of freshly sheared ice blocks covers the steps Dwayne carved, and the toilet seat is nowhere to be seen.

Jane's eyes grow wide. "How could we have slept through *that*!"

"Pretty messy remodelling job if you ask me," Albi says. The boys laugh and joke as if they are watching a comedy on TV.

Jane says, "And I say it's pretty terrifying to think this happened so close to us. You guys are all acting like this is just another day—on Mount Everest."

"It *is* just another day on Everest, if you haven't noticed," Dan replies.

Jane takes a step back. "Look at us standing here in our identical long underwear looking like a bunch of big babies with our sleepers on." She grabs the sagging material from the backside, "And with a diaper full. And you," she says to Chris, "with your surgical mask and a bloody wad of toilet paper sticking out of your nostrils. What a sight we all are!" Then she points over at the crevasse. "And sometime in the middle of the night this crevasse cracked wide open, no more than a few metres from where were sleeping. Do you not think that is even a little unusual?"

Albi says, "How about we put our new shitter somewhere different for starters?"

"Is it safe to even camp here is what I want to know," Jane says.

Dan says, "I'll probe around after breakfast and make sure there aren't any other crevasses that have opened beneath us, and I'll dig a new hole on the other side of camp."

"That's a good start," Jane replies. "And I'm going to move our tent today." She turns toward the shelter. "Now, how about breakfast?"

Albi puts on his best upper-crust British accent. "If it's eggs Benedict on the menu, I'd like my eggs medium-soft, please."

Soon after, we are all assembled underneath the orange tarp, which casts a jaundiced tint on our faces. Jane slides a pancake out of the pan and into my empty cup and looks for another taker. She passes me a cup of syrup, homemade from butter and brown sugar.

"Who's going back up today?" Dan asks.

"I am," I say. "Anyone interested in getting this over with sooner by going all the way to Camp Four in one go—two days in one?"

"I'm in," Albi says. "Chris and I are due to move into Three today. But anything's better than sleeping in that refrigerator. Let's give it a go!"

Thirteen hundred metres is a big day in the Rockies, let alone on Everest. But we're all roused by the prospect of trying something new and raising the bar, which is more invigorating than a good day's rest. We talk about the strategy, our loads and how long it might take us. Fuelled by dopamine, I feel as though I'm under some strange spell of mania on this day.

I saddle up, load my cassette player, clamp an ascender on the rope and start up with a piqued sense of wonder. After multiple trips over this ground and the ground before this, I begin again an elegant dance, practised and lived into, of weight shifts, cross-steps, back steps and toe-ins, all in what seems a concert of pistons, pulleys, levers, pumps and bellows. I am certain that all these moves will alter my movement on steep ground for the rest of my life.

I pull up over the headwall in half the time it used to take. I look back down to see all three boys making their way up the ropes. Now, at the beginning of the hardest day yet, I load up *Tattoo You*, slip on my headphones and turn my player on. The first few bars of electric guitar twang loud in a world-altering riff. Mick Jagger snarls the initial lines of "Start Me Up" as I punch my ascender up the rope. Fuelled with these lusty lyrics imbued with grit and testosterone, I start up the spur of the highest mountain in the world.

The tempo of "Tops" lulls me into a rhythm, which pulls me through the rest of the day. Long after the batteries in the player die, I am still accompanying Mick.

Albi, Chris and I set a new standard by stringing the two carries together. None of us will ever stay at Camp Three again.

* * *

A few days later, Camp Two is empty but for Dan, Laurie and me. Jane left earlier that morning to pick up a load of supplies from Camp One, and I wake to a calm, sunny morning. The frost on the tent has melted into rivulets and trickles down the walls into pools on the floor. I put our sleeping bags out to air and remove everything else but a sleeping pad and zip the tent up tight. Dressed in my one-piece base-layer, I pad over to the cook tent. I step down into a layer of knee-high cold air. There must be a twenty-degree temperature difference between the upper air of the shelter, warmed by the sunshine through the tarp, and the floor.

Pots of water sit on both the stoves with a half-kilogram can of bacon thawing in one of them. I stew it up and eat a third of it, saving the rest for Laurie and Dan. I make tea in Laurie's measuring cup and take it over to his tent.

"Hey, Laurie, time to rise and shine. You still up for another carry today?" I tell him that I have water on to boil and breakfast waiting.

"Lots?" he asks.

"Yes," I say. "I'm off to the baths."

I return to my tent, which is warm enough now to strip off my clothes for a complete scrub down and a shampoo. With about six litres of hot water, I work from visible to less visible parts. First I wash my face and then I immerse my head into the full pot of warm water and lather up. I rinse my hair with cups of clean water, which drain into an empty pot. Then I combine the clean water and the rinse water and dip my underwear in to wipe down the rest of my body. Finally, I squat over the pot and wash my nether regions. I wring out my underwear and hang it to dry on the cords strung across the ceiling of the tent. I wrap my small towel around my head and lie naked atop my sleeping pad to air-dry in the sauna-like luxury of my tent.

Rarely naked, I survey my new physical landscape of angles and hollows. I run my gaze down over my atrophied breasts, lamenting how they are always the first to go when I lose weight. When I lift my head to look below my ribcage, a six-pack of well-defined stomach muscles ripples. Smudges of purple and yellow bruising from my pack's hipbelt colour my hipbones. I caliper the skin on the inside of my thighs with forefinger and thumb, gauging how much is left to burn. A pair of long, sinewy muscles parallels my thighs, running from my groin to my knees. I admire my toes and pink nailbeds. These small feet, despite the minus-fifty-degree days of Denali and the many sub-zero days spent bashing them into frozen waterfall ice, are still all here. I wonder if Everest will exact a toll, as it did with Willi Unsoeld when he was benighted near the summit and subsequently lost nine of his toes to frostbite. I examine my fingers, thick as sausages from years of gripping ropes and holds. Thick, maroon-coloured blood oozes from my cracked cuticles, which I think is a sure sign of anemia. Red puffy skin around cuts that never seem to heal tell of malnutrition.

Once dry, I sprinkle baby powder all over my body. I sniff the layers I have been wearing for the last several weeks. Despite all this time, they have little to no odour. Cursed with a good nose, I can usually detect the scent of others and myself. But in the high-altitude semi-arid desert air, it seems I sweat less. We lose our fluids through breathing and evaporation, leaving little to cling on our clothes. Or is it that bacteria can't survive this high?

I remember the leg of goat that hung from the rafters in the cook tent of our Makalu Advance Basecamp at 5,500 metres. Despite the warm daytime temperatures, bacteria didn't seem to grow in the dry and rarified atmosphere and the desiccated goat leg only emitted a mild gamey smell. Over the course of a month or more, our Sherpa cook sliced off slabs to put in stews and we never suffered any intestinal problems. I might be wrong in that theory, but it worked for us.

However, bacteria still thrive within our wasting bodies. This high, where vital functions work at fractional capacity, it is nearly impossible to heal once broken. As if in testament, I hear Dan hacking.

I slip my base layer back on and step out to see Dan rooting through the stores under the tarp.

"You seen any cough drops?" he asks. "This fucking cough kept me up all night."

"I've got half a box here."

"Thanks. Think I'll put a little more work in around here before I leave for Camp One," he says. He clears his throat, turns and spits a gob of thick yellow phlegm on the snow. "Be careful, eh?"

"What do you mean?"

"Don't burn yourself out. We've still got a long way to go. And I'd say, you've got one of the best chances of reaching the summit out of any of us."

I step back. "Me?" It seems like a long time ago when Laurie and I mused about my standing on the summit. Since then I had slipped into a comfortable routine, put my head down and carried my loads just like everyone else.

"I haven't been thinking that way," I say.

He snorts. "Well, you might want to start. Isn't it obvious? You haven't been sick once and you're going strong."

Dan's view startles me and snaps my head up. I watch him trudge off to his tent. Back in the Rockies, I saw Dan, a burly six-foot-five mountain guide, as a sure bet for the summit. At the first expedition meeting I attended, I remember rocking onto my toes beside him and Dave and Jim, trying to be taller, to believe that I measured up to the others on this team. I had thought and felt smaller then.

In need of a talk, and wondering what is taking Laurie so long to get ready, I go over to his tent to find him sitting in the vestibule with a pot of hot water in front him.

"Hey, Sharon, got a towel I can borrow? I haven't shaved or washed for at least a couple of days and I forgot mine down at One."

I return with my only towel, which is still damp.

"Thanks," he says, then hesitates. "This been anywhere I don't want to know about?"

"Nope." I'm disappointed that it isn't the right time to talk to him and turn to leave.

"So, what does that mean?" he asks. He is sitting cross-legged and naked from the waist up, holding out my towel pinched between his thumb and forefinger.

I can't help but smile. "It means it hasn't been anywhere on a woman's body that you aren't familiar with."

He laughs. "There you go again, Sharon. I know, I know, you're just trying to get the upper hand by embarrassing me."

"Hurry up so we can get back before dark," I say. "Whether you're ready or not, I'm out of here by eleven!"

"Hey, since I'm working with just you today, could I use some of that baby powder you've got that makes you smell so nice? I can smell it from here."

My chat with Laurie will have to wait for another day.

CHAPTER 12

Ya Gotta Want It!

THE DAY LAURIE, DWAYNE and I carry to Camp Four together marks close to the halfway point of our time on Everest. We climb a rope-span apart with Dwayne in the lead, Laurie second and me last. Although we speak little on carries because of the distance between us, we read one another by the way we move. The wind increases in intensity through the day, making Dwayne and Laurie look as though they are pinned to a clothesline. Dwayne sways in the wind but stays on his feet, pausing for the stronger gusts to pass before he continues. In contrast, Laurie, who is usually solid and steady, stumbles and falls to his knees when the stronger gusts hit us. The length of time he remains down, or hanging from his ascenders to recover, grows longer.

I wonder if we are pushing too hard and if conditions are nearing the point of unreasonable. Laurie and Dwayne slip in and out of view through clouds of spindrift. One gust blows all three of us over with a fierceness that feels like rage, as if it is trying to tear us off. *This is it*, I think, *this may be the first day I will have to turn around.* There is only one thing I can be certain about: worse is to come. Someday soon we will be higher and it will be harder. I wait to see what Laurie and Dwayne do. Laurie looks down at me and shakes his head. He has given up. Then he turns to look up at Dwayne, who staggers to a stand and punches his ascenders up the rope. Laurie shakes his head again and then gets to his feet and does the same. We complete our carry that day with our mentor sandwiched between us.

* * *

Mute light presses through cracks in the snow-encased walls of our tent the next morning. Malaise ambushed me sometime in the night. Storm days are difficult for anyone, but they tend to be a little worse for me. I know I'm cursed with bouts of depression and have learned to rise out of them with a good run or climb—an activity that alters my brain chemistry and gives me a sense of progress. But I can't escape it here, pinned down for the day or longer with nowhere to go, and nothing to do but wait. When I'm under depression's spell, I feel like I've always been this way and always will be.

I find Jane in the cook shelter reading by headlamp. Drifting snow covers the tarp overhead, dimming the light and muffling the maelstrom outside. I had hoped for a mood lift when I see her but I know I'm in trouble when I don't feel anything.

Jane fills me in on the news from the morning radio call, which I missed because I was trying to sleep. "Jim's back in Camp One already." He'd been in Zegar, a half day's travel from Basecamp by jeep, to extend our climbing permit for another week, to May 25. "Said he got worried when no one answered his call at seven this morning. Then, when I came on at eight, he asked why I was an hour late." She explained to him that we'd switched the radio call times to eight o'clock in order to make best use of the daylight hours. "I didn't get a chance to say anything more before he started yelling, saying how dangerous it is to make random decisions without group consensus. And since he wasn't here, it wasn't a consensus decision." Exasperated, she asks, "What's his problem anyway?"

"Ghosts is what," I say. "He attributes the three deaths on their '82 Everest expedition to their leader switching a radio time without notice so he could sleep in. But I'm not the one to tell you that story. You ask him sometime."

"Well, Jim and his ghosts are on their way up here today and he's hopping mad. Says he wants to go to Four tomorrow to replace Chris, who's coming down sometime today. Sounds like Chris's ribs are giving him grief. He thinks they may be broken because it's really painful on every intake of breath, and he wants Dr. Bob to check him out. They say they're not getting much done up there in this weather except home improvements. James wants to stay up at Four and wait it out." Jane pauses until I look up at her and she catches my eye. She tilts her head and asks, "What's with you this morning? You seem kind of depressed."

"Yeah, a little."

"Want to talk about it?"

"Not really—I know it'll just get worse if I try right now. I just need to move."

That afternoon, Kevin and Chris arrive after retreating from Camp Four. They tell us the wind was too strong to fix rope on the ridge. We are all in the cook shelter finishing up dinner when Jim arrives. He tosses an envelope of mail on the floor and says, "What the hell were you guys thinking when you decided to change the call times?"

Kevin starts to explain that the Chinese time zone we're working in doesn't coincide with our work schedule. Seven in the morning feels like we could use another hour of sleep, and seven in the evening feels like late afternoon.

"Fuck! Thanks for telling me! Where's an empty tent?" He snatches up a silver surprise and I lead him out to a vacant tent, where he keeps to himself through to the next day.

The weather, Jim's mood and my state of mind are no better the next morning. But Jim is determined to carry to Camp Four and asks me to join him. I would bolt out of here if I could. Usually when I am under this black cloud, friends don't hear from me for days. And when I can't hide, I suddenly transform from a vibrant force into a pathetic trickle, which is humiliating and, I fear, another reason Jim hesitated to invite me onto the team. I don't want him to see me like this on a day when he will be relying on me.

At the bottom of the ropes, I load my player with a cassette of Handel's *Messiah* that my erudite university professor client–turned–friend, Dixon, has sent me in the latest mail delivery. In his letter, he explained the three parts that the work expresses—the prophecy of salvation, the redemptive sacrifice and the promise of resurrection.

He told me not to try following it too closely and to let the music convey the transitions. Dixon instructed me to wait for a difficult day to play it, promising elevation and bliss. The music soothes me and carries me up the headwall to the spur. Then the rising "Hallelujah" chorus begins as I step into the full force of the storm—the music renders it into a celestial tempest.

Again I position myself on the windward side and allow the wind to help me. I look below to see Jim struggling on the leeward side of the rope, and I realize I have learned something from all the time spent in these gales. Fresh off a long rest, Jim is keeping up. But he is less accustomed to the force of the wind, and he fights it.

When we reach our halfway point at Camp Three, I tuck in behind a snow wall to wait for Jim and pull my watch out to check the time. I sag when I see it has taken an hour longer than usual to get to this point. When Jim arrives, I shoot him a look suggesting we drop our loads and return on a better day to finish the carry. He answers by transferring his ascenders to the next rope and pointing upward.

A few rope spans higher, I look down to see he has switched to the windward side of the rope and is gaining on me. When he goes to pass me at the next anchor, a rogue gust hurls him against me, and we topple together. Once we untangle ourselves and clamber to our feet, Jim squints at me through ice-encrusted eyelashes and yells over the howl of the wind, "Ya gotta want it!"

Those words echo through my memory, taking me back to a dismal day in Toronto. The whole team was attending a press conference shortly before we left for Everest. Jim cajoled me into joining him on his regular training regimen of running—three times—up the CN Tower, then the tallest free-standing structure in the world. On that grey, brittle February day, I attempted to follow him up the 1,776 steps. Broken glass grated under my feet as I ran up those stairs littered with cigarette butts, used condoms, syringes and tampons. By the third lap, my legs had turned leaden and I slowed to a plod. I could hear the patter of Jim's feet on the metal treads many flights above me. How could he do this day after day? Just then, he yelled, "Ya gotta want it!"

We have come a long way from that depressing day in Toronto. Riding on that same memory perhaps, Jim shoots me a wry smile and steps into the lead. Still on my knees, I watch him stagger the first few steps upward as the refrain of "Hallelujah" comes around again. Clouds roil and part, revealing patches of deep blue space. Soon I am blinded to all but my feet and the rope in front me.

Ten hours after we began, Jim and I pull into Camp Four. The boys have carved out a tent platform on the steep snow face just below the West Ridge and built a fortress of snow blocks around it. But the storm kept burying the tent, and over the course of several days of poor weather the boys tunnelled into the ridge and built a snow cave.

James has been watching for us and pops his head out of the cave entrance to greet us. He shouts over the wind's roar, "Welcome home, kids! Wow, good job getting up here in this today." He waits at the entrance as we unload our packs, then pulls them into the cave ahead of us.

I feel like I can't breathe as I slither up through a body-width tunnel, and only once my head is inside a surprisingly spacious cavern do I gasp for air. The cave feels like a sanctuary from the violence just a few feet away rather than the tomb I feared it would be.

"I've been fixing up the place, doing a little interior designing in my spare time," James tells us. The cave floor is higher than the entrance to allow cold air and off gasses to drop, and heat to rise and warm the dome-shaped space above, which is now much bigger than when I first checked it out. I can stand hunched over but Jim has to stay on his knees as we look around. James sits on a snow bench that is big enough to sleep four and about a metre higher than the floor. A stove and a couple of candles warm the cave and light it well enough that we can see one another. A small deep hole in the floor is the urinal, lined with the telling dark yellow signs of dehydration.

James gives me a hug and wraps a sleeping bag around me. "Have a seat," he says, pointing to the foam pad on the platform, "and make yourselves at home while I serve up the drinks and hors d'oeuvres." Steam billows from the pot and we dig out our cups from our packs.

He pours in some hot water, stirs in a few tablespoons of powdered milk and hot chocolate crystals and hands us our drinks. Then he scoops some snow out of a stuff sack and into the pot to make more water.

Stunned from our ordeal, Jim and I sit together under the sleeping bag with our backs against the ice wall and our boots sticking out in front of us. In the vacuum-like silence of the cave, my ears still ring from the din outside; otherwise all I can hear is the occasional muffled boom of a gust and the hiss of the stove.

James hands us a package of Fig Newtons. "How'd it go out there?"

Jim wraps his hands around the hot cup and tells James about the day. James lets out a throaty chuckle that I've come to know and that somehow diminishes any crisis. As they talk, I sip my hot chocolate and nestle into the warm sleeping bag and the reassuring presence of James. I look around at the neatly stocked shelves he has carved and the stitching on his homemade overboots and I rest, contented. High altitude can cut a person down to the basest level of coping. James has a way of making the environment work for him rather than him working to fit it; he has a knack for rendering comfort from the inhospitable.

Between coughing fits, James updates us on the progress they've made up high over the last few days while Jim has been away. But he looks thin and drawn from working too high too long. Even James is wearing out.

I call Jane on the radio for a check-in and to let her know I'll be on my way down soon.

"You with Jim and James now?"

"I'm sitting here with them in the snow cave."

"How is everyone up there?"

"It looks like James has been on a diet and I'm probably looking a little wasted from a hard day." I keep my fingers on the transmit button and glance over at Jim, then say, "And it looks like the boss is the only one better for it."

Jim holds his hand out for the radio. "Jane, this is a day I will not forget. Woody is understating the worst day we've had on this mountain yet. At one point the wind picked me right up off the ground and threw me against her. I know, I know," he laughs, "you think guys are always falling for her." I marvel at the change in Jim as he chats and jokes with Jane, when earlier he had been so broody. *And me too.* The thousands of breaths we drew to the bottom of our lungs, and the firing on all cylinders to get here today, were a sure cure for what plagued us both.

In her standard sign-off, Jane drawls, "Remember, darlings, it's not how you feel; it's how you look that's important—and you look marvellous." I smile over how hard days like this bring out the best in us. *Why else would we do this?*

CHAPTER 13

Small Plans

Two days later, the weather clears and Albi and I head up for a lead shift and to spend our first night at Camp Four. On that calm and sunny day we reach the camp in a record time of five hours. Rather than stay in the snow cave, we resurrect the tent.

Over the last couple of days we have resolved the radio call issue by altering our time zone again by yet another hour to make best use of the daylight hours. During our call that evening, we learn that Dr. Bob has diagnosed Chris with sprained intercostal muscles from coughing so hard, and Dan with pleurisy. The news is a death sentence for their summit dreams. Despite their misfortune, our proximity to the summit shifts Albi's and my mindset from the ground beneath our feet to heady possibilities. As we work together over the next several days, events and speculation shape a plan to go to the summit together.

I lie in my sleeping bag half asleep, 1,300 metres higher than the night before. The wind teases, pelting erratic bursts of snow against the tent walls. What starts as envy for Albi's ability to fall asleep turns into resentment once he starts to snore. With the hope of distracting my busy mind, I turn my headlamp on to read, but I'm too addled by the altitude to concentrate and I give up by the second page. The drifting snow begins to build up, pushing my side of the tent inward and me closer to Albi. I toss and turn, and the combination of the shrinking space between us and the swishing and crackling of my sleeping bag in the cold soon wakes him.

He snorts and rolls on to his side. I whisper, "Albi, are you awake?"

"I am now."

"Want to talk?"

"No, but why do I have the feeling you do?"

I sigh. "I can't sleep."

"I can tell."

"Remember when Charlie and I did that carry to Camp Four on Makalu? God, I felt terrible. I'm not sure how I'll do at higher altitudes."

"Well, we won't find out any bloody time soon if you don't let me get some sleep."

A shot of white light flashes from his watch and he says, "It's all-good-girls-should-be-asleep o'clock. Take a pill." Soon after, he is on his back and snoring again.

I'm too tired to rein in my thoughts, and the memory of my first time near 8,000 metres plays through. My teammate Charlie Sassara and I had carried a load up to our high camp. We were surprised at how strong we felt after a strenuous day of climbing fixed ropes up six hundred metres over steep rock. Although the plan was to turn around once we'd delivered our loads, we decided to stay because it was our first time at that altitude and we wanted to find out how we would do sleeping that high. I woke the next morning with a pounding headache. I threw up after the first brew and couldn't stop retching. Dizzy and off balance, it was all we could do to stand up. We took one good look at the ground above Camp Four before we slid back down the ropes as fast as our sluggish brains and bodies would allow. I was alarmed by how hard it was to think straight and how much extra time it took to check and double check my systems as we transferred from one rope to the next.

I ask myself now, *Why would it be any different this time?* The ground is easier here on Everest than it was on Makalu, I reason. But that offers little comfort.

* * *

Albi's voice pierces my sleep. "Wakey, wakey, sleeping beauty. I'm going outside to dig us out." He rolls me like a log and presses me into the wall to scooch past to the door and get his boots on. I drift back to sleep and wake once more when I hear him shout. "It's a beautiful day out here, totally calm again!"

After he climbs back into the tent, I sit up and reach outside to light the stove in the vestibule while Albi fires up the hanging stove inside. The pot of water we melted the night before is frozen over with a thick skin of ice. He breaks it with a can of bacon and drops it in to thaw.

Kevin's voice comes over the radio. "Good morning to all you campers out there! Anyone up and at 'em yet?"

"Hi Kevin," Albi says, "this is us at Four. You copy?"

"Five by five. How's life above seven thousand metres?"

"Just peachy, Kevin."

"You guys heading to Five today?"

"You betcha."

A raspy whisper comes on. "This is Jim and James at Five. We're out of here and down for a rest today."

"Holy shit, Jim!" Kevin says. "Are you putting on your best sexy morning-after voice, or are you sick?"

"Lost my voice yesterday," Jim says. "James and I had a rough night last night. Couldn't keep anything down. Over."

"This is Dan from Basecamp. Copy?"

"Yep, read you five by five, Dan," Kevin says. "Are you and Chris going to lie low?"

"We're going to take a slow walk up to Camp One and see how it goes."

Jim rasps, "Why not stay in Basecamp and rest for a few days?"

"Cuz I'll go fucking crazy is why."

Albi pulls the can of bacon out of the boiling water. He pours the water into a bottle for us to start drinking and puts the pot back on the stove. Then he upturns the can and a pork popsicle slides out and sizzles when it hits the bottom of the pot.

"This is Jane at Two. Dave and Laurie are headed up to Four today and they want to know if you need anything."

I hold up the empty bacon can and point at it. Albi says, "More bacon, please."

"Copy that," Jane says. "They also asked if there are enough sleeping bags up there for them tonight."

"Yep, Woody and I are returning to Two tonight after we carry to Five. Jim, do you need anything up there?"

"Keep those spools coming," Jim says. "Hopefully you guys can finish stringing out the ropes to Five over the next few days."

"How much do you figure is left to go to reach Five?"

"Maybe three hundred metres—two spools should do it. James and I thought it might be easier to finish it from this end rather than working out of Four." His voice dwindles to a whisper. "But after last night, we're not sure about that. Too soon to be this high. And yeah…we need a snow cave. Lotta work to do. We'll see you guys somewhere on the ridge. This is Five, over and out."

I empty packets of instant oatmeal into our cups and add boiling water, a dollop of butter, and a couple of spoonfuls of brown sugar and powdered milk. The scent of bacon wafts thick and heavy in the confined space of the tent. Albi serves it into our cups on top of the oatmeal.

"Want this? He tips the pot to show me the crispy bits floating in a centimetre of fat. I hold my cup out. "I hope any worries you might have had last night will be put to rest with your appetite for bacon at 7,300 metres, Woody. Just keep eating this way and you'll do fine."

"Yeah," I say, "I hope you're right."

Once we turn the stove off, we start to stuff our sleeping bags and pack food away between bites and gulps of water. Albi mutters and cusses as he rifles through the piles in search of his sunglasses. "I give up," he sighs and flops back on the mess for a rest. A few minutes later he says, "You ready?" I nod at the door then push everything aside. I scooch around to put my feet out the door.

"Aha," he says as he plucks his glasses from where I was sitting. "You hid them on me, didn't you?"

He joins me at the door and between more gulps of water, we bend to put on our boots and strap on our crampons.

I feel sluggish from the sleeping pill I took a few hours before. I lean against Albi and groan, "I don't feel so good this morning." He plucks at my crampon straps, like guitar strings, to check that they are taut then lifts my jacket to look at my harness, and gives me a nod.

In the same breath it takes him to lurch onto his feet and out the tent, he grunts, "Come on, old girl, you'll feel better once you press the pedal down to burn off some of that bacon." He reaches down to give me a hand up, and I look up at him and pause.

"What?" he asks as he waits with his hand out. His face is peppered with spotty growth, flakes of burnt skin and tooth paste lines at the corners of his mouth.

I let out a weak laugh. "You're looking a little rough."

"Yeah? Well, if you haven't noticed, I'm the one on my feet and raring to go. I may not be pretty but I can lift heavy things." I grab his hand and he pulls me to my feet. "Hmm, not so heavy anymore." He puts his arm around me and gives me a squeeze. "Let's hope this weather holds out for us to get up this sucker by your birthday." My birthday is in three weeks, on May 18.

It is calm enough to hear my crampons bite into the snow. Grateful for the ski pole I use as a third point of contact, I teeter through my first few steps before I find my balance. The ridge starts out wide and narrows to an airy catwalk where we straddle the border of Tibet and Nepal with a 1,500-metre plunge off either side. When the ridge grows too narrow, we walk below the knife-edge and push against the sidehill with a ski pole to keep us out and over our feet.

Although the two-kilometre-long span between Camps Four and Five is the easiest ground on the route, it feels like the hardest yet. The effects of the altitude increase exponentially above 7,300 metres in terms of the time and energy it takes to do anything.

Halfway across the ridge we see Jim and James coming toward us. Every dozen or so steps they double over and droop. When we meet, they collapse onto their packs and sit with us for a few minutes.

James brings his head up from his knees and says, "Oh, man, that's a lot of up and down and walkin' sideways. Going by how shitty we felt over there, it sure feels like a heck of a lot more than just three hundred metres higher. One night at Five feels like enough for us right now." He coughs, then turns and retches. We all have that high-altitude hack by now, but some have it worse than others.

Albi and I reach the end of the ropes a couple of hours later. By then the ridge has broadened out again on a section we will call the Football Field. It is easy walking, but we know by now that if the wind is strong enough to blow us off our feet, it could blow us off the ridge, so we run a rope out and walk the remaining distance to get our first look at Camp Five.

A low wall of snow blocks surrounds the single tent that Jim and James have collapsed and weighed down with spools of rope. The handle of the carpenter's saw they used to cut blocks out of the rock-hard snow sticks out from a chink in the wall. Just beyond camp, the summit pyramid—a whole other mountain—rises another 1,200 metres into an ink-blue sky.

On our way back, we see Dave and Laurie appear on the spur, coming up from Camp Two and making their way toward Camp Four. They are already at Camp Four digging out the tent by the time we arrive.

"How'd it go over there?" Dave asks.

"Good, but harder than I thought it would be for such easy ground," I say. "I think I was still dehydrated from coming up too fast yesterday. The new altitude starts talking to you about halfway across, probably around that 7,400-metre mark. We were lucky with the weather, though. Sure glad to be heading down."

"We'll probably do the same as you guys after we haul a load across to Five tomorrow," says Dave.

Laurie points at the tent still half buried in drifted snow. "I can't believe you guys spent the night in that. I went to move in and the tent floor is like a hole. How'd you sleep in there?"

"Some of us didn't," I say.

As I prepare to leave, I give Dave a hug, then Laurie. I hold onto him a little longer and say, "Don't work too hard on digging out that tent, eh? You guys have a long day tomorrow and like I said, it feels hard."

About an hour later, Albi and I arrive at Camp Two in time to catch the tail end of the evening radio call. Kevin and Jane are standing out beyond the cook shelter in order to get line-of-sight reception from Camp Four.

Dave says, "Laurie just gave this place a major remodelling job. He's got a real bad headache and I'm worried that it might be something more."

"This is Dr. Bob at Basecamp. I assume you've got some Tylenol up there?"

"Better than that. Laurie just took a couple of Diamox and is working on downing a couple of litres of water. We'll wait and see how he feels in an hour or so."

"This is Jim at One. How about we keep our radios on and do another check-in at eight?"

An hour later, Dave reports that Laurie's headache is getting worse. Dr. Bob suggests he take some Tylenol and check in again at nine.

We talk among ourselves in the cook shelter as we wait for the next check-in. Kevin says, "Laurie's been up to 7,300 metres several times and is well acclimatized by now. He should be feeling better after drinking all that water, not worse. This is serious. If they wait around any longer he may not be able to walk—let alone get down the ropes. He's got to get out of there while he still can."

Headaches are a common symptom of acute mountain sickness, which we all suffer to varying degrees when we gain a new altitude. But the urgency in Kevin's voice jolts us onto another track of thought. Random as it may seem, we realize Laurie is likely suffering from high-altitude cerebral edema (HACE), a condition in which fluids leak into the cranial cavity and compress the brain. It can be fatal unless the climber gets to a lower altitude immediately. But Laurie is stoic and dismisses it as nothing more than a dehydration headache. Denial and irrational thinking, however, are also symptoms of HACE. Kevin says, "Let's get on the radio."

Barry pre-empts us. "Hello all camps! This is Camp One, can you read me?" Once we all respond, Barry says, "It is the opinion of four high-altitude climbing veterans here at Camp One that Laurie needs to get down—*now*."

"Dave here. Right-o, we're getting suited up. I'm going to accompany Laurie and we've both got fresh batteries in our headlamps. We'll leave our radio on and keep you posted."

Dave later tells us that by the time he managed to get Laurie dressed, out the door and clipped into the rope, he was dopey, confused and unable to stand on his own. Dave draped Laurie's arm over him and they descended locked together for about 150 metres. By then, Laurie's condition had improved enough that he was able to start descending on his own, with Dave checking his rope transfers. Halfway down, Laurie was fully functional and when they arrived at Camp Two, he had no sign of a headache.

The randomness of Laurie's affliction rattles me. If it can happen to the high-altitude veteran who has been to the top of Everest, it can happen to any of us. Had he been higher on the mountain and above the fixed ropes, he could have died.

Jim calls a meeting at Camp One to discuss strategy. In just two weeks we have gone from being ahead of schedule to being behind. He has vowed to bring everyone back alive, and the odds of accomplishing this on the formidable West Ridge are starting to look grim. Our team is wearing down; Laurie's emergency evacuation and Chris's and Dan's health issues, which have hobbled them to the lower camps for the time being, have pushed Jim to propose we change our route from the West Ridge Direct to our Plan B, the Hornbein Couloir.

From the first time we saw the West Ridge Direct route, Albi and I believed the Hornbein was the only viable option for our small team. We assumed time and attrition would make it obvious. But half our team is adamantly against the switch. James is among the protesters, saying he would rather fail trying than compromise. I hear their objections as a threat. I think, *This is going to divide us, and it will be all over if they don't start being realistic.* From high on the mountain, Albi and I rail and argue that the Hornbein Couloir is hardly a compromise. It is a far cry from a hike by anyone's stan-dards. Although Jim is in favour of changing to the alternate route, he doesn't press us for a consensus vote now. *We haven't got time to waste on this!*

In the end, however, it is by honouring the dissent—hearing everyone out, and giving everyone the time they need to let go of the old plan and grab hold of the new one—that Jim reunites us. A few days later, after dinner on our first night at Camp Five, Albi and I hear the radio come alive with an inaudible voice that sounds more like radio static.

"This is Barry at Four. I think that noise was Jim's voice."

"This is Jim," he rasps. "Better now?"

"Yeah," Barry says, "but it sounds like you're not."

"Saw Dr. Bob before he left this afternoon for Camp One. Says I've got laryngitis. Looks like I'll be lying low for a few days to try and beat this, so we'll be down one more climber. Relay to Albi and Woody that we're all on board to switch to the Hornbein now. And ask them if they can start fixing tomorrow?"

Albi says, "We can hear you, Jim. That's good to know that every-one's on board for the switch. Woody and I will try fixing at least one spool. We're down to two."

"That's what I thought," Jim says. "The Americans are looking pretty hungry. I've arranged a trade of food for rope."

Albi says, "Sounds good, Jim. Unless anyone has anything else to say, it's nighty-night for us." He tosses the radio on top of my sleeping bag and asks, "You and Laurie gained six hundred metres of vertical and fixed, what, a kilometre in three days?"

"Maybe so," I say, "but that was all below 7,300 metres in perfect weather conditions. Look how slow we moved across the ridge today and we were just walking."

"There's not much technical ground through the Diagonal Ditch," he says, referring to the long gully slanting upward above Camp Five toward the North Face. "So stay with me here. Our window for the summit bid is May tenth to twentieth, ten days from now. Three teams split a thousand metres between them, each fixing two spools per shift. That's doable. So in an ideal world, we've got six days of work left before we're ready for the summit."

"I think you're being overly optimistic."

"Perhaps, but then I've factored in four days of compensation for the altitude and weather. Even if it takes us the full ten days, that puts us right on schedule. Dwayne and Barry are right behind us, so we can safely assume they'll be the first summit bid team given they've been working together for some time now and Dwayne has the most experience above eight thousand metres."

"Okay," I say. "Sounds like a plan. Barring any miracles, Dan's out with whatever he's got. Laurie's out, Jim's out with laryngitis, and Chris surely won't be able to work high with the state of his ribs. So, as it is now, that leaves you and me; then Barry and Dwayne, who are right behind us; and a third shift of Dave, James and Kevin to cover those six days of fixing."

With the anticipation of starting up new ground the next morning, and our first night at Camp Five, I take a sleeping pill to get a good sleep. But it never kicks in soon enough, and I find myself hovering in the in-between. Pinpricks of light, like stars, fade in and out of sight.

Two years ago, close to the day, our Makalu team stood at Advance Basecamp staring hard and long into the night at a place 2,700 metres above our heads for the faint twinkle of headlamps. Dwayne and Carlos had moved up to Camp Five the day before. They started their summit bid the next morning at 3 a.m. Twelve hours later, Carlos was in the lead when he discovered the body of a Czech climber who had hunkered down on the ridge two years before. The grim reminder and late hour turned them around one hundred vertical metres from the top. That small distance over easy ground to the summit, but above eight thousand metres, could have led them to the same fate. Their descent seemed endless. Exhausted and hypoxic, building anchor after anchor, rappelling pitch after pitch, became a fight for their lives. I grew still as I watched, overcome by a powerful prescient thought, *That fight will be mine one day.* Ever since, I had sensed I was on an inexorable course toward that same nightmare, benighted on an eight-thousand-metre peak. Although I am safe now, I feel haunted. I follow those pinpricks of light into sleep.

When I open the tent to empty my pee bottle the next morning, I notice a cloud cap on Nuptse and a distant roar, indicating high winds aloft. I scrape the frost off the walls and prepare breakfast while Albi nurses a headache. The thought of bacon triggers an instant gag reflex, so we stick to oatmeal and force it down. We pull on our insulated one-piece suits for the first time, and I am first out of the tent, trussed and ready to go.

This time, I offer Albi the hand up. "Come on, old boy. What do you think, shall we start and get out of here at the first sign of that wind dropping down to this level?" He groans as he pushes himself to his feet. "I take that as a yes?"

It is the last time we will talk to one another until the end of the day. Knowing how wind can come up suddenly, we collapse the tent when we leave it and weigh it down. I load a spool into my pack while Albi slides the other one onto a broken ski pole for me to run out.

Within fifty metres I am climbing diagonally up and across loose shale and snow on the North Face. New ground pulls me on and distracts me from all else but my goal to run out the rope and search for the next point of solid rock to build an anchor. The wind picks up a bit over the next couple of hours, but I give it no further thought, as this is the norm not the exception. I am maybe 150 metres out now and focused on hammering another pin in, when a deluge of spindrift knocks my goggles off my face and me off my feet. I hear a shrill whistle over the wind and look down the line at Albi, who is waving madly at me to come back. Then he disappears behind pulsing streams of spindrift. I scrabble to my hands and knees, tie the end of the rope to the pin and start back across the face. Between ever-increasing gusts and the rock that skitters out from under my feet like loose shingles, I stagger toward Camp Five.

I find Albi sprawled atop the tent, which flaps rapid-fire as he shoves our belongings into his pack. Snow crystals sandblast my face and the wind slaps at my hood as I crawl around pinning the tent down with snow blocks. A jacket plucked from Albi's grasp shoots upward, whips sideways and is gone. Once packed, we lean headlong into the wind in retreat.

Hours later, Barry and Dwayne pull us into the snow cave at Four. They cover us with sleeping bags and fill us with tea. I look over at Albi and say, "So much for our small plans."

CHAPTER 14

The Meeting

May 6: Camp Two

BARRY AND DWAYNE MOVE from Camp Four to Five the following day. Instead of fixing ropes on their high shift they exhaust themselves building an igloo to ensure we have shelter that will withstand the kind of wind event Albi and I had just experienced.

Twenty-one days have passed since Laurie and I first sat atop the west shoulder. We thought then it would take less than a week to establish Camp Five at the other end of the ridge, but in the end it takes three weeks. The storms have grown worse and closer together. Our bodies are breaking down, and Kevin, James and Dave have all been forced to take sick days. We have now been on Everest for fifty days—too high, too long—and the ravages of altitude are outstripping our hard-won acclimatization. Less than half our team can consistently work at Camp Four or above.

Although we were all aware of the high attrition rate on eight-thousand-metre peaks before we came to Everest, all of us but Dr. Bob and Jane came aiming for the top. We knew that everyone would not summit, and those who did would get there only by all of us throwing everything we have into the pot. By now, we know that Albi, Dwayne, Barry and I are considered the team's best bets for the summit because of how consistently we can work above 7,300 metres and remain healthy. Albi and I are a tight team, as I assume Barry and Dwayne are by now, having worked together for the last ten days as well. The team planned to make our first attempt by the tenth of May, but the route up the mountain isn't ready. I am beginning to doubt we will be able to pull it together.

Jim has called a meeting to discuss our strategy for preparing the upper camps and timing for the summit bid teams. Albi, Dwayne, Barry, Jim and I meet at Camp Two on May 6, when our rest and work rotations intersect. It is another stormy day. The light is muted, the wind a constant. Snow patters and metal zipper tabs tick against the drum-taut tent walls. I find Dwayne, Albi, Barry and Jim in the cook tent, clustered around the radio for the morning call.

Jane bustles, cooking bacon, flipping pancakes and filling pots with snow and mugs with hot water. She stops to listen when Dave's voice crackles over the radio. He is waiting at Camp Four for Dan and Laurie, who are coming up from Camp Three. Dave reports that he spent the night alone battling spindrift that kept blocking the entrance and trapping the poisonous off-gases from the stove. Jim grips the radio. By the end of the call, he tells us the meeting is postponed until the boys are down safely.

I sit amidst the others, yet lost in a dismal world of my own making. I stay in the cook shelter as long as it takes to force down a pancake before I slink out. Jim follows me and motions me to join him.

Perhaps Jim has noticed my awkwardness in the cook shelter: he is perceptive and checks in with me periodically to ask after my well-being. I feel a flush of shame and wonder what to tell him as we huddle with our backs to the wind. But he has something altogether different in mind.

He holds out his package of throat lozenges. To suck on a candy whenever we have to breathe hard or talk has become necessity, especially for him. "There's talk that Annie and Todd are ramping up for the summit," he says. "I think you should go on the first bid— with Dwayne."

I stagger backwards as if he has just taken a swing at me. I cross my arms and blurt, "That's not the plan! It's been obvious for weeks now that Dwayne and Barry are a unit. They're on their way to Basecamp for a rest and I'm slated for another shift up high with Albi.

There's no one else ready or in place to work with him. This isn't a race, Jim. It's a team effort. Just let it play out."

"It has played out and you four have risen to the top. You're the obvious ones for the summit bid."

I wrap my arms around myself. "The timing isn't right, Jim."

He grasps my arm. "Just hear me out. Dwayne can still go down for a rest. Barry can rest here and replace you in two days—so you can rest."

"Have you talked to anyone else about this?"

"Just Laurie. He agrees. He thinks you should go for it. But—I can't be seen as favouring one person over another, particularly you."

"Oh, that makes me feel special. So why team up with Dwayne rather than Albi for first bid?"

"Dwayne's a different case."

"What's different?"

"You know the story. There's an unpaid debt from when he gave up his turn for the summit on the '82 trip and he's got the most experience up high. Besides—" His voice fades into a whisper. My thoughts race to catch up to all that he has said. "This isn't about Dwayne," he continues. "It's about you—and something way bigger."

I think about Albi and all the conversations we've had to piece together our plan of going second—together. "No, I don't feel right doing that," I say.

He pulls me in. "Part of our vision is to make history. We can do that—by putting the first woman from North America on top of Everest. It's been a part of the plan since you joined the team."

"No, our vision was to climb a harder route in good style, and if I happen to be one of the climbers who is in the right place and right for the job, then so be it."

"Well. Guess what? You are. Here's our chance to realize the other part."

I turn to face him. "'The other part'"—I stab out quotation marks—"was just a way to attract a sponsor." I have made sure to quash any special status since the beginning of the trip to avoid alienation.

"None of us have given it any further thought or mention. Thank goodness." My gaze drops to our feet, toe to toe in the same purple plastic boots—his twice as big as mine.

Jim grasps my arm. "This is what I'm trying to tell you. I've been very careful to never single you out, to treat you as an equal, and to expect no more, and no less. And if we're talking about seeing how things play out, you've earned this chance through merit. You're strong and an obvious choice for a summit team."

We stand in front of a cache of supplies covered by a tarp. An avalanche probe, strung with a Canadian flag, marks its location in a snowdrift. It leans as if tired, bowing and swaying as the flag whips in the wind. I say, "How would you propose the switch at the meeting?"

"That's the tricky part. I can't say anything at the meeting. You guys are going to have to work it out among yourselves."

"Right," I snort. "I can hear myself now: 'The plan has changed, boys. It's my turn to go to the top.' Not happening!"

"What if Annie gets there first?"

"Then good on her. Like I said, it's not a race. We'll get there when we get there."

Jim says, "We might not get a second chance, let alone a first one." The flag snaps overhead. My gut leaps as the ground drops out from under me.

"I'll think about it." Now I really can't face the others in the mess tent and I plod back to my own tent, heavy with conflicted thoughts. *A man in this same position wouldn't dither like me.*

I wake sometime later to Laurie, Dave and Dan's voices and the crunch of snow as they pass my tent on their return from the upper camps. But I remain in the tent, staring up at the ceiling. Sometime later I hear someone approach and then Laurie's voice.

"Hey, Sharon, you awake?"

"Yeah."

"Open up. I just want to say hi before I head down to Camp One." I sit up and unzip my door. His smile vanishes when he sees me. "You okay?" he asks.

"Oh, yeah, just tired is all. Sounds like you had a rough night."

"Yeah, effing cold up there. For some reason"—he looks over his shoulder and then back at me, and lowers his voice—"Dan wouldn't let me spoon with him like you did." I can't help but crack a smile. He squats down and keeps his voice low. "What's with you? Jim told me to come over and talk some sense into you. He said something about you being too nice and that you'd tell me what that means."

"Hmm, I've never been accused of that before. I don't feel nice."

"What's wrong? You should be happy that you're going to the summit with Dwayne."

If I can't understand, then how can he? "I think I'm just exhausted, and I don't know how to handle this."

"Handle what—saying yes to an opportunity of a lifetime?" His eyebrows shoot up, then he narrows his eyes and looks straight into mine. "Listen." He sets his lips in a straight line across his broad face. "Remember what I told you about recognizing your turn when it comes around? Jim and I aren't just telling you to go for it because you're a woman, Sharon. These expeditions are a karmic playground and you've got a lot of allies here. This is as close as it gets for a turn to be handed to you on a platter. Hell, you and Dwayne have been through a lot together and I think you'd be the strongest team for the job."

Dan shouts, "Hey, Laurie, we're out of here. You coming?"

"Yeah, just give me a second!" He reaches in and puts both hands on my shoulders and plants a cold wet kiss on my cheek. Then he rocks back on his heels, springs up and shouts over his shoulder, "Take it!"

I arrive last to the meeting. Dwayne, Albi, Barry and Jim are sitting on the benches, chatting idly. Jane is there too, ostensibly to mind the stoves. Albi flashes a smile at me and pats the seat beside him in invitation. Everyone grows quiet. The air crackles with anticipation. Thoughts throng in my head. Laurie's voice whispers, *Take it!* Another voice counters, *Who said anything about it being your turn to take?*

Jim says, "So, who's going to start? His eyes tick on each of us, ending with me, and he gives me a barely perceptible nod.

In the instant I hesitate, Barry begins. "What have we got with the extended permit now, Jim? Until the 25th?" Jim nods. "That should be enough to get two teams of two to the top, maybe more. We've got what, four more days of fixing to reach Camp Six? So, Dwayne and I figure, given the higher altitude, there are two shifts left above Five."

Albi says, "Providing this storm breaks, we'll head up tomorrow. Then Dave, James and Kevin can replace us. Chris is going to give it a shot too, so that should set you and Dwayne up for the first bid, and give Woody and me a chance to rest before our turn. How many days do you think you'll need for the first bid?"

"I figure four days," Dwayne says. "One day to get to Camp Four, the second to reach Five, the third to Camp Six, which will hopefully be as high as eighty-two hundred metres, and then on the fourth day we attempt the summit. Regardless of the outcome, we'll be done by then. No rest to be had at eight thousand metres. We'll need to get as low as possible that same day."

"Do you think you'll start using oxygen?" Albi asks.

Dwayne says, "We don't know yet; it'll depend on a bunch of unknowns."

Jim remains passive, as he told me he would. I feel impotent and alone with my knowledge of our talk that morning. Jane's eyes meet mine to say she is listening and with me. Just as I thought, the plan was already too well established to change now. We discuss what will be required to support two people at Camp Six: one bottle of oxygen per person per day, one tent, 150 metres of the lightest rope we can find to fix through the crux and six canisters of fuel at minimum.

Jim interjects, "And there must be a team in place at Camp Five ready to help the summit team in case there's trouble—or it's no go."

The meeting is over. Paralyzed with regret, I watch the others file out.

Jim is waiting for me outside. Mute with self-defeat, I watch my feet rearrange the snow. "Woody, what's with you?" he says. "Do you know what you're doing? I thought you had decided to step up! I told you I couldn't do it for you."

Allison Andrews climbs below me on the first pitch of Air Voyage at Lake Louise in 1985. *Pat Morrow photo*

The 1984 Makalu West Ridge Team, left to right: Charlie Sassara, Ken Bassett (expedition doctor), me, Dwayne Congdon and Albi Sole. The upper part of our route is directly behind Albi, half in shadow. *Carlos Buhler photo*

I lead the first pitch of Bourgeau Right-Hand in the Canadian Rockies in 1985. *Pat Morrow photo*

The 1977 Mount Logan Canadian Women's Team, back row, left to right: Kathy Calvert, Lorraine Drewes, Judy Sterner, me and Diana Knaack. Cathy Langill is in front. *Photo courtesy author's collection*

— Everest Light Route
Nepal/China Border

A   Makalu
B   Lhotse
C   Hornbein Couloir
D   Nuptse
E   Diagonal Ditch
F   Everest
G   Western Cwm
H   Changtse
I   Headwall
J   Khumbutse
K   Rongbuk Glacier
L   Lingtren
M   Rongbuk Valley

0   Basecamp
1–6   Camps

Everest Light Route. *Google Earth; Image Landsat / Copernicus, US Dept. of State Geographer, Image © 2019 CNES / Airbus, Image © 2019 DigitalGlobe*

The Canadian Everest Light Team: Standing, left to right: Laurie Skreslet and Kevin Doyle. Back row, left to right: Barry Blanchard, Dan Griffith, Dwayne Congdon, James Blench and Dave McNab. Front row, left to right: Jim Elzinga, me, Chris Shank, Albi Sole and Dr. Bob Lee. Jane Fearing is missing from the photo. *Courtesy of the Continental Bank*

We are the first team to arrive at Basecamp in the pre-monsoon season of 1986. Mount Everest is fifteen kilometres due south at the head of the Rongbuk Valley. The American Great Couloir team and Spanish Northeast Ridge team will arrive a few days later. About forty of us will occupy the Rongbuk Valley. *Jim Elzinga photo*

Albi hefts a box onto our cargo trucks in Lhasa, bound for Basecamp. *Jim Elzinga photo*

Yaks shuttle approximately two tonnes of our supplies the first six kilometres to Camp One. *Team photo*

A view of Everest from Camp One. Our route winds through the penitentes (ice pinnacles) of the Rongbuk Glacier to Camp Two which is located at the bottom right end of the north face. *Jim Elzinga photo*

A team member walks up the Rongbuk Glacier between Camp One and Camp Two. *Jim Elzinga photo*

Team members walk down the glacier at 6,000 metres. Camp Two is hidden in a hollow, centre page, near the lowest point of the rock face. Our route follows the left-hand edge of the rock to gain the snow arête (spur) above. *Jim Elzinga photo*

Dr. Bob prepares to operate on Dwayne's sore throat at Camp Two. *Jim Elzinga photo*

Jane makes pancakes in our kitchen shelter at Camp Two. *Jim Elzinga photo*

Chris Shank shows the ravages of the sun and altitude. Many of us wore light disposable surgical masks to protect our airways from airborne silt down low, and at the higher altitudes, to retain moisture in the arid and often windy climate. *Jim Elzinga photo*

Team members carry loads on the headwall above Camp Two. *Team photo*

A climber carries a load on the spur above the headwall at approximately 6,300 metres. *Team photo*

Kevin Doyle is near Camp Three talking into one of our massive radios. *Jim Elzinga photo*

Team members are on their way down the West Ridge and nearing Camp Four at 7,300 metres. *Team photo*

Dan is left of James at Camp Four at 7,300 metres on the West Ridge. *Team photo*

A view from around 7,200 metres shows the 1.5-kilometre-long stretch of ridge we follow to reach Camp Five at the base of Everest's upper pyramid. *Jim Elzinga photo*

The summit bid meeting is held in the Camp Two kitchen shelter. Left to right: Barry, Dwayne (hidden behind Barry), Albi and me. *Jim Elzinga photo*

Dave McNab climbs at 7,700 metres across the Diagonal Ditch above Camp Five. *Sharon Wood photo*

We reach the summit at 9 p.m. *Dwayne Congdon photo*

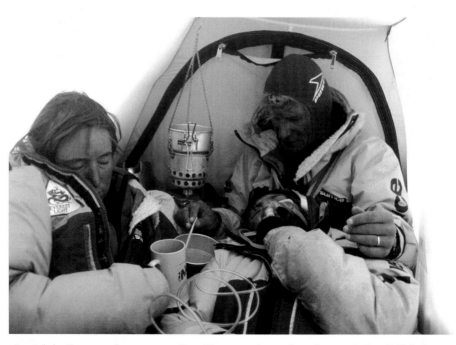

Laurie helps Dwayne and me recover at Camp Five on our descent from the summit. *Dan Griffith photo*

Kevin, Jim, James and Barry (left to right) are delighted to hear from Dwayne and me that we are twenty feet from the summit. *Chris Shank photo*

My son Robin, in utero, and I pose with Canmore's Three Sisters in the background. *Barbara Woodley photo*

My son Robin is five years old on a family climbing day in Cougar Creek in Canmore in 1995. *Colleen Campbell photo*

My son Daniel is twelve years old on this scramble up Schaffer Ridge in Lake O'Hara in 2004. *Pat Morrow photo*

I stare at our boots and mumble, "When could I have said anything? Like I told you, there was already a plan."

"What do you mean? I gave you the perfect cue!" I think back to the nod he gave me as I watch his fingers roll a lozenge. "Come on, Woody. Stop being so Canadian! So polite! What's the difference between Americans and Canadians?" He doesn't wait for me to respond. "Americans are always first! Here's your chance to make history. For us—and for Canada!"

I glance over my shoulder and see Jane poke her head out of our tent and shoot me a look. I meet Jim's eyes and say, "I need to go think about all this."

The air whooshes out of my sleeping bag when I flop onto my back in the tent. Jane peers at me. "Well? What's going on with you and Jim?"

I look up at the ceiling and sigh, "He told me to quit being so Canadian."

"What the hell does that mean?"

"He urged me to speak up and tell the guys I want to go on the first bid with Dwayne." I pause, bracing myself for Jane's shock over such an idea—her disapproval.

But instead, she leans over me to pry my eyes off the ceiling. "Go on, I'm listening."

I explain Jim's rationale, and Laurie's pep talk about this being as close as is possible to being handed my turn on a platter. As I tell her, it's as if I'm hearing it for the first time—and clearly. "Oh, Jane, I guess what I'm really trying to say is, I think I blew it by not stepping up. I just didn't think it would play out like this."

"Do you really think you've made a mistake?"

I draw a deep breath through my teeth and sigh. "It's too late now. It's done—settled. Isn't it?"

Jane rubs the bridge of her nose. "Okay, let's talk this over. Who's to say you don't deserve to go first? You've worked as hard as anyone, if not more—that much is obvious." She pauses. "Albi will understand. He can make the second bid with Barry. I thought you said the chances of success are better on the second bid, once everything is in place. He'll be okay with that."

I sit up. "How do I tell them?"

"You don't tell them. You *ask* them. Don't do it as a group; ask them one at a time. You start with Dwayne because he's the one who has to agree to climb with you. If he doesn't, it's a dealbreaker, right? If Dwayne says yes, then you go to Barry, and then Albi. What's the worst that can happen? You won't be any farther behind than you are now if they say no. In fact, if they do say no, it might make it easier in some way." Marni had applied the same reasoning to asking my teammates if I could join Everest Light. Why must I ask for permission again, but this time to go to the summit first? It doesn't seem fair. Jane says, "You're dithering," and gives me a nudge. "Don't hesitate. Go *now!*" And she shoves me out the door.

When I ask Dwayne if I can speak to him, he unzips the door, pulls an extra sleeping pad out from under him and pushes it to the other side of the tent to invite me in. I crawl inside, pull my knees up against my chest and wrap my arms around them. "Why is it that we have only climbed together once on this trip?" I ask.

He pops a cough drop into his mouth. "I don't know." He clears his throat. "I guess it's just the way things worked out."

"This is awkward," I begin. "Before I tell you what's on my mind, I need to know if you have any objections to climbing with me."

"Of course not. Why do you ask?"

"Jim had a talk with me this morning before the meeting and he thinks I should go with you on the first summit bid."

"Yeah, so?"

I blurt, "I want you to tell me I should join you on the first summit bid."

"I can't tell you that. But I'm okay with it if Barry is."

Next, I go to Barry's tent. Without hesitation, he says, "Go for it, Woody. I'll be here till August if that's what it takes. Besides, I owe you one." He reminds me that I took his place to help Dwayne complete the packing while he went off on his honeymoon. My heart pounds and my mind reels over what I'm setting in motion as I leave him.

I stall at the door of Albi's tent, having left the hardest conversation for last. "Hey Albi, can I come in for a minute?"

"Sure, more than a minute if you like." I open his door to see him curled up on his sleeping bag, smiling up at me. His smile fades when I don't reflect it back. Albi bolts upright. "Uh oh, what's up?"

I climb in and get settled. I can't meet his eyes. "Albi, I've decided to go on the first summit bid with Dwayne." I glance at him and wince.

"What!" Albi falls back onto his sleeping bag and cradles his head in his hands. He sighs. "I thought something was amiss between you and Jim." He shakes his head, still gazing at the ceiling, "Fucking Jim. That conniving bastard!" He looks through me, as if I've already ceased to exist, and says, "Well, I guess you've got to do what you've got to do."

"I'm so sorry." I unfold myself and leave as carefully as I can so as not to break anything else.

Steam billows out of Jim's tent when he opens his door. "Quick, get in." He is bent over a steaming pot with a jacket over his head, breathing in the moisture as I tell him what I have just done. "Great. Can I assume, then, that you'll head back up with Albi for a couple of days tomorrow?"

"If he'll have me."

I return to the tent, stunned by how I've just upturned our world. I go over each conversation I've had with the boys with Jane because it seems an event has not completely happened until I tell her.

* * *

After waiting out another storm at Camp Two, Albi, Dave, James and I set out to carry to Camp Four. I'm last in line, trailing behind Albi to the bottom of the ropes. He clips his ascender onto the rope and looks at me. "Come on, Woody, quit sulking. It's time to get back to work. It's the mountain, not our little plans, that will run this show."

When I arrive at Camp Four, James waves me over to the tent and says, "Albi and Dave are in the cave. You're bunking with me for the night." I crawl in and flop down on the sleeping bag James has fluffed out for me. As he hands me a cup of tea, James says, "Having fun yet? Just think, I could be handing you a cold beer about now in Yosemite Valley. Yep, we'd be in our shorts and t-shirts settling back into our lawn chairs."

"Dreaming about being in just that place is my favourite pastime these days, James."

"But you know what we'd be dreaming about if we *were* in those lawn chairs?" James pauses while the wind gives our tent a good shake. "Our next Himalayan expedition, that's what!" He laughs. "Dreaming is more than half the fun."

"You're not kidding."

We all carry to Camp Five the next day where Dave and Albi will stay to work in lead. But Albi falls ill the next night with a stomach ailment and descends to Basecamp to recover. With no one else rested enough to take Albi's place, I remain at Camp Five to work with Dave.

I remember what Albi said to me two days ago and am relieved when the mountain takes charge. It is easier when all there is to do is work and not give up.

Dave and I work two days fixing six hundred metres of rope through the remaining distance of the Diagonal Ditch, across downsloping shale and cross-loaded gullies, and all the way to the beginning of the traverse across the North Face. The cost of our effort becomes apparent by the end of that second day when Dave notices a black spot in his left eye's line of vision. He reports his symptoms over the radio that night, and Dr. Bob, suspecting Dave has suffered a retinal hemorrhage, tells him to get down as soon as possible before any further damage is done. Dave tosses the radio aside and drops his face into his hands. The next day, Dr. Bob confirms the diagnosis and Dave is confined to Camp Two and below for the rest of the expedition. With no one in position to replace Dave, I descend with him.

It will take ten days instead of the four we had hoped to prepare the mountain for a summit bid. Over that time the Spanish team quits when their high camp on the North Ridge is decimated in a storm. In addition, a few members of the American team, worn down from the altitude, leave for home. Every time a team quits or a member gives up, they take with them a part of our resolve. I am afraid that most of my teammates, having lost their personal chances for the summit by now, will want to follow. But perhaps the Spaniards know what a toll deserting at this time can take on those who remain, because they choose to wait out the rest of the time on their permit at Basecamp to cheer the remaining Americans and us on.

The Spaniards' sportsmanship, and news that Annie and Todd are planning to start their summit bid any day now, spurs our team. Our loyalty to the vision is still stronger than the pull homeward, which surprises me given how beaten up we feel by the altitude and weather. Despite the pain Chris suffers with every breath, he makes three carries between Camp Four and Camp Five. Against Dr. Bob's advice, Dan makes several more carries to Camp Two. And the chronic laryngitis that hobbles Jim focuses his fierce determination to lead from behind. But poor weather and a shortage of supplies and manpower at Camp Five postpone the next shift above Camp Five and the American's attempt on the summit is delayed as well.

Just days before, I had thought I'd lost my place on the first summit bid team when I had to go back up for another high shift. But with the storm forcing everyone off the mountain, I descend to Basecamp. While the delay is disappointing, I will get a rest and perhaps be ready if the mountain gives us a chance.

CHAPTER 15

Glory or Death

A MONTH HAS PASSED since I was last at Basecamp. As Dave, Jane and I step onto the floodplain, we breathe in a pungent earthy scent. The brown grass we camped on now looks like a golf green.

The courier arrives after dinner that night. Dressed in jeans and a leather jacket, and green with nausea, he nearly falls out of the jeep when we open the door to greet him. We help him with the mailbags and steer him into the mess tent, where we give him a cup of tea and a couple of Tylenol. Soon after, we are slouched in our favourite boxes with our feet up, tearing into the packages, magazines, newspapers and letters he's brought, and savouring the luxury of news from the outside world.

I open my Mom's letter first. Tears well in my eyes at the sight of her impeccable cursive script. I can feel her fingers stroking my head, hear her melodic voice reading *Grimm's Fairy Tales* and smell her homemade apple pies fresh from the oven.

"How's my girl?" she writes. "It seems like yesterday when you climbed your first mountain with your dad. I remember how he suited you out at the army surplus store. I had no idea it would lead to this!"

I was eighteen and long gone by the time my parents finalized their divorce. I believed my mom got the short end of the stick. At the age of fifty, she faced starting a career with a resumé filled with chores and children, while my dad enjoyed a full and liberated life. So in an act of sisterhood, I moved into her little place in West

Vancouver for a winter, camping on her hide-a-bed sofa. It was not that she had invited me but I knew I had to be there for her *and* for me. And in that short time we spent together, I came to know her as a woman of pluck and class. She never uttered a negative word about Dad. She rose from the wreckage and up the ranks of her new job to executive assistant in a national firm. It has been long since I thought she was *the* queen, but she will always be *my* queen. And although she can't fathom what I'm up to, she always made me believe I could do anything I put my mind to.

Next is Dad's card, which makes me smile. On the front is a picture of mice, each one dressed in a little jacket and top hat, or dress and apron, in a tree with houses on every limb. "Dear Mouse," he begins, "I thought you would get a kick out of this card…" He writes that he and his partner Peggy are travelling and checking Reuters newsfeeds every day for updates on our progress. "Who thought my mouse would climb Everest one day. I did! We're both so proud of you."

Albi shatters my reverie when he says, "Uh-oh, Woody. This isn't going to make you happy." He is perusing the latest pile of newspaper clippings.

"What's that?"

He holds up the newsprint page, which reads in bold letters: *2 Women in Everest Foot Race.* There, side by side, are head-and-shoulders pictures of Annie and me. The caption under Annie's photo reads, *Annie Whitehouse: Buhler's partner* and under mine, *Sharon Wood: no grudges.* I snatch up the article and read it:

The siege of Everest is a race between two nations, two women and two ex-lovers. Carlos Buhler, former boyfriend of Burnaby native Sharon Wood, is helping a U.S. woman, Annie Whitehouse, race Wood to the top.

The winner will be the first woman in the western hemisphere to stand atop the world's highest peak…

"This can't be happening," I croak. Jim has been careful to keep tight control over what information is released to the media, but obviously someone has leaked our pathetic soap opera to the press. I bolt out of the mess tent and up to the memorial cairns, where I slump down and drop my face into my hands.

Albi arrives a few minutes later and sits down beside me. I feel his arm slide around my shoulders, and we sit together and listen to the shouts and laughter from below where the Spaniards are playing soccer. We watch as they steal the ball with deft swipes, kick it, chase it and dodge around one another. They cheer and raise their fists in victory as someone scores a goal.

"Oh, Albi, am I being a drama queen?"

"Not really. I'd be right pissed off if someone did that to me, but I'd probably hit him or smash something."

"Remember the last time when we sat like this on top of a moraine?" I ask.

"Oh, yeah," he says as his voice softens, "I sure do. We were at Advance Basecamp on Makalu."

On that day, Carlos was exhausted and shaken from his and Dwayne's near miss in joining the dead Czech on the summit ridge. He blamed Charlie and me for his failure because we stayed at Camp Four after carrying a load instead of descending that same day. I couldn't understand how we had impacted his summit bid, but then I rarely understood Carlos. He moved out of our tent and wouldn't talk to me for days afterward. I was beside myself with guilt and grief, and Albi comforted me.

"I regret that patch job I did," Albi says. "It worked so well that it got you two back together again." "Yeah," I sigh, "I regret that too." I brighten for an instant. "Remember what we did right after that, when we trundled those giant boulders?" Albi and I pried and pushed refrigerator-sized rocks off the edge of a steep sidewall of the moraine and watched with glee as they barrelled down three hundred metres to crash into the boulders on the valley bottom. "God, that felt good!" I laugh, then instantly sink back into despair.

"Let it go," he says. "This is the price of fame, my dear. And you better get used to it, because this is just a little warmup for worse to come." He nods at Everest. "Once, and if, you reach the top of that, people will be looking under your skirts for whatever dirt they can find on you. It's not that bad, really. You think it is because the news is about you. But news is like scenery and readers are like passengers on a sightseeing bus. You catch their eye as their bus rolls by and then they drop you for something new that comes into view."

I snatch the article out of my pocket and read a line aloud: *"The winner will be the first woman in the western hemisphere to stand atop the world's highest peak."* I growl, "This makes me mad enough to want to be the winner. If for no one but myself."

"Atta girl." He peers at the clipping. *"No grudges,"* he reads. "The best revenge is to be classy about this sordid business."

What he says ignites a fire in me. *The article is already written, and I don't have to take it so personally. What is the point of worrying about it when it takes so much from me? And Carlos is merely an obstacle—an obstacle that I alone have the power to transform.*

* * *

Albi and Kevin leave for a high shift the next morning, and I spend the following three days eating and sleeping as much as I can. The day before I leave to go back up the mountain, I'm rifling through my pile of stuff sacks, examining each item I plan to take, and rereading my letters and journal entries one last time. Packing feels different this time—now I wonder who will pack up my personal belongings if I don't come back.

I put that thought aside for the moment and smile when I discover an unworn pair of birthday undies and imagine them giving me superpowers. As my dad often said, "It's what's *underneath* that determines strength and beauty." I throw the Tuesday undies in my pack, planning to slip them on before I leave Camp Two for the summit. When I finish packing, I wonder if I should talk with Jane in case I don't make it down, or write her a note and leave it in my journal under my sleeping mat. Talking to her seems too melodramatic, and in the end I do nothing.

I choose to walk alone on the final trip back up, going the long way to pass through the Spanish camp to say goodbye to the caballeros. The Spaniards assure me they will stay for a few more days yet and come to our victory party. From their camp, a straight line to the trailhead leads past the American camp. I usually skirt wide around it, but the Spaniards tell me that Carlos is on the mountain, so there is no need to avoid it. On my way through, I find Todd Bibler sunbathing on a rock in just a pair of iridescent tights and mirrored glasses. He lolls his head as I stroll by and says, "So, you're off to the summit?"

"Yep."

"Glory or death," he drawls and then rolls his face skyward again.

"Thanks."

Camp gossip has it that Carlos caused a rift between himself and his teammates when he pressed them to designate a new leader—him. Apparently, Annie has moved out of Carlos's tent and into Todd's— and she and Todd are due to start their summit attempt any day now. That possibility, and Todd's cavalier blessing, spurs me on.

My walk back up to Camp One becomes a ritual. I am acutely aware today of this ground I have passed over so many times. I know its features as intimately as I might a lover's: the patch of silt where I leave the imprint of my boot sole every time; the sound of my shoes on bedrock, on gravel, on ice; the slot between two boulders that echoes back my passage; the halfway rock I rest on or, at the very least, run my hand over as I go by. Will I see all this again, and if so, will I experience it differently? What will this mountain make of me or take from me?

I am nearing the final rise to Camp One when I see Carlos standing atop the moraine, watching me. I feel a momentary catch in my step, my breath—a bracing—and then a release. An unthinking, unplanned sense of calm guides me through the time it takes to reach him. I glance at the pack at his feet, which is loaded with his sleeping bag and a sleeping pad strapped on the outside. *Is he leaving?* When I raise my eyes to meet his, he says, "I just thought I'd tell you that I believe that you and Dwayne have the best chance of anyone I know of pulling this off."

I have forgotten how Carlos can be my champion. I drop my

shoulders and shrug my pack off, letting it drop to the ground. "I don't think we've got a chance, Carlos. There's no high camp in place. We're all so tired."

He looks at me with the most intense gaze, listening to me as if what I am saying is the most important thing in the world. He understands me in a way no one else ever has. I have forgotten this until now. "You've got to believe in yourself, Sharon. You've worked really hard for this. I've seen you on so many climbs. And from everything I've heard, you're going strong. I know you can do this! I'm going to stick around as long as I can to cheer you on. Good luck up there."

"Thanks. We'll need all the luck we can get and then some."

"Be careful." He opens his arms and I step in.

* * *

That night at Camp One, Albi reports that he and Kevin have fixed eight hundred metres of rope in a single-day effort to reach the base of the Hornbein Couloir. It is the biggest push yet on our expedition, and the last of our rope and our efforts to prepare the route.

Jane tells us that Colleen, Dwayne's partner, has arrived at Basecamp. Jim banned all visitors over the last few weeks to protect us from illness or disruption, and he asked her to wait until Dwayne had left for the summit bid before she came. It is a comfort to know she is with us, as she was on Makalu. As much as I've missed her on this expedition, I have long since seen the wisdom in Jim's decision to bring Jane instead. He is right that there is no room amidst a team and an objective like this one for the exclusive intimacy that couples share.

The next day, Jim, Dan, Dwayne and I walk to Camp Two together. Another system blows in, bringing with it a few squalls. My thoughts are as mixed as the weather. When it grows dark and daunting, I retreat into my hood and think, *We haven't a chance of pulling this off*. When it brightens, my thoughts turn. *I can't believe my luck; I've made it onto a summit team!*

CHAPTER 16

Commitment

May 17 to 19, 1986

THREE DAYS OF STORMS take us to the edge of the window we have to make our summit bid. The constant drone of the jet stream pounding against Everest grows stronger each day, and we grow weaker waiting for a break in the weather. The delay scrambles our small plans once again.

Kevin has recovered enough from his last big push with Albi to join James in climbing in support of Dwayne and me. Even though Kevin and James have lost their own chances for the summit by now, their commitment at this time in our long siege when everyone must be thinking of home astonishes me. Barry steps forward too, despite knowing he has his own summit bid to rest up for in four days' time.

May 17: Day 1

A lenticular cloud hovers over the summit pyramid. With no time left to wait, we choose to begin, hoping that the weather will improve by the time we are in place at Camp Six in three days' time. In four days, successful or not, we will have played out all our time and strength and will descend in order for Albi and Barry to move into place.

In early afternoon we shoulder our packs. Jim comes out of his tent to see the five of us off. As we lean in for a huddle to hear him, he rasps, "I've got one piece of advice for you that might help keep you alive. Treat this like any other mountain. It's not worth dying for."

We all know that climbers have made irrational decisions to stand atop the world's highest mountain—and died because of it. I know he is warning us to not allow this mountain of mountains to skew our judgement, though he himself has put aside his family, his job and four years of his life for this expedition. No one would do that for any other mountain, nor would any one of us have pursued a summit for so long. I sink under the burden of our teammates' hopes.

We step into the wind at the top of the headwall. Barry insists that he take the lead to preserve Dwayne's and my strength for the summit. The rope is buried beneath drifts of wind-hammered snow that have set like cement, and Barry stops every few steps to wrench it free. Then, for the rest of the way to Camp Four, he'll fall to his knees to recover and repeatedly rise again to fight his way a few steps higher.

Halfway up, we stop at our abandoned Camp Three to check in with one another. Barry, James, Dwayne and I hunker down on the lee side of the snow wall to wait for Kevin, who is coming up last. We don't speak, to spare our breath and raw throats. I fish for the string of the watch around my neck and pull it out to look at the time. We have been going for five hours already—twice as long as our best time to this point.

My gaze is pulled to the plume of airborne snow seething over the summit and spilling down the North Face, which makes my stomach lurch as if in sudden free fall. Everything is telling me to turn back, including Jim's voice that whispers, *Treat it like any other mountain, treat it like any other mountain.* Dreading worse to come, in my mind I am already up there, days ahead and hundreds of metres higher, inside that maelstrom.

I watch Kevin below as he leans into the wind and still it lifts him and slams him against the face. He struggles to his feet only to get blown over again. His battle mirrors ours. It is the worst day yet, and I am sure we will turn around soon. If we do, it will be over for Dwayne and me, and our retreat will put a serious dent in the team's resolve. I wonder too why Kevin has volunteered to support Dwayne and me. We haven't climbed a single day together on this expedition. Once one of the strongest, Kevin is now the weakest among us today. The cost of that last push with Albi had finished him. So why is he here now? He seems angry, or is it fed up? I read it as resentment for my having taken Barry's place in the order of summit bids. Or am I just losing my mind, thinking this way? Are his motives simply noble?

When Kevin finally arrives, instead of joining us out of the wind, he stops a couple of steps downhill. He plants his feet wide to brace himself and then looks at me and yells over the wind, "Well, what are we waiting for?"

"Jim told us to treat this like any other mountain," I shout. "I wouldn't be out here in these conditions if this was any other mountain."

Kevin yells, "To hell this is like any other mountain. This is fucking Mount Everest! I didn't spend all this time working my ass off to come this far and turn around. Look at me, I'm the worst of the lot of you and I'm goin' on!" Then he pushes a shoulder into the wind as if to shove it aside, clips his ascenders onto the next rope, punches them upward and steps into the lead.

As I watch Kevin pull ahead, I resign myself to a new reality: we will keep going until we physically can't. I drop my face into my hands and feel James's arm slide across my shoulders and pull me in to let me know I'm not alone. Then we follow in Kevin's willful wake.

It takes ten hours to climb to Camp Four. My heart sinks when I discover Dwayne and Barry have moved into the tent together, leaving the snow cave for Kevin, James and me. I keep watch for James, who pulls in a distant last—just after 10 p.m. The wind swipes at his pack as he shrugs out of it. He pushes it toward me, and I grab a strap and pull it through the tunnel entrance into the cave. When James doesn't follow it in, I poke my head outside to find him doubled over, coughing and retching. He falls to his knees and holds his hand out to keep me back as he vomits. Once he is in the cave, Kevin and I peel off James's puke- and ice-encrusted balaclava and strip him of his insulated oversuit before we get him into a sleeping bag with me. Kevin's face is flushed red in contrast to James's waxy grey pallor. Glassy-eyed, James shivers uncontrollably and his teeth chatter. Kevin mans the stove while I help James sip hot fluids. Between spasms of coughing and retching, James lapses into an unfocused lifeless stare. Kevin and I exchange glances and wrestle with the unspoken question: should we get James down while he is still conscious—keep him moving? Or wait out the night, praying he will recover?

I have never seen James so helpless. He has often been the one to look after me when I get into camp. Through that fitful night, we watch over James like fretting parents over a sick child. We check to see if he's worsened each time we wake, and to our relief, he finally falls asleep toward the end of the night.

May 18: Day 2

Once, on a day filled with hope, I had dared to dream I would turn twenty-nine atop this twenty-nine-thousand-foot peak. But on this morning of my birthday, I don't give the significance of the day a second thought.

Although James is weak, he is strong enough to be his stubborn self and insist that he can retreat without our help. We watch as he descends the first couple of ropes to be sure. He keeps his feet under him as the wind kites him across the slope to the limit of the rope's arc and stretch. Soon we lose sight of his frail form as he dissolves into the blizzard.

Sometime on this day or perhaps the next, we learn that Annie and Todd started their summit bid and retreated when Todd fell ill at a higher camp. Then Annie made a second attempt with another teammate, Andy, but they turned around as well: too windy, too much avalanche hazard. Everyone else has given up. *What makes us think we can still do this? What will it take for us to turn around?*

The skies grow calmer through the day, but still, rogue gusts taunt us. We reach Camp Five late that afternoon. The only sign of it are the two snowdrifts that conceal the igloo and tent. Dwayne and Barry start digging them out while I search for the cache to find food and fuel for the night. I find six fuel cartridges. *Not enough!* I think, and I call Dwayne and Barry over. Dumbstruck and slow-witted from exhaustion and hypoxia, the three of us stare at the six canisters lined up on the ground. Not enough to last us tonight and tomorrow.

I thrust my hand out and say, "Where's the radio?" Dwayne pulls it out of his inside jacket pocket and hands it to me. I grip it possessively as I raise Jim.

"Did you make it to Five?" Jim asks.

"Yeah, but where are the fuel cartridges?"

Jim tells us that Chris brought some up on the last carry.

Albi comes on the radio from Camp Two and confirms, "There were a bunch when we were last there."

Jim adds, "Then there should be enough, somewhere else."

"Well," I say, "there aren't."

"Look around."

"We have."

"Count again."

I snap, "We can count to six! Isn't it obvious we have a problem here?" Dwayne and Barry back away as I unravel.

Dan's voice comes on. "Sharon, I hear you've got six cartridges, right?"

I stomp and pace. "Come on, guys, this bid is off. I'm done!"

Kevin arrives and Barry nods his head toward the igloo, where they are sleeping for the night.

Dan says, "Just stay with me here, okay? Have you counted the ones on the stoves?"

"No, but—"

"Okay," Dan speaks slowly. "Albi says that he just replaced a canister on one of the stoves before he left the other day. So at least one is new. That makes seven. You'll use two tonight, at the most. So at the very least you'll have five cartridges left for Camp Six."

Barry, Dwayne and I stand together with our backs to the wind.

They tilt their heads back to peer out at me from under their hoods. Barry holds out his hand to ask me to surrender the radio.

"Thanks, Dan," he says. "I think we've got it sorted."

I drop my head and rub my temples. "Guess I lost it there, eh?"

Dwayne smiles and rolls his eyes upward. "Just a little. I guess."

Barry laughs, clasps my shoulders and shakes me. "Just don't let it happen again!" He speaks into the radio, "Jim, so yeah, we're all here now."

Now painfully aware that I have just behaved like a child having a tantrum, I walk away to calm down. I didn't expect Dan, who has lost his chance for the summit and is kilometres away, to step up as he did. Will I look back at my actions twenty years from now and feel proud of my part in this expedition as Dan, or anyone else, might? Dan's example shifts my perspective: this is not just my climb—it is the whole team's climb.

* * *

Dwayne and I lie on our backs, staring at the ceiling of the tent. Any movement feels as if it is in slow motion and takes a monumental effort. I wave my arm in front of my face, as I used to do to check out how high I was after dropping acid, and sure enough, it jerks across my field of vision in a series of delayed still-frame shots. In silence, I hold up our dinner options of freeze-dried chicken stew or ramen noodles. Dwayne points at the noodles. At this altitude, we have no appetite: we eat for fuel and sip warm water for our headaches, waiting for the stove to melt enough snow to get us through the night.

The blood in my head thrums to the count of my pulse. Every breath of air and word uttered aggravates our dry throats, causing us to cough constantly. We speak little and in single sentences between breaths.

"Kevin looked pretty wrecked this afternoon when he pulled in," Dwayne says.

"Think he'll have the guns to make it to Six tomorrow?"

"Hard to say if any of us will."

We drift in a state that erases time. The tent walls suck in and push out with the ebb and surge of the wind. I pull an envelope from the top flap of my pack. The sight of my mom's perfect cursive handwriting makes me smile: *Do not open until May 18!*

"What's that?"

"Birthday card from my mom," I say.

"Oh shit, I forgot."

"No worries, my mom didn't." *Ha*, I think, *too bad I feel like I'm turning eighty-nine rather than twenty-nine.*

I doze off when Dwayne slips out of the tent, and then wake when the door zipper rips open and an oxygen cylinder thuds down on top of Dwayne's sleeping bag.

"Let's party," he says.

I sit up, turn off the stove and look at Dwayne, who is grinning. He shrugs and says, "I found a bottle that might have belonged to the Yugoslavs and it won't fit our mask system. Someone may as well use it."

We hadn't planned to use oxygen during our ascent but we've brought some in case of an emergency. I question the wisdom of climbing above eight thousand metres without it. But by now we are pulling out all stops, and the plan is to turn the oxygen on tomorrow for the first time.

Dwayne cranks the valve open and oxygen hisses out into the confined space of the tent. Within a few minutes my head clears. The lines and colours grow sharp and vivid. I feel a smile crease my face and my fatigue lifts.

Dwayne says, "Good stuff, eh?" He pulls out the radio and speaks into it. "Okay, Jane, hit it." And a chorus of voices sings me "Happy Birthday." We leave the oxygen on just long enough to know what we are missing.

The boost of oxygen and a sleeping pill put me to sleep. I have never used oxygen before and am heartened by the difference it makes. We plan to carry two bottles each, enough for both tomorrow and summit day if used sparingly. But will it make up for the extra weight on our backs?

May 19: Day 3

The sleeping pill takes me through half the night. I wake, mulling over questions and doubts. *How hard will the rock climbing be through the Yellow Band? Can I climb technical ground above 8,500 metres in sub-zero temperatures with a heavy pack on my back? Will I be able to climb off the end of the ropes tomorrow after I have become so accustomed to the security?* Surely one of us won't make it through yet another night above 7,600 metres. By the way Kevin dragged himself into camp yesterday, I am convinced he won't have the strength to carry to Six. *How will Dwayne, Barry and I carry over 120 kilograms of gear and supplies for Camp Six and beyond between the three of us? Camp Six doesn't even exist yet. Where will we put it?*

Blowing snow has drifted in overnight and packs in between the wind barrier and the tent. The walls judder under the hammering wind. When I punch through a snowdrift to look out, I see Kevin already outside divvying up loads. I don't know what to expect anymore, but to see Kevin first out and ready is the last thing I imagined. He paces between the four piles he has started, checking each item for weight and bulk. Stunned, I watch him for a few minutes as he dumps a food bag into one pile and picks up a tent from another.

When Kevin notices me, he straightens and looks me in the eye with a fierce intensity. "Well," he says, "I don't know about you but I'm going on till I can't. What's the worst thing that can happen to us by trying?" A gust knocks him off his feet. He scrabbles to his knees as it tears at him. "Fucking hell is what this is! But if I turn around now I'll be wondering for the rest of my life whether we could have done it." *He's right. We can at least go to the end of the fixed ropes.* That would be a kilometre. We have to at least try after all we've done to get here.

Later, we stand mutely looking at the piles of gear. Barry plucks the radio out of his inside pocket and hands it to me with a knowing smile. More interested in lightening my load, I pause. The radio will be useless once we leave the ropes. If anything goes wrong, it will be everyone for themselves if one of us is in trouble. Rescue is not an option at eight thousand metres. So I reason, *Why bother with the extra weight of the radio?* I just want to chuck the thing, but the expectant look on their faces reminds me that the rest of our team is connected to this radio. I'm not thinking straight. I turn it up to full volume and tuck it in next to my body to keep the batteries warm and alive.

We pack up, each piling oxygen bottles on top of tent parts, sleeping bags and mats, stoves and pots, ice axes, hammers, snow stakes, pitons, ice screws, rope, two full water bottles each, and personal gear and food. I drag my pack up my leg and balance it on my knee, slip one arm through the strap and swing it onto my back. Then I slip my other arm in and stumble backwards under the weight. Our loads are the heaviest they've been yet. *This weight could finish us.*

I slide my oxygen mask over my mouth and nose and open the valve on the regulator to a two-litre-per-minute flow rate. If everything functions perfectly, a single bottle at that modest flow rate will last us ten hours. It takes all I have to shift my weight from one foot to the other, let alone make forward progress. Whether the low flow rate, the heavy load or exhaustion is the problem, I am alarmed at how poor my balance is. We each use a ski pole as a third leg to push ourselves out from the uphill side of the traverse and to help keep our weight directly over our feet. To push myself away from terra firma on a thirty- to forty-five-degree slope with more than a 1,500-metre drop below my feet is counterintuitive. Instinct urges me to lean into the slope. But when I do, my feet skate out from under me and the fight to stand up again on the loose down-sloping shale wastes too much energy. The more I push myself out from the slope, the harder the wind tears at me.

We climb one behind the other as we move up the Diagonal Ditch. Glimpses of the boys ahead of me wash in and out of view between gossamer sheets of snow. Spindrift avalanches pour down the face, streaming off our hoods and shoulders. Shrouded in three layers of one-piece suits, hoods cinched and face covered with bala-clavas, masks and goggles, I feel like I am in my own cocoon. My sole focus is on the next step in front of me. Each shove from a gust and each jolt from a slip or a deluge of spindrift exacts a cost I can't afford. Calm is the only way through. But I know we are moving too slowly; all it will take to turn us around is for one of us to say we've had enough. I'm convinced we'll turn around once we reach the end of the ropes.

I am in the lead when we exit the Diagonal Ditch and climb out onto the vast expanse of the North Face. Jane's voice wafts up from inside my jacket, cutting through the thunderous din of the wind. "We've spotted them! We can see two, no three, coming out of the rocks onto the face!"

I halt to pull the radio out from inside my jacket, and the boys and I huddle around it to listen.

"This is Bob at Camp One. Looks like all four are on the snow now and clear of the rocks."

Jim says, "Thanks, we see them now."

"Hi," I croak, "we can hear you guys."

We hear cheers. "Way to go, guys!" Jane says.

Jim says, "How's it going up there?"

We look at each other and I hand the radio to Dwayne. He slips his mask off and says, "Slow, but it sounds like you guys think we're getting somewhere."

"You're going to do it!" Jim says. Other voices come on and I understand that they have divided into three different viewing parties at different vantage points. I envision some of them at the cache site over two thousand metres below, passing the binoculars back and forth; another group taking turns looking through the tele-scope at Camp One; and others peering through Dr. Bob's telephoto lens mounted on a tripod at Camp Two. That is all I need to know. They are watching us. They are with us. I step away and rest my load against the slope to ease the strain on my shoulders. For the first time in what seems a long time, I bring my head up to take a look at the world beyond my feet. The sight of Dwayne, Barry and Kevin bent over the radio, their faces lighting up as they listen to our teammates, lifts me out of myself. I marvel at the difference in our perspectives. Ours is a plod from one foot to the other; theirs is convinced we are going for it. Our teammates' voices transform what feels like an exercise in futility into progress. At well above 7,900 metres now, I lean back and look out from higher than I ever have before.

Barry and I are the first to reach the end of the fixed ropes near the entrance to the Hornbein Couloir at eight thousand metres. We take off our packs for the first time that day and clip them into the anchor. I feel so light I could blow away and am glad for the anchor to hold me down. I peer up into the deep gash that cleaves the North Face. Shaped like an hourglass, it starts wide and narrows to a body width before it fans out three hundred metres higher into a yellow band of rock. Spindrift cascades down and funnels through the narrows. Surges of flotsam spurt out the bottom, dispersing into rock-peppered spray that whistles by our heads.

I think of Tom Hornbein and Willi Unsoeld, who pioneered this route. Guided by a single black-and-white photo, they traversed the North Face to the base of the couloir and left their ropes behind them. They must have stood close to this same spot we are in now, looking up at the very same sight. I remember Tom's first impressions: "The prospect of entering the gully was too much like becoming tenpins in a high-angle bowling alley."

I put my head down, force my thoughts away from what lies above and bend into the task of unravelling a spool of rope into usable portions for the next day. Grateful for the distraction, I wrestle the kinks and tangles into coils while Barry turns the spool. Suddenly Barry shouts, drops the spool and flattens himself against the face. Trapped in my sluggishness, I freeze in confusion. Then, over the roar of the wind, I hear the telltale sharp cracks of rockfall, as startling as gunshots. A flush of adrenaline snaps my head upward as a barrage of rocks the size of basketballs barrels down the couloir. They explode against the walls and are heading straight for us. There is nowhere to hide. I grab Barry and tuck in beside him beneath our hanging pack. My body flinches as the rocks thud into the face nearby. I watch them hit, bounce, fly and vanish, along with countless irretrievable heart-beats, into the airy abyss below. Numbed and spent, we say nothing and resume our task.

Minutes later, Dwayne pulls in and Kevin drags in soon after. Kevin's body heaves with each ragged breath as he slumps over his pole and ice axe. He is out of oxygen.

Dwayne, calm and unaware of what has happened minutes be-fore, says, "Well, what are we waiting for?"

In a brief glance between us, Barry and I opt to not tell them about the near miss. There is no room for drama—and in any case I used up my quota over the cartridges. Now, I am stoic and all busi-ness.

"Right, then!" Barry says. He hefts his pack onto his back, unclips from the last of the rope and starts up.

I lean back against my pack, slip into the shoulder straps, roll onto my hands and knees and push up to stand. I leave my pole clipped into the anchor, unclip myself and start picking my way up the rock-pitted and wind-strafed face. Ironically, the craters from the rockfall I step into are like stairs, which eases my straining calves. The face steepens as we move up into the outwash of the couloir. We thrust the shafts of our axes into the slope for a sense of security but that is all it provides. Now, with no fixed rope, we are tenpins at the mercy of a rock that finds its mark, or a gust of wind or an avalanche that sweeps us off. But, I reason, we have all survived and thrived in these unforgiving places before. We won't fall—can't think about it. Although each move upward takes me closer to what I have feared for years: being benighted on an eight-thousand-metre peak, I don't entertain this thought because I can't afford to. Instead, each step upward is a step in numb resignation, a new normal I would never accept on any other mountain.

As if conjured by a malign presence, spectral veils of spindrift envelop us. Pulses of ice and rock, beaten and tumbled into sugary grains, stream down the couloir and hiss as they part around my boot tops. This, I think, is John Lauchlan's kind of day out. John was a friend, a talented, committed and visionary climber who defined a new generation of bold alpine climbing. He used to say, "Go big or go home," and he would have bared his teeth to this mountain as if it were a blustering adversary. I can imagine John now, his eyes narrowing behind his pop-bottle-thick frosted aviator glasses and his wiry body leaning hard into the fight. But John went big on a solo climb several years ago and didn't go home. I feel his spirit with us now.

Fatigue and oxygen starvation make me feel detached from all that is happening, and time is suspended. I have lost all sense of how long we have been climbing when Barry stops. I wake as if from a trance. We are in a small bay below a steep rock wall off to the side of the couloir. It is only when I see an old oxygen bottle, some splintered tent poles and pieces of tattered nylon sticking out of the snow that I understand why we have stopped. I recall our plan to camp for the night and it snaps me back to attention. I nod at Barry and we both start chopping into hard snow to set anchors and get our packs off our backs.

The view between our feet and the valley floor disappears into roiling snow. When I stand up straight and extend my arm, I can touch the face in front of me, which makes it about forty to fifty degrees. With no ledges to be found anywhere, we start to chip a platform into the face that is big enough for a small tent. We have forgotten a shovel, and without it the task will cost us hours. But we find one in the first few minutes of our excavation, which would seem miraculous anywhere else. Nothing surprises us anymore, and we pick it up without comment and keep digging and chopping.

There is only room for two of us to work at the same time, so we take turns resting with Kevin. In his all-or-nothing style, he cranked his oxygen to the full flow rate of eight litres per minute this morning and ran out halfway through the day. Now he sags, folded over his knees, sides heaving—spent. He has given his all to us even though he knows his chances to summit are over. Years later, I will apologize for saying nothing then—I didn't have it in me. And he will say, "It's just what I do, Woody. It's what we all did. The whole team gave our best."

Kevin and Barry stay longer than I thought they would to make sure we are well dug in. Our teammates will tell us later that they saw them start climbing down at 9 p.m. Dwayne and I watch them briefly as they descend the ground we worked so hard to gain, but we have nothing left for sentiment. We do know that regardless of the night ahead of us, and our dwindling chances, we cannot turn around tomorrow morning without trying. We owe them at least that for their commitment.

We work into darkness. Dwayne climbs into the tent to get the stove going while I stay out to tighten, check and recheck every attachment of the tent to the mountain. I prepare leashes for us both and clip them to an anchor for insurance. A scenario plays through my mind: a hit in the night, our tent swept off the face and us dangling in our harnesses off these anchors. I need to remain outside and occupied rather than give my imagination idle time to spin worst-case scenarios.

Once I climb inside the tent, we radio the rest of the team. Dwayne wheezes and coughs before he speaks. "We've just sort of got ourselves thrown in here. We're kind of cold—pretty breezy still—still a factor as to how things might go tomorrow. Everybody did a fantastic job—put out lots of energy. I hope we get a shot tomorrow."

Jim says, "You will get a shot tomorrow. Just remember, you've got to want it more than it wants you." We startle as a rush of snow spills over our tent.

"Well," Dwayne sighs, "I tell you, we put up with a lot of pain today to give it a shot."

"That's why you'll get it."

Laurie comes on from Camp Four. "How's Sharon doing?" I am relieved to hear his voice in the mix.

"She's hot."

James says, "It's a pretty long birthday climb for her. We'll gab later, Dwayne. I hope you feel all the good energy we're sending up to you."

Jane comes on from Camp One. "How are you guys up there?"

Dwayne hands me the radio and I tell her, "We could be better."

Dan says, "You're supposed to have a plastic thingy over your face right now."

"We just got the stove going and I don't want to blow us up. That would be embarrassing."

"How's Dwayno?" Dan asks.

"About the same. He's got cold feet. He can't decide whether to fill his water bottle to warm them up or have a hot drink."

"How's the wind?"

"Real strong."

"No protection, eh?"

I tell them we have the tent tied down so tight we aren't going anywhere. "It's bombproof." But that vision of us hanging from our harnesses keeps playing through my imagination.

"Are you guys comfortable?" Jim asks.

"It's all relative, I guess."

Dan comes on. "You guys have the O's on?"

Small sharp teeth gnaw inside my temples. "We're using it when we can. It's a contest between the oxygen and the stove. The oxygen is working excellent, except Kevin's bottle gave up a few pitches below the Hornbein."

Jim asks, "Is that why he was so slow?"

"We were all going slow because the wind was beating us around and we figured we were carrying thirty kilos each."

"The main thing is, you did it. You got up there."

I turn my headlamp on to look at Dwayne lying on his back staring into the void, his face swollen from surface edema. I sigh. "It's going to take a wonder to make men out of us again."

Jim reminds us to keep hydrated and get a good rest. He suggests he spot for us the next day through the telescope from out on the glacier near Camp Two. He can help guide us to the safest, most direct route to the summit once we exit the couloir.

I hand the radio to Dwayne and pop another lozenge. Dwayne says, "Yeah that would be helpful, Jim."

"With any luck, it'll blow itself out tonight." Jim's voice fades to an airy whisper.

A part of me can't believe we are talking about still going on. By the way I feel and Dwayne looks, I think we'll need a lot more than just the wind to die down. I can't imagine how much strength we will need to simply stand up, let alone climb unroped six hundred metres higher over the hardest ground yet to reach the summit.

Laurie must be reading my mind when he comes on from Camp Four. "Even if you get no sleep tonight, with oxygen you'll be okay. In '82 we climbed nine hundred metres on our last push to the summit. I know it's more technical ground, but you're only six hundred metres from the top. If you're feeling lousy, crank up your oxygen for five minutes at a time to get a richer flow. It makes a big difference. The fact that you've got oxygen might make up for the lack of sleep tonight."

"Look," Jim says, "I know you're really tired and you've had a hard day, but don't let that get you down. You guys are in a real good spot. Be positive about what you've accomplished."

Dwayne says, "Thanks a lot, Jim. We need to hear that. We're pretty psyched, or we will be as soon as we go to bed with our oxygen masks on."

Jim says, "Be proud of what you've done and if it happens tomorrow, it happens. There's no sense worrying about it tonight. Just relax and get some brews in you, collect some O's and tomorrow will take care of itself."

Dwayne sighs. "Yeah, it had to be done."

"It had to be done and you did it. You've got everybody down here beaming you up as much positive energy as they can."

Dwayne falls back on his sleeping bag. "Well, we'll get an early start and even if the wind is up, we'll see what happens."

It must be close to midnight by now. When we first discussed our summit bid, "early start" meant 1 a.m. But with our long day up to Camp Six, we still have hours before we'll be rehydrated.

Recovery is impossible at 8,200 metres above sea level. No one can survive at this altitude for long. We estimate that we have twenty-four hours to get up and get down to a lower altitude before our time is up. Our oxygen will help, but we only have a partial supply for the night and one bottle each for the summit push. Even as acclimatized as we are now, we know that vital functions steadily deteriorate.

Death is imminent.

Bile rises in my throat at the thought of food. My stomach is shutting down. We both fear if we eat anything that we will throw up and lose even more energy and fluids, but we need fuel and force down a few raw cashews and some chicken noodle soup. We know we must drink as much as possible. We turn the stove on and off through the night, alternating between its off-gases and water, and oxygen and dehydration. It's more apparent than ever that we and the stove compete for the same oxygen.

Spindrift avalanches pour over the tent and fill the gap between the outside tent wall and the mountain face. We punch the wall back in a fight for space but the buildup of snow is winning, reducing our space and pushing us closer to the edge of our platform. My consciousness drifts. A faint twinkle of Dwayne and Carlos's headlamps in the night on Makalu stalk my memory. I sit up and turn my headlamp on to banish the eerie sight. Dwayne lies covered in a fine layer of frozen condensation and spindrift that has pressed through the walls and small openings. I'm relieved when he stirs and the white shroud cracks and slides off. His eyelashes are white with frost. We don't need a thermometer to know it is minus twenty or thirty degrees.

We talk in abbreviated and disjointed fragments between dozing and waking through the night. Dwayne asks, "Are you going to wear two one-piece layers under your down suit or will that make it too tight?"

"Yeah, I tried that last time I was at Five and I couldn't move very well. Do you think we should try our one-piece insulated suits over our down suits?" Small details can make the difference between success and failure, right down to a suit that even slightly constricts the thousands of moves we'll make that day. Once we're out there and moving, changing our clothing layers won't be an option.

I say, "Think I'll wear a mitt on my left hand and a glove on my right. You know, for a combination of dexterity and warmth?"

Time slips before I hear his voice again. "How long do you think it'll take to get up to the Yellow Band?"

"Maybe an hour?" I top up the pot with more snow. "I don't think it's that far, and there's no changing our minds once we start up." I repeat the advice Annie gave me: "Trend right at first even though it looks harder. Don't get sucked into the weakness on the left side of the Yellow Band."

"Yeah," he says, "that jibes with what Todd told me. Better not blow it. Guess we'll solo to the narrows, eh? Whoever gets there first can stop and wait if we need to rope up."

Sometime later, I wake up gasping. A sickly green flame sputters above our heads. "Are you awake?"

"Sort of. I don't know what you call this state, but I'm hoping it's rest," he murmurs. "I'm thinking we should take all the pitons we've got."

Every time we turn off the stove for a few minutes and turn on our oxygen, the conversation starts to make more sense. I ask, "What time do you think we should turn around?"

"Let's take it one step at a time."

"How much rope do you think we should take?"

"I say we take all of it. I coiled about 150 metres or so."

"What's your strategy for the O's?" I ask.

"Turn it on for the first few minutes when we start, to get moving and get warm, then turn it off to save it until we get to the Yellow Band."

"Dave says it will last ten hours if everything works perfectly," I say, "which is hardly likely."

"Yeah," Dwayne says, "those valves freeze and the flow is inconsistent."

"Do you think we'll even be able to get out of this tent in the morning?"

He doesn't answer.

CHAPTER 17

Summit Day

May 20: Day 4

THE SAME TACIT AGREEMENT that has brought us this far, to keep going until we can't, pushes us out of the tent this morning. Dwayne leaves first at 9 a.m. I sit at the threshold with my top half inside the tent and my feet outside. The door flap whips and slaps at me as I strain, bent over my four layers of insulation, to reach to my boots. Hands that seem not my own fumble to fasten my crampons. A stream of spindrift pours over my legs and I pull back to wait until it passes. I chant to myself, *Be calm, be patient.*

Aware of the fatal consequences of the smallest oversight, I cinch the straps with meticulous care over the two layers of overboots. One loose crampon could send me on a one-way trip down the North Face. At the very least, a strap come undone could cost me my hands. The glove on my right hand and the mitt on my left hand are working as a combination so far, and I pray neither one will have to come off until the end of the day—or tomorrow. Bare hands for even just seconds can freeze, rendering them useless. No hands—no way to get down.

When I jerk forward and rock to a stand, the radio slips off my lap and skitters toward the edge of the platform. I catch it with my foot. An ache throbs to the pulse in my head when I bend over to pick up the radio. I peer up to see Dwayne fade in and out of sight behind sheets of spindrift. He reappears a little higher as if moving in single frames, roughly spliced, like in the old black-and-white films. Thirty metres above him, the strip of snow he follows tapers into the narrowest part of the couloir. Another thirty metres above that, and as if a curtain is lifted, a sudden solid patch of yellow rock looms—the Yellow Band.

Dwayne said he'd take it slowly so I can catch up. *Is there any other speed at 8,200 metres?* I zip the tent shut, wondering what state it will be in when we return—if we do.

The slope in front of me is pitted with rocks and craters, and the snow varies in consistency from ice to Styrofoam. I convince myself that the odds of a rock hitting me are slim. I kick one foot and then the other, dagger the pick of my axe in the snow and press my other hand against the slope for balance. Anywhere else I could stand up without my hands, but this high, with such poor balance, I can't. I aim to find a rhythmic flow to my movement but instead I stop and gasp after each step. My lungs fill and empty, but still I feel desperate for air. I cannot close the gap between Dwayne and me.

The couloir deepens, and narrows to a body length. Carabiners and strands of frayed rope dangle from pitons on the steep walls that flank me. The height of the pitons tells of more snow in previous years. *Spooky*, I think. The place feels haunted. I know men have fallen here—died here. Last year, a team of Australians and New Zealanders led by Peter Hillary attempted the couloir. Peter told me he was climbing up behind his team when suddenly one of his mates clattered past and disappeared out of sight below. Minutes later, Peter watched in horror as another climber cartwheeled past him. Peter and his team went home.

But I think of Tom and Willi, who succeeded with heavier gear. I have read the passages in Tom's book over again and again looking for information about the route, but he reveals more about his heart and mind than about specific technical details. Tom has given me what I need—a friend and a mentor in spirit—rather than what I wanted. When he heard we were attempting to climb his namesake route, he sent a telegram wishing us well. That means more to me than he can know.

Rocks whistle by my head, stirring my sluggish thoughts into a frenzy like a startled school of fish. My gut recoils as a rock cracks, explodes and ricochets off the walls. *I'm in a shooting gallery.* I keep moving because Dwayne is up there, yet I realize with dread that each move upward is another step we will have to take to get back down—and in what state of awareness?

I bend forward to disconnect the batteries to my electric socks—now that my feet are warm I want to save the batteries for when I will really need them, at the end of the day—and my oxygen regulator dangles into view. The needle hovers over the zero. The near miss with the radio at the tent had distracted me and I neglected to turn my O's on, which I hope explains my slow progress.

The Narrows is a vertical chasm maybe six metres high and less than an arm span wide. Back at the tent we thought we might rope up here, but Dwayne has gone ahead. With no sign of him or a rope, I assume it must be all right. In anticipation of the burst of exertion ahead, I check my oxygen flow regulator. It is still at zero. I thought I'd turned it on. How could I have forgotten again? I turn the dial to two litres per minute and start up. I press my back against one wall of the Narrows and my feet against the opposite wall to wedge myself in. I push with my feet, wriggle my back up, lever my body and push again to inch my way up like a caterpillar. My body is jammed so tight into the crack that if I slip I won't go far. It is the most secure I have felt over these past two days and the need to concentrate has squelched my mind chatter.

As soon as I reach the top of the Narrows and resume the monotonous steep plod up the final patch of snow, the internal chatter resumes. Then I hear Jim's voice hiss over the radio, "We just spotted one of them on the snow patch below the Yellow Band." *That must be me! They're with us!* And then a few minutes later I pull in beside Dwayne at the base of a steep rock wall of the Yellow Band.

"How's it going?" Dwayne asks.

"Slow," I say breathlessly. "Here." I fish the radio out of my jacket and hand it to him. "Jim's in there."

I tug my watch out and am surprised to see it is noon. If it's taken us three hours to climb less than a hundred metres of easy ground, how long will it take to climb the harder ground above?

Dwayne glances at me for confirmation when he tells Jim that we are going to keep going. I nod.

"Good luck," Jim rasps. "Remember, ya gotta want it more than it wants you!"

Dwayne signs off and turns to work on an anchor he's started. He scratches at a crack with his axe pick to check its depth and chooses a piton from the cluster hanging from his harness. The pitch above is the hardest yet and, by any standards outside of where we are, is unjustifiable without a solid belay. I think, *Just a few pitches of mixed rock and snow and we'll be above the crux—it'll just be a steep walk from there.*

I study the fractured rock cross-hatched with veins of snow and ice, looking for where best to begin, where we can place pitons and a route through. I am rehearsing the moves I'll need to make but my mind refuses to believe, morphing the cliff into a maze of dead ends. *I can't do that.*

I recall what Tom said to his teammate Jim Whittaker, who spoke with him by radio from Basecamp on the other side of the mountain: "There's no rappel points in the Yellow Band, Jim, absolutely no rappel points. There's nothing to secure a rope to. So it's up and over for us today." His words haunt me; it won't be up and over for Dwayne and me today. In order to get back down, we have to find anchors and rappel points where Tom and Willi did not.

I can't visualize rock climbing in sub-zero temperatures, with crampons on my feet and a fourteen-kilo pack on my back, and at an elevation above 8,300 metres. But what I can easily imagine are several good reasons to turn around—reasons that anyone will accept: we are out of time, spent and in unsafe conditions. I turn to deliver my this-isn't-our-time speech, but Dwayne thrusts the end of the rope at me and says, "Your lead?" He must know what I am thinking. *Bless him,* I think, *we're in this together and he's got to get me in the game.* I accept his gift of confidence and tie into the rope.

Dwayne is anchored to the rock and prepared to give me a make-believe belay. We both know the rope will not hold a fall; the setup is only strong enough to descend on. Instead of climbing rope, we are using a static cord. It's slightly thicker than a bootlace and will snap under an abrupt load, sever over an edge, or it won't absorb the shock of a fall and will pull the anchors out.

I crank my oxygen regulator up to a four-litre-per-minute flow— the highest yet—as Kevin's voice echoes in my mind. "What's the worst thing that can happen to us by trying?" Dwayne's confidence, the oxygen, Kevin's prod and a doable plan to make three moves upward are enough to get me started. The alternative, to fail without trying, will leave me wondering until the end of time if we could have done this. *If the climbing is too difficult,* I tell myself, *I can still back down.*

Dwayne hands me the carabiners loaded with pitons and says, "On belay." *Just three moves. Then I'll know.* My focus narrows to a single action at a time. I reach up to probe the depth of an edge and pull down to test it. I tease my crampon points into a horizontal fissure. *Not deep enough.* I try a little farther over to get a better purchase. I ease my weight onto the new foothold and step up. "One," I say aloud. My mind chatter hushes as a benevolent voice begins to coach me with patient precision: *Okay, now bring your axe up, reach high and wedge it in that crack. That's it. Now pull down. Ah, it seats nicely. Move up on it. Now bring your other foot up and try putting it just there, on that shattered block.* The hollow sound that my crampon points make on the rock tells me it is loose. I try putting my foot on another rock and it shears off. A loud crack rings out as the block hits the sidewall below. *That's all right, you're okay; that's what the other three good holds are for. Keep going.* I stop counting. *You're doing it! You are climbing perfectly.* Something beyond me is propelling me upward.

I glance down at Dwayne. His eyes are on me. His hands are on the rope, ready to feed as I move up and down testing holds. The impossibility of this rope saving us intensifies my focus. I find a soft iron piton driven into the rock. I smile at the thought of it belonging to Tom and Willi, and I clip a carabiner to it to run my rope through. I am relieved to find a few more, as well as places to drive in my own. With each placement I pray for the high-pitched ping of a tight and sound fit as I deliver the final blows with my hammer. I reach a ledge perhaps thirty metres higher that's big enough to stand on and where I can build an anchor. Once I fix the rope to the anchor, I give Dwayne a wave to signal he can weight it. I watch the rope cinch tight and the pitons hold firm. It is when I slump back against the rock wall to rest that I realize the key to getting through this day isn't more strength—more than anything, it is removing self-imposed obstacles.

While I wait for Dwayne to reach me, I draw my camera out of my jacket. As I look through the viewfinder, my awareness opens. Sometime in the last hour, the wind has died to an occasional nudge. Its absence accentuates the taste of the cashews I graze on, the sound of Dwayne's crampons scraping over rock and the sensation of the ice water sluicing down my throat when I take a sip from my bottle. With no spindrift to obscure my view, over three thousand vertical metres of space drop away beneath me.

We leapfrog one another's leads for a few more pitches, fixing 120 metres of rope that will be our way home at the end of the day. We have moved steadily and without any exchange of words. And so we are surprised when we finally step out of the couloir and hear Laurie's voice: "The summit team is through the hard section and is in the upper snow gully! I repeat, Dwayne and Sharon are through the hard section and in the upper snow gully!" We realize we have cracked the crux. We hear it is 3 p.m. I didn't expect to get this far, and if there is any talk of a turnaround time, I don't hear it.

Dwayne and I stop and pull out the radio. I say, "Are we really in the upper section?"

Laurie says, "That's a confirmation. Yes."

"We're still a long way from the top, eh?"

He doesn't hear me. "Laurie to Sharon, click twice if you can hear me." I click the transmit button. "Okay, Sharon, I'm going to assume you can hear me. Jim wants me to relay that you should keep heading up the snow that you're on until you hit a broken section of rock. Start to trend right along that snow band, which will lead you to the West Ridge."

"Okay, thanks." I click twice again.

Without further thought, Dwayne and I climb on. We reach the broken section that Jim has guided us to and the exit of the couloir. Dwayne motions for to me to pull the radio out.

I say, "Hello, Jim, can you hear us now?"

"Loud and clear. We can see you too!"

Dwayne looks at his watch and holds up five fingers.

I say, "Good to know. This is the ramp you spotted for us, eh?"

"Yes, correct. Trend right and up it."

"Got it. We can see the upper snowfield now. It looks lower angled than we thought it would be. I think we're going to make it after all." The wind has died or maybe we're on the lee side of the ridge. I didn't expect that.

"You guys are going to make it! You've got less than 150 metres to go, Sharon. Hang in there!"

"That's what we like to hear. It sure is beautiful up here."

Jim whispers, "Take lots of pictures."

With the exception of a few words, the only conversation that Dwayne and I share that day is with the team. Spurred by their optimism and the improving weather, we climb upward. All we have to do now is traverse an easy slope to reach the summit ridge.

At 8,650 metres we begin a traverse toward a break through the final grey rock band of the West Ridge. But what appeared to be a snowfield from a distance is a wind-crust overtop sugary snow on friable down-sloping rock slabs. Every few steps one of my feet will break through the crust and skate down the rock before I find my balance again. My gaze gravitates to the dropoff just below me and I wonder, *If I fall, could I stop myself before launching into the abyss? How much longer can we keep this up and remain alert at this altitude? Have we been above eight thousand metres for over twenty-four hours now?* The steady tick-tock of an old-fashioned clock fills my ears, its rhythm quickening and getting louder, but with each step my focus resumes, blocking out all other sounds—including the radio.

Later, I'll read the transcripts: "What are they thinking? —Four hours of light left. —Bivouac. —Benighted." But at the moment we are in different worlds. I hear bits of conversation through my jacket, but I am not registering the gravity of their words. Dan says he is back at Camp Four after attempting to cross the ridge to Camp Five. "You wouldn't believe it, Jim. The fucking wind picked me up off my feet and I wasn't sure I was going to get down again." I take another step and his words are gone from my mind.

It is only when Jim says, "Dan! You and Laurie have *got* to get to Camp Five. Dwayne and Sharon are going to need help getting down," that I jolt to attention. I think, *We're in trouble. We've gone too far.* But the next step cancels out those thoughts again.

Sometime later, we find a break through the rock band above us and stop to check in with the team. We huddle in the lee of the cliff. The wind rumbles in warning overhead and plumes of snow roil off the summit ridge, spreading into tendrils as if reaching for us. We'll be lucky if we can remain on our feet, let alone talk on the radio up there. I yank on the aerial of the radio to pull it out. Dwayne holds up seven fingers and mouths, "Seven o'clock." I think, *How can it be? Where and when did we agree to keep going?*

"Hello, Jim?"

"Go ahead, Sharon," he says.

"Yeah. It's so cold up here it's hard to get the radio out. We're ten metres from the top!" I'm surprised by how much it sounds as if we're talking about a walk in the park. I think, *You're not!* Then, *We will beat the darkness; we will be okay.* The team must think that we'll be okay, so we continue to believe the same.

"You guys," Jim whispers. Dwayne and I lean our heads together with our ears to the radio to hear him. "We're all really proud down here. We're all in tears."

"Hi guys, it's Colleen here at Camp One. We're beaming you up lots of energy!"

I hand Dwayne the radio. "I wish I had more time up here," he says. "It's outrageous."

I look down from this impossibly high perch. Thousands of metres below and kilometres away, a faint grey outline of the glacier curls like a serpent's tail and tapers to a tip; Basecamp lies amidst the murky shadows.

Barry says, "Do you want us to keep supper on for you?"

"Can you see us?" I ask.

"Not really, but Kevin says he can make out a guy with buckteeth and a girl in a bikini."

Kevin shouts in the background, "Get some clothes on, girl!"

Why can't they see us? I reason that we must be blending into the rock, which makes us much harder to see than when we are on the snow.

Barry says, "Congratulations, Sharon and Dwayne, on your first Himalayan summit—it's the right one."

Dwayne says, "We'll try talking to you once we're on top. We better get going."

"Don't forget that photo!" Jim says. We hear cheers, whoops and hollers.

I start out first. Thinking it will be easier to climb up the rock without my axe, and certain that we are close enough to the summit that I won't need it, I leave it leaning against the rock to pick up on my way back down.

When I crest the top of the rock step, the wind greets me and drives me to my hands and knees. My stomach drops at the sight of the summit ridge stretching upward and out of sight—not ten metres, but hours away. When Dwayne comes over the edge, he lunges into the force, stabbing the pick of his axe into the hard snow to pull himself upright. He starts up the ridge. I follow him but without my axe I am staggering. *I must be really out of it to leave my axe behind! What was I thinking?* I reel like a drunkard.

Over the next ninety minutes, the wind ebbs as the sky fades to twilight. Dwayne and I plod, unfeeling, unthinking, like automatons. He finally stops and I follow his finger toward the summit a few paces away. We take the final steps side by side. Jim will tell us later he saw us through the telescope—two tiny yellow specks on the highest point on earth at 9 p.m.

When I visualized reaching the summit—in what now seems like a lifetime ago—I imagined we'd hug and cry, raise our arms above our heads in triumph. But right now all I care about is that there is no more up. I glance down at Makalu, in shadow to the east, but I feel nothing. If we had allowed for any emotion over the last days, we would not be standing on the summit now.

One of us says plainly, "Let's tag the top and get the hell out of here."

The radio is dead and we take no time to find out why—there is none to waste. Dwayne crouches while I hold up one flag after another: Canada's, China's and the Bank's. The wind plucks the last flag from my grasp and I watch it jerk upward then sideways until it takes a sudden plunge into the shadows and disappears. My thoughts follow it down there to our teammates who are safe and warm and getting ready for bed. All I know is we are here, alone—and the day is about to leave us behind. Dwayne and I switch places and it is through the camera lens that I see him illuminated in this thin slice of sunlight on top of Everest. We are spotlighted in this moment, suspended between heaven and earth. We are in limbo. We have gone too far.

PART 2

And once the storm is over you won't remember how you made it through, how you managed to survive. You won't even be sure, in fact, whether the storm is really over. But one thing is certain. When you come out of the storm you won't be the same person who walked in. That's what this storm's all about.

—Haruki Murakami

CHAPTER 18

Into the Dark

WE COBBLE OURSELVES TOGETHER and strap our headlamps on. We will need them—soon. It is far too late to be here. I know we are in trouble. Although it feels like we've been on top for only five minutes, our teammates will tell us later it was half an hour.

Dwayne stands waiting for me. I roll onto all fours and struggle to stand as the ground shifts and rocks like an unsteady boat beneath me. I know I have broken a cardinal rule of mountaineering by abandoning my axe and the oversight rattles me. Without it to provide balance, I'm not sure I can walk anymore. Dwayne seems more confident than I am and I don't want to know otherwise. I'm counting on his strength as much as he is on mine to get us down.

I take a long look at him to measure the cost of what I'm about to ask. "I feel a little wobbly without my axe. Would you mind short-roping me to the top of the first rock band?" I am admitting I'm weak in a place I can't afford to be. I wonder if this admission will kill us or save us.

Dwayne tethers me with a short line of rope and falls in behind as if it is business as usual guiding a client in the Rockies. The slight tug of the rope is all I need to find my feet and head again. Dwayne keeps telling me to slow down. He seems calm and deliberate, and I force myself to mirror him.

We arrive at the top of first rock band in less time and with less effort than I thought it would take, which buoys my confidence. While Dwayne prepares the rope for our rappel, I hammer in the last of our pitons and connect the last of our rope to them. The fact that I can build a solid anchor is evidence that I can still think and function. I feel a rush of relief when I surrender my weight to the rope and it holds. At the bottom of the rappel I see my axe leaning against the rock wall waiting for me, and I push the vexing mistake out of my mind as if it has never happened. I watch Dwayne slide down the rope slowly and in control. It is just the way I want to see him—solid.

The footing back across the snowfield is better than I feared. With my axe in hand now, and pushing it against the uphill side, I pull ahead of Dwayne. It is all I can do to hold back from scrabbling. Threat propels me: we've been too high too long, we're going to run out of oxygen and it is going to get dark. That clock is ticking louder and louder inside my head.

We turn our headlamps on halfway across the traverse. The arc of light limits my focus to one step at a time. Easier. I stop frequently to wait for Dwayne. Is he going slower or am I speeding up? Each time I wait for him to catch up, he reassures me with a nod and a wave. *He's stronger than I am. This is good. Use his pace to slow yourself down.* My faith in him is my only comfort.

I imagine our teammates watching and willing us down safely, just as I did for Dwayne and Carlos two years ago. Here I am now, behind one of those faint and twinkling lights, living out the premonition that has stalked me ever since. It isn't as terrifying as I feared it would be—at least when I am moving and focused.

I arrive first at the top of the Yellow Band and the fixed rope. Dwayne pulls up a few minutes behind. I study him again, and he reassures me that he is doing fine. It seems he is shepherding me ahead.

We need to descend the rope one at a time. Will the single strand of thin cord sever when loaded? Will the anchor fail? Relief follows when the first rope and anchor hold. As it does each time, resignation precedes surrender through a half dozen or more anchor transfers until I reach the end of the ropes.

The desire to sit and to sleep pulls at me as I wait for Dwayne at the bottom of the ropes. I know that if I fall asleep in the open in these sub-zero temperatures above eight thousand metres, I may never wake up again. Or that if I do, hypothermia or a paralyzing apathy will kill me. This threat keeps me standing, leaning against the cliff.

Fatigue overcomes me and I doze. The next thing I know, I am peering into the dark at Dwayne's headlamp. His light streaks and swirls then disappears. *Am I hallucinating, am I dreaming or am I awake?* My mind slips and jerks between dreaming and lucidity. Cold seeps into my body. I swing my arms and legs, urging warm blood to reach my fingers and toes, but they stay cold.

I tell myself, *I have descended climbs in the dark, been very cold, pushed past exhaustion, gone without food and drink for days at altitude. And I've survived acid trips gone bad. I have experienced all of this before—just not all at once.*

Where is Dwayne? How much time has passed? Has he passed me? How could he have without my knowing—that is impossible.

I can't trust what I see or think: I must have run out of oxygen some time ago. *Tick-tock, tick-tock, tick-tock!* goes the clock, and then its old-fashioned alarm clangs and my thoughts clamour: *I better go down and get the stove on and the place ready for when Dwayne comes home. He may be in trouble up there. How can he be? He was so strong, so in control. I can't climb up there. What if he's on the rope?* I am running on empty and losing my hold on reality. I hear Jim's voice in my head: "You have to want it more than it wants you!" *If I wait here any longer, I am going to be here for good.* I start down.

I descend the couloir facing in, as if inside a bubble, until a silvery wash of moonlight jolts me out of my trance. I have no sense of how much time has passed and I panic. *Have I passed our tent?* I pan the beam of my headlamp across the widening expanse of the couloir for any sign of it. *Should I start going back up? I can't. I'm too tired.* I continue down, stopping every few steps to look. The harder I stare, the more my vision blurs. Then I catch a glint of an oxygen bottle. It is all I can see of Camp Six.

My heart thuds when I open the tent and find it empty. Impossibly, I hoped Dwayne would be here. The tent looks long deserted— a home with its contents draped in white sheets. Spindrift has all but buried the tent. I start to dig, spooked by the way the mountain is erasing us and reclaiming itself. When I finally climb inside the tent, an overwhelming fatigue pulls me down onto my sleeping bag. My mouth feels as though it is lined with cotton wool. I fire up the stove and begin to feed the pot with snow. I lie back and fall asleep.

Later, our teammates will tell me it was around midnight when they saw our lights separate as I descended into the Hornbein Couloir. They locked their attention on the light stalled at the top. They knew one of us was in trouble and willed that person down for the longest time. It was 2 a.m. when they saw the first headlamp reach Camp Six. And another ninety minutes before they saw the second light get there too.

The crunch of Dwayne's crampons outside the tent rouses me. It is the best sound I will ever hear, but my relief ebbs at the sight of his waxen face and glazed eyes.

He looks through me and speaks in a monotone. "Will you take my crampons off? My fingers are frozen." As I guide him into the tent and sit him down, he says, "I ran out of oxygen and my mask was clogged with frost—suffocating me. It took me a long time to figure out what to do with my bottle. I couldn't find anywhere flat enough to leave it so it wouldn't fall down the couloir and maybe hit you." Later he tells me that he sat down—gave up—didn't care. Then something woke him and pushed him on.

No sooner do we settle in than the stove flame sputters and dies. I thread the last fuel canister onto the burner. It takes several flicks to get the lighter to spark, and when it does, the tent lights up in a sudden blinding flash. The walls suck inward then blast outward. I watch this happen, and our reaction, as if from a great distance. We unzip the doors and jettison the stove, pot, hats, gloves—everything that is on fire and then some. I am amazed at how fast we respond despite our exhaustion and hypoxic sluggishness. With the same degree of dispassion, I think. *What irony—we've made it to the top and all the way back down to die, now, in a fire.* I wonder what this spectacle looks like from below: the flaming stove streaking through the dark like a comet's tail. *Do they think it is one of us? Is anyone still watching?*

CHAPTER 19

Coming Down

LIGHT PRESSES THROUGH MY EYELIDS. When I open them, I can't understand why I see the couloir until I realize that I am looking through a basketball-sized hole in the ceiling of the tent. My sleeping bag is half open and I am fully dressed. Both ends of the tent are open, and Dwayne and I are covered in spindrift.

Dwayne is staring up at the ceiling when he feels my eyes on him. He takes a long time to clear his throat before he says, "What?"

I unstick my tongue from the roof of my mouth. I cough.

"What, is right."

"Nice skylight feature we've got here," he says.

"Yeah, the place has an airy feel to it."

He moves to prop himself up on one elbow, and the stiff coating of spindrift cracks and slides off his sleeping bag. He glances back up at the hole in the ceiling, "How'd you do that, anyway?"

"Best I can figure is I must have cross-threaded the new canister onto the stove and the fuel leaked out."

With no food, water, fuel or oxygen, we have nothing more to do before we leave other than dig through the ruins to find replacements for the hats and gloves we lost in the fire. The radio, left for dead, surfaces in the search. We both look at it for a long moment, recalling that it went silent after our last transmission to the team, just below what we thought was the summit. The aerial is missing. Then Dwayne reaches into his pocket and plucks from it the aerial; a rabbit from a hat. He holds it between his thumb and forefinger and says, "I thought we could use this. I found it lying on top of the snow on my way down." He goes to hand it to me and then draws back, pauses. "Don't lose it again, eh?"

I thread the aerial onto the radio, turn it on, push the transmit button and croak, "Hello. Is anyone out there?"

Nothing seems to amaze us anymore—until Jim answers. "Sharon! Where are you? Is Dwayne with you?" It's a miracle to hear Jim's voice—light years away. Dwayne and I grin at each other. I feel elation, but then I realize that Jim may as well as be on another planet and somehow we've got to get there.

"We're together at Camp Six, or what's left of it." I say.

"What do you mean by what's left of it?"

"The stove blew up last night."

"You guys okay?"

"Alive, it seems."

"Let me talk to Dwayne."

As I pass the radio to Dwayne I notice that his face is still swollen—all the hollows filled in. "Hi, Jim," he says.

"Oh my God," Jim's voice cracks, "we're so relieved to hear from you guys! How are you?"

"Glad to be alive." Dwayne glances at me. "But not looking so good. Woody lost her eyebrows and eyelashes in the fire and she's got soot on her face." He hands me the radio and falls back, exhausted.

"Yeah, I'm a real doll," I say.

"Why didn't we hear from you guys last night?"

"We lost the aerial but found it again this morning," I say.

"Think you can make it down?"

Good question, I think, and hand the radio to Dwayne.

"We're pretty wrecked but we're going to give it a try," he says.

I don't even know if I can stand up yet, let alone climb down. A piercing ache thrums in my head. Each pulse killing another brain cell.

"Help is on its way," Jim says. "Laurie left Camp Five about an hour ago to see if he could get up there." I feel my heart jump. We couldn't have hoped for a better person to meet us.

"That's great news. We're going to need it." Dwayne holds his hand up to examine. "I frostbit my fingers and we're out of O's."

Barry says, "I think there's a full bottle where the ropes end."

"Okay," Jim says, "save your energy to get down safe. Let us know when you're leaving Five."

We move slowly as we pull ourselves together for one more push. We find neck tubes for our heads and mismatched spare mitts and gloves. First, exhaustion lays us back down and shuts our eyes, then hope prods us to sit back up again. Hours evaporate as we ready ourselves to descend.

I sit bent over my legs, panting and spent from tightening my crampons.

Dwayne stands at the door of the tent looking down at me and says, "You up for this?"

My head drops to rest on my knees. After a few deep empty breaths, I look up at him again and he offers his hand and pulls me to my feet. Stars fill my vision. I sway and teeter. "What's our choice?" I say as I exhale. "Let's do this."

Dwayne moves in slow motion as if floating. He turns around, daggers his axe in and steps down. I think to myself, *This is going to happen. Just a thousand more moves like this and we'll be with Laurie.* As I turn to start down, I say to myself, *Don't blow it now, not after we've come this far.*

Two days before, it was as if the mountain was enraged and trying to shake us off, but it now feels like it is releasing us. I am relieved to find I can still move, focus and function well enough to climb down. It is only when we reach the base of the couloir, where it fans out onto the wind-strafed North Face, that I stop to bring my head up and look for any sign of Laurie. I squint through scratched goggles. *There!* A patch of yellow wavers against the black of the cliff band like a mirage, then disappears behind sheets of spindrift. I wonder if I'm hallucinating again. I rest my head on the top of my ice axe and look down through my feet, watching the distance grow between Dwayne and me. Then he stops, looks across the face and his pace quickens. He must see it too. This time, I see the yellow patch wave. Hope hurries me to where Laurie stands waiting, laughing and crying.

"Oh my God, I'm so happy to see you guys!" he says, wrapping his arms around both of us. We linger in his embrace for a long minute. "I can't tell you how proud I am of you. You pulled it off. You really did it!"

I am too tired to feel any emotion.

"You're going to be okay now," Laurie says as he helps us clip into a cluster of old ropes. We shrug out of our packs, lean against the rock wall and slide down to sit. Tied to the same point is our rope, which stretches down and across the face toward the west shoulder, leading the way home. Laurie pulls out a big thermos and pours a cup of tea for us to share. "I won't make you talk now. Keep drinking and rest while I get Jim on the radio."

When Jim answers, Laurie keeps his eyes on us and tilts his head like a proud father.

"I've got Dwayne and Sharon with me now."

"Wonderful! How are they?"

Laurie hands us the radio. "I'll let them tell you." He films us with his video camera as we talk to Jim. We perk up by the minute as we sip on tea, talk to Jim and draw deep breaths of oxygen from the tank we share.

Soon, Laurie presses us to get moving. We slide an oxygen bottle each into our packs, slip on masks and saddle up. Dwayne starts down first, facing away from us, his skeletal form halting momentarily between each step as he wobbles, leans against his inside pole and then recovers enough to take another step.

When we reach Camp Five a couple of hours later, Dan is waiting for us. He ushers Dwayne, Laurie and me into the tent and tends to us, making sure we drink and fuel up for the next leg. Both Dwayne and I fall asleep and have to be woken by Laurie, who urges us to get up and keep moving.

We thought we would get as far as Camp Four today, but when we reach it Dwayne keeps going. As we lose altitude, bit by bit my balance improves and my vision and my mind grow sharper. We move faster. I have no idea how long our day has been, but by the time we meet Albi, Kevin and Barry at the bottom of the ropes at Camp Two, we have descended close to three thousand metres in the past twenty-four hours.

The boys push us into a tent lined with layers of insulated mats and extra sleeping bags, where they bring us food and drinks. We are more tired than anything and sleep into the next day.

* * *

The sound of a zipper wakes us. Albi's face appears in our tent door. "Wakey, wakey! How are you children feeling this morning?" I blink and look at him dumbly. "You're looking better but you've still got a dirty face, Woody. Better clean up for those photos."

I sit up and rub my face. "Ouch," I cry.

"Hmmm, methinks you've got a bit of frostbite on the side of both cheeks, old girl, or war paint perhaps. Maybe there was a gap between your balaclava and goggles?"

"Let me see," says Dwayne. I turn my face to him. "Yep, but it's nothing cosmetic surgery can't fix."

Albi laughs. "Good to hear you're back with us on the same planet, Dwayno. If you let me come in, I'll give you these cups of tea. Think you've got enough brain cells left for a chat?"

He wriggles in and lies down between us while we sip our tea. I snuggle up to him and rest my head on his shoulder while he strokes my head. *So warm and kind*, I think, *and now we've paved the way for his turn.* He plies us with questions about what to expect from Camp Five to the summit. Dwayne and I doze off and when we wake again, Albi is on his way up to Camp Four with Kevin, James and Chris in support.

A few hours later, we see Barry off. As I hold him, I whisper into his ear, "Thank you. It's a much gentler world up there now. Everything's in place for you to pull this off."

Dwayne hugs Barry, then pushes him back to grip his shoulders and says, "Thanks for everything, brother. You've got this one in the bag, man. And you deserve it."

As Albi and Barry head up the mountain, Dwayne and I continue our descent. When we reach the edge of the glacier, Colleen stands waiting for us with tears in her eyes. My heart lifts as I see her—a teeny thing with wiry springs of black curly hair pushing out from beneath her toque. I have been waiting for this moment, the first of our homecoming, to feel relief and joy, finally safe.

As Colleen and Dwayne linger in quiet embrace, I realize our mission is over and I feel a strange sense of loss. When Colleen hugs me, tells me how proud she is of us and weeps, I don't—can't. *What's wrong with me?* Colleen and I are friends and have shared many chapters. We held vigil on Makalu for Dwayne and Carlos and greeted them on their return just like this. I know I should feel something. But I've shut down my emotions to get through, get up and get down. I've been in overdrive for days now, and I'm still on guard. *Am I just tired?*

Partway down, the radio crackles. We stop and sit down to listen. First Chris, and then James and Kevin, too spent to go on, turn back from their way to Camp Four, which leaves Barry and Albi unsupported. Then the radio conversation between Jim, Barry and Albi begins.

"You know the agreement we made," Jim says to Albi. "It's off."

"But everything is in place, Jim," he says. "The weather is perfect. The camp is there. All we'll need to carry is our personal gear, a tent, oxygen and a stove."

Jim says, "If no one but you and Barry can get to Five, then you'll have no one to back you up if something happens. Having backup is what we all agreed upon as a team."

Barry comes on. "Hey, Jim. It's a completely different world up here than it was three days ago. It's as calm as it can be. Albi and I are feeling strong and we're ready to go for the top."

"That's not the deal we made. There's no one to support you. Don't you get it? Dwayne and Woody barely got off alive." Jim's voice cracks. "I'm sorry, man."

"Yeah, I know, Jim, but right now it's about the safest mountain I've ever been on! We've got fixed ropes most of the way up it, and camps in place. You've gotta let us go for it!"

Albi shouts, "Jim, think about it, man! You can't pull the pin now!"

"No," I say to Dwayne and Colleen, "this can't be happening."

Dwayne speaks into the radio. "Barry, Albi, remember what we said, everything's in place. You've got to go for it!"

"I need time to think about this, Jimmy," Barry says. "Sorry, but I'm feeling the pull. Do you know how hard this is for me? Over and out."

That evening at Camp One, Dwayne, Colleen and I walk up the hill for the radio exchange. The call is already underway when we turn the radio on.

Barry's voice breaks. "I'm not happy about this, Jim. I've decided to come down because I love you, brother, and I'm going to stand by my word."

I can tell Jim is crying. "You don't know how hard—this is for me to do. I love you too, brother."

"This can't happen," I say, and I push the transmit button.

Dwayne lays his hand over the radio and pushes it down. "It's done. They're fucked."

I want to feel grateful for how the team has helped Dwayne and me—and for what we have all accomplished. Against all odds we made it to the top through sheer bloody-mindedness, their noble efforts and talent, and have been granted safe exit from the highest point on earth. But instead, guilt and despair weigh on me for our teammates who are being denied their own summit bid.

Dwayne spits, "Fuck! I can't believe this! What the fuck? Fuck, fuck, fuck!" He shrugs Colleen's arm off his shoulder. "I gotta deal with this." And he strides off. I have never witnessed such vehemence in him before.

I sleep alone for the first night in a long time, and I wish Jane was here. I wake in the night in a panic, half out of my sleeping bag and with my head pressed up against the door of the tent. I have to get up, get out, keep moving, get down from here! It takes a few minutes to shift from this dream to where I am now. I lie awake, telling myself I'm safe but still, I am not able to relax. Despite my exhausted state, I sleep poorly.

The next morning, I step out of the mess tent after breakfast to see Carlos across the meadow, dismantling the last of the American team's tents. Instinct draws me to him—someone who knows me, knows that harsh world above, knows what I have been through. He meets my eyes for a long minute as if to get a good read before he walks over. We embrace, and it is a warm and soothing comfort. Tears stream down my cheeks.

"Congratulations, I knew you could do it," he says. "I'd like to hear all about it, if you're willing to tell me. How about we walk to Basecamp together?"

"I'd like that."

As I begin recounting the story of the last few days to Carlos, I feel as though I'm finally coming down and everything will be okay. Talking to him is so familiar—so comforting. He is interested in every detail: what kept us going, the rock climbing through the Yellow Band, the sound of the clock in my head, my magical thinking that we would beat the darkness, and the loneliest feeling I've ever experienced at the top. He listens intently. But when I get to my dilemma at the bottom of the ropes, over whether to wait for Dwayne or move on, he tells me what I already know but don't want to hear: "You never abandon your partner on a mountain. Never." And I crash. I will wrestle with that decision for years.

As we near Basecamp, I see Jane bounding up the trail to greet me. I know by the look she gives Carlos that I will be giving her a full report by day's end.

Homecoming at Basecamp is anticlimactic. Everyone is subdued because of Barry and Albi's defeat. My focus on their disappointment and the part I played in it dampens any sense of accomplishment I might feel. There's nothing left to do now but remove the ropes and the camps and pack up. Yet my mind and body lag days behind: I am shell-shocked and exhausted, still trying to catch up with all that has happened between ramping up for the summit and this letdown. Yet when Albi and Barry return a few days later, they appear to be excited about a victory party. They've moved on, and I haven't.

Laurie can tell something is up with me, and late that afternoon he seeks me out for a walk to the memorial cairns. On our way, he tells me I should feel proud of what I've accomplished.

I say, "I do feel proud of what *we've* accomplished, but I'm not sure how Barry and Albi see it."

"Well, get over what others think," he says. "Believe me, I know. All kinds of shit was going down when I came back from Everest in '82: the grief over the deaths, the conflicts, some of the team members' resentment toward the leader or me being the *one* to reach the summit. I had to rise above it all to serve a higher purpose. Now it's your turn."

"What's the higher purpose?"

He laughs. "Well, for starters, quit feeling sorry for yourself! That doesn't do anyone any good. People want to hear about the courage, endurance and teamwork that will inspire their own stories. Your world is about to change, Sharon, and I want to make sure you're ready for it. The media will ply you with questions. Let's talk about that."

When we get to the memorial cairns, we stand quietly with our own thoughts. On our way back, Laurie pretends he is an interviewer and fires questions at me. He laughs when I stumble over my answers and says, "Ask them to rephrase the question, or you repeat it in your own words to give yourself time to think." Once again Laurie makes me feel I have something to rise to.

That night, the Spaniards and the half-dozen remaining Americans join us to celebrate our victory. Someone on our team got a sponsor to donate a case of White Horse whisky, and the amber elixir softens the edges. A boom box blares tunes in the background. We dance, laugh and chat late into the night.

The party and the anticipation of the trucks arriving in the next few days help to improve everyone's mood. One afternoon while I am lying in my tent reading, Barry comes by. "Hey Woody, Albi and I have been talking about going to Nanga Parbat next year. It's the highest vertical face in the world. Wanna come?" I marvel at the way these men can move on so quickly.

CHAPTER 20

Lost

WE ARE ON OUR way home at last. I am looking forward to getting back to Canada, but we first spend a night in Shanghai before catching our flight. The phone is ringing when Jane and I reach our room—and it doesn't stop. One of the first callers is Jane Sharpe from the Continental Bank. She lists off a string of calls to expect from national networks and radio stations requesting interviews.

I try to sound gracious with each caller, but it isn't until I get off the phone each time and take great gasps that I realize I am holding my breath. I think of the letter I wrote to Chris just before our summit bid: "I'm yearning to return to you and a normal life back home, but I fear it will be completely different if I make the summit." I only have to look at the stack of messages for interviews, public appearances and presentations I was handed at the hotel's check-in to know that "completely different" is beginning to unfold.

One of the last messages I read is from John Amatt, the business manager of the Everest '82 expedition and now the owner of a speakers' bureau in Canmore. He told me before I left for Everest that a lucrative speaking career awaited me if I summited, and that he'd be glad to help. For a girl with no fixed address and whose entire belongings fit into a duffle bag, "lucrative" sounds appealing, and help fielding requests now sounds even better. I call him and sign on. I'm terrified of public speaking, but that fear fades to make way for a new one—one that niggles at me. *Who am I to be personally rewarded for our team effort? Am I becoming an opportunist?*

Chatter and laughter echo off the walls as we stride down the arrivals corridor at Vancouver International Airport toward our families, lovers and friends. After three months away, all we can talk about is the first things we'll do when we get home. Most of us are dreaming of food because we all weigh eight to ten kilograms less than when we left.

I am daydreaming about soaking in a steaming bubble bath and sipping on a cold glass of Chardonnay, when ahead, the exit doors slide open. I stall, causing the other travellers to eddy around me. Jim bumps up against me and leans in. "It's show time, Woody." I catch a whiff of shaving lotion and notice he has changed into a clean white t-shirt and his Everest Light team jacket for the occasion. Jim is bringing everyone home alive, and it dawns on me that this is *his* summit day.

As our team steps across the threshold, the clapping begins. Flashbulbs pop. A woman reaches out, clutches Jane's arm, thrusts a microphone in her face and asks, "Are you the woman?"

Jane looks back at me. "No, she's the *one*." She shoots me a raised eyebrow as if to say, "Are you ready for this?"

From all directions camera-ready reporters shout questions at me:

"How does it feel to be the first woman from the western hemisphere to climb Mount Everest?"

"Did you ever think you were going to die up there?"

"When did you know you were going to reach the top?"

"Did you see any dead bodies?"

The arrivals lobby clamours with media teams and I am pulled from one interview set to another. "Jim, will you hold a corner of this flag? Hold the other end, would you, Dwayne? Sharon, would you please get in the middle? Don't look into the camera, just pretend you're having a conversation with Monica." I look beyond this sphere of frenzied hubbub and lights and see my teammates reuniting with friends and family.

A hand grasps my bicep and a man says, "Hello, Sharon, I'm Michael with the CBC." Keeping his grip on me, he says, "Congratulations. There's someone who has been waiting to welcome you home." He steers me to where my mom, my dad and stepmom are waiting. The camera is rolling as my dad steps forward and we embrace.

It seems no more than seconds before I feel a hand on my shoulder, pulling me toward another set. "Can we get you over here beside Dwayne; he's the one that went to the top with you, isn't he?"

I catch sight of Chris standing at the edge of it all, dressed in a suit and holding a bouquet of red roses. He gives me a nod as if to say, "Keep doing what you're doing. I've waited this long."

Later, I will regret how these first days unfolded: I will wish that I had paused to look into my mom's tearful eyes and lingered to hear what my father whispered after he said, "Welcome home, Mouse." I will wish that I had greeted Chris. But, wide-eyed and stunned, I comply with the media's requests, swept up in their urgency to show and tell.

* * *

From the airport, the entire team and our families are taken to a four-star hotel to spend the night before attending a welcome-home party the following day. My parents, who live in Vancouver, return to their own homes for the night.

Chris and I are treated to an extravagant suite. We open the door into a main room filled with bouquets of flowers, a stack of cards, a fruit basket, a bottle of champagne and a separate bedroom with a king-sized bed. Chris closes the door behind us, reaches for me and kisses me deeply. I slip out of his embrace.

This is what I've been waiting for—dreaming of. *What's wrong with me?* I look at this prince of a man who stands by the door, gazing at me in adoration. "I'm sorry," I say. "I think I'm just a little rattled by it all." I can't explain then that I've just spent the last couple of months in a secluded world of rock, ice and snow, lived intimately—

intensely—with twelve people, and moved only as fast as we could walk. From that to this is too much.

What I do know is that Chris feels like a stranger to me. For weeks, I have been looking forward to the feel of soft satiny sheets and of him. But I shut my emotions down at the airport to manage the onslaught of media attention. I yearn to debrief this day with Jane as we have over the past few months. Instead, I lie awake churning over the week-long blitz of appearances, events and interviews ahead of me.

The next morning I sit with Chris, watching my teammates trickle into breakfast with their partners and families and sit at their own tables. They are drifting away and I miss them. I know they would rather be with their friends and families than the media—so would I. Never has normal looked so good, and I envy them.

It's been a long time since I've spent any time in this city I once couldn't wait to leave. Vancouver is at its best on this June day, saturated with sun and oxygen, dripping with blossoms—and so verdant the place feels like it breathes life and moisture into me. We make our way to Vancouver Harbour where the Continental Bank is hosting our welcome-home party on a luxury yacht. They invite our full entourage, as well as our sponsors, and prominent business and community members, including the mayor. My sister, Barb, is dressed in a diaphanous pastel-pink silk pantsuit, which in its entirety could fit into the palm of my hand. I marvel at how she kibitzes and sidles up to the men and flirts her face off. Chris and my parents beam as we chat with the guests. My parents adore the notion of Chris and me as a couple. Jim is beaming too, and comes over now and then, resting his hand lightly on the small of my back to escort me to meet another guest. The expectations make me swallow hard and step back.

Meeting those expectations starts at five the next morning, when Dwayne and I are crammed together in a small padded cubicle. We are talking to a camera for a remote interview. We nudge each other with our knees as we take turns answering questions volleyed at us through our headsets by an interviewer in Toronto. I cherish this last bit of teamwork with Dwayne—this last link to our expedition. Afterward, we climb into separate taxis. I ache for the life he is returning to. His car turns toward the airport and disappears, while mine takes me to the next interview. I sink back into my seat and remind myself to breathe. *What have I done?* I've long accepted myself as an introvert and I struggle to embrace the emerging expectations of this public persona.

A short while later, I'm seated in another padded room with the host of a local radio morning show. The man operating the switches on the other side of a picture window counts down from five. The host begins, "Today, I have with me in the studio an amazing woman who has just made history. Her name is Sharon Wood, and she is the first woman from the western hemisphere to climb Mount Everest! And people, Sharon is a Canadian, and she's from our city! Sharon, you must be over the moon about your conquest. Tell us what it was like to step onto the highest point on earth."

I want to bolt. Try as I might to remember Laurie's advice, the channel between my brain and my mouth shuts down. I stutter, "It felt like a privilege. When I reached the top, I mean when my partner Dwayne Congdon and I reached the top, we were together. Well, ours was a fraction of the team effort that went into climbing that mountain..." And I blather on.

Every interviewer, it seems, has already written my story—one about me being "over the moon" that I have "conquered" Everest. But I'm wondering if it has conquered me, leaving me bewildered. I hadn't expected all this attention, and for people to put words in my mouth. But why wouldn't they when I can't find my own words? As another cab whisks me off to the next engagement, I wish it would keep going all the way to Canmore.

I call John Amatt. "Please remind me why I'm putting myself through this?"

"For your team, for your country and for your business!" he tells me. "Fame is fleeting and you've got to capture it while you can. You should feel proud!"

Later, when I ask Laurie the same question, he says, "Snap out of it! Make it your goal to become as comfortable and articulate with this new world as you are with the mountains."

The cab pulls up at the Expo 86 entrance and I am escorted to stage. There I stand in front of thousands of people while the whistling champion of the world warbles "Climb Every Mountain" to me. I'd thought the simple off-white short-sleeved blouse purchased in China would be appropriate—classy, in fact. Now I wilt in the wrinkled travel clothes, two sizes too big. My eyes dart between the audience and the whistler as I wonder how to stand, what to do with my arms, and whether I appear as terribly awkward as I feel. I can see the organizers of this special event standing off to the side. And the look on their faces tells me they suddenly realize this idea of matching the whistler and me is a bad idea, but it is too late now.

The most fun I have that week in Vancouver is when I go shopping with Mom. Usually I buy clothes from thrift shops, which reflect my budget and my priorities, but occasionally Mom and I share a ritual of going shopping where she buys me a thing or two. So she is delighted when I tell her I need something to wear to presentations and ask her to come shopping with me. After three months without a mirror, it is still a novelty to look at myself in one. Mom sits in an upholstered chair as I strut out of the dressing room in one outfit after another, pretending to be a runway model and striking poses. We laugh at the bad ones and she *oohs* and *aahs* at the good ones.

While I change, Mom tells me how the media ambushed her when the news broke that we had reached the summit. Two men were waiting outside her apartment building as she arrived home after enduring a root canal. She hadn't heard the news yet.

"One man put a camera up close to my face while the other asked me, 'Peggy, how do you feel about your daughter becoming the first woman from the western hemisphere to climb Mount Everest?' Were you still alive is what I really wanted to know!" She continues, "But I tell him something like, 'Well, I'm just stunned. I don't know what to say!' So the interviewer told me I must be so proud of you. And he kept prodding for answers until finally I blathered something about how strong-minded you were as a teenager."

"Why did you even agree to talk to them, Ma—of all the times?"

"Oh, because I couldn't say no, of course. It all happened so fast."

"I know what you mean." I didn't feel like I could say no either.

We pick out two suits, one robin's egg blue with a knee-length pencil skirt with a slit up the back, and one navy blue double-breasted blazer with a matching pleated skirt. As well, there are a pair of houndstooth pants, a casual pair of black slacks, a white blouse—and a pair of low pumps. "I can't do heels yet, Ma," I say. But I will.

Straight after shopping with Mom, I visit my sister, who helps me "clean up," as she puts it. I'm not used to wearing anything more than mascara, so Barb plucks my Groucho Marx eyebrows and shows me how to put on makeup. "Don't worry," she says, "I can make it look subtle." And she does. Yet despite her efforts, all I can see is clown.

"Okay, well, let's see the new clothes," she says. I tell myself that I am no longer the little sister who used to worship her opinion. Yet I am reluctant to model these new clothes for her because I love them and know I won't after she has her say. She spins me around to get a better look. "Very nice—a little roomy, though. But then you'd look good in anything right now, even if it's Mom's taste." I wince and back out of her place.

At dinner with Dad that night, I tell him about my session with Barb. "I thought, after all I've been through, that I might have gained some confidence. Grown up a bit, you know? But still I take whatever she says so personally."

Dad has been a mender of all things family, the mediator, the smoother of feathers, the lay philosopher and now minister. He laughs, as he often does when I complain—he's a bit like Laurie that way. Then he says, "If you think you've evolved, come spend a week with your family."

The last thing I do after the week of interviews and appearances before going home to Canmore is spend a few days with Chris up at Whistler to decompress and try to get reacquainted. I haven't been able to look him in the eyes when he tells me he loves me. One night after we've made love he tells me again. But this time he gently cradles and tips my face to bring my eyes up to meet his, and I crack—slowly at first. "Sorry," I say, then I start blubbering, "I'm just not ready for this—yet. I think we just need to start over again as friends."

He is underway packing to move his business to Canmore. "Friend, lover or neither," he tells me, "the train is already in motion. If and when you're ever ready, I'll be there for you."

CHAPTER 21

On Stage, Off Stage

I RETURN TO CANMORE in early July. By now I've been away for four months and it feels good to be home. And even better when I move in with Marni, and our friends Colin Rankin and Dave Stark. All four of us are in one stage or another of breaking up with partners, so we call our place the Heartbreak Hotel. We share three bedrooms, counting on one of us being away at any given time, and sleep in whichever one is vacant when we get home. Now and then the system fails, and after trying each door and then swearing under their breath, the latecomer ends up on the floor. A floor is all I have anyway, until Chris builds me a bed and buys me a mattress. "With no strings attached," he says.

It's hard for the four of us to tear ourselves away from the breakfast table when we're all home at the same time because we all have so much to talk and laugh about when it comes to our sad state of affairs. This is as normal as I've felt since life after Everest began.

I soon fall into a routine of guiding and training for my upcoming Full Alpine Guide's exam next summer. I rise as early as 3 a.m. to climb and work through long days that will also include giving corporate presentations.

It takes me a month to prepare for my first presentation and audience. Chris, who is well versed in making slide presentations, coaches me: "Don't spend more than a minute talking about each slide. Too many slides, too much talking, so pare them down. Use the images to cue you for every point. Write your points down on recipe cards." I wake in the nights, my mind rehearsing, and write down ideas on a notepad I keep at my bedside. Although I thought I would be ready for anything after Everest, speaking to an audience for an hour is unimaginable. When the day comes, pure will marches me to the podium and sees me through. Will is all I can count on for now.

Barry asks if he can come to one of my talks, and how can I say no? I wince when I glance at him at the back of the room. His being there underscores the collision between my life as a member of the tribe who believes modesty and understatement are mandatory virtues, and my life as a perceived hero with a story to tell. It helps when the lights dim and I can't see him anymore. I begin, "Ours is a story of ordinary people accomplishing extraordinary results." And I take the audience through the expedition over the next sixty minutes. Although I receive hearty applause, I have an uneasy sense that it is Everest earning the applause.

As people file through to talk to me after the presentation, they say, "That was incredible." And I know they are referring to the mountain, as if all I need to do is show up. Or they say, "That was an amazing feat you pulled off," and I hear this as an accolade for what *I* have done, not the team. I know Barry is hearing these comments and I feel embarrassed. Once the room is empty, and as I am collecting my slides and papers, Barry approaches me. He smiles, grasps my shoulders, tilts his head from one side to the other, examining the woman in front of him, and says, "You're not ordinary! We're not ordinary!" His words sting, as they echo my own thoughts. I am uncertain how to get past the awe of Everest to reach an audience with my own voice. I know as he does that my gratuitous self-deprecation isn't the answer. But I do believe I am an ordinary person trying to accomplish the extraordinary task of meeting my own expectations.

For now I skulk out of town in my businesswoman's disguise, hoping none of my tribe will see me. Moving between these two worlds—the one I know and the one where I feel like an imposter—I begin to separate myself into two women: the one who guides and climbs, and the one who gives motivational speeches.

I first get a sense of my own voice late that fall on a day when I'm delayed and arrive fifteen minutes late for a presentation. This predicament forces me into a state of mind I know well from when things go sideways in the mountains and there is no choice but to take charge. As I enter the meeting room, I hand my slide carousel to the audio-visual operator and ask him to start fifteen slides into the presentation. With no time to ease my way out of my self-consciousness, I launch right in. Within minutes I become aware of the hush in the room. For the first time, I make eye contact with the audience instead of gazing over their heads. I pause to let my words sink in rather than scrambling to fill the space with noise. Soon I feel these five hundred people are in the moment with me.

When I finish, however, nobody stirs, claps or utters a word. I hover in that silent void for what seems an eternity. Then a single clap breaks the silence. One person pops up, followed by another and another until the whole room is standing, whistling, cheering and clapping. This time, I sense that my message may have earned some of this applause. A thousand butterflies are taking flight inside me. I want more of this.

* * *

The conference season ends in November and I work as a heli-ski guide in the Interior of BC through the winter months. Chris has been hired by the same company to visit their six lodges as a snow safety consultant, but that winter he spends a disproportionate amount of time at the Bobbie Burns Lodge where I'm based. He glides effortlessly through the powder snow, his skis a natural extension of his feet. He coaches me: "Keep your hands in front, get out of the back seat." And he gives me tips on how to lead groups of guests who will always be right on my tail. At the top of a run, he will slide up beside me, lean in and whisper into my ear, "Take that line"—and I do.

As my speaking engagements start up again in March, Chris becomes my bridge to the business world. My Everest acclaim parachutes me into galas and receptions that precede presentations with blue-chip corporations. Groomed by an upper-class British mother, Chris tutors me in the etiquette of formal tables: the order of utensils used for each course, the right side to take my napkin from, the need to use my butter knife. He adds, "And stop swinging your fork in the air like you're conducting a symphony!"

He reassures me when I receive a call one morning from a woman representing the University of Calgary Senate telling me that I have been nominated for an honorary Doctor of Laws degree. In panic, I wave madly at Chris to listen in on the conversation.

"I'm not sure I understand," I tell her. "Are you saying that the university wants to grant me an honorary degree for climbing a mountain? Why?"

"Why, my girl, is because your accomplishment is symbolic for all women—and men for that matter—who are aspiring to greater heights in the world."

I put my hand over the receiver and hiss at Chris, "I'm a high school dropout! I can't accept this!"

He whispers, "No one needs to know. Just say yes!"

Public recognition is a deceptive mirror. Close on the heels of the doctorate, the American Alpine Club and the Explorers Club of New York jointly recognize me with the inaugural Tenzing Norgay Award for exceptional mountaineering. As I settle into the back of the limo at LaGuardia Airport, I puff up with the thought that despite being Canadian, these prestigious American organizations deem me worthy enough to fly me to New York City to receive the award from Sir Edmund Hillary himself. I'm heady with the thought of being united with this great man by our historic ascents of Everest. But as Hillary's huge hand envelops mine, his mouth is smiling but his eyes are not. I read Hillary's look as confirmation that I am just one of the more than two hundred climbers who have summited this beleaguered mountain. Instantly, I deflate. I should have known better than to fall for the opinions of strangers. The mountain has lulled me into this false sense of greatness, and I begin to resent it.

* * *

Everest becomes uncontainable. The carefully constructed box in which I keep it bursts open at unexpected times and places. Chris takes me to dinner one night to celebrate our engagement. And as the maître d' leads us to our table, a diner grabs my arm. "Are you the woman who climbed Everest?" he asks.

"Yes," I reply, as Chris and the maître d' stand by entirely ignored.

"Let me introduce you to my clients," he says and proceeds to present me to everyone at the table.

Once Chris and I are seated, he leans in and hisses, "I can't believe how rude that man was!"

"I'm sorry, I should have said something—at the very least, introduced you. It's just that he caught me by surprise."

"No, no," he says. "It's not up to you. *He* should have known better."

I suck the air in between my teeth, and run my fingers through my hair, thinking, *No, I should have known better. I could have prevented this spectacle.*

I become increasingly wary of Everest. It opens doors, then elbows me aside. I start out poised and articulate in my presentations, then the mountain takes over. I finish bewildered, as though I'm waking from a spell.

More often than not, an hour of storytelling rouses a standing ovation. But I feel more embarrassed than exultant. The audience rises from their seats for Everest.

I hope to find my feet by returning to the mountains, where I've always felt grounded. In the spring of '87, James and I set out to climb the Paragot route on the North Face of Huascarán Norte in Peru, a dream route that demands our rock- and ice-climbing skills and high-altitude experience to pull off. On our second day out, a softball-sized rock hits me square on the top of my helmet and knocks me senseless. For the rest of the four-day climb, I feel more nervous than engaged—a sure sign that I've had enough.

A new problem to solve or a new route to climb used to fulfill me. Every climb was an investment in attaining greater mastery. The passion sustained me—defined me. The realization of what I have lost is frightening.

I count on the comfort of the familiar when James and I return to a summer of guiding and training for our upcoming alpine guide's exam. In September when the examiners summon me to tell me whether I've passed or failed, they are quiet. They don't look at me, and I know the news isn't good. Everest, looming and omnipresent, is impotent in this room of qualified men who don't care.

"It didn't seem like your mind was on the exam," says the first examiner. The others nod in agreement. "However, we are granting you a conditional pass. If you can meet these conditions, we will approve you for full alpine certification."

Although I know my heart isn't in guiding or in high-altitude climbing anymore, I am disappointed. Later that fall I spend a few days climbing with an examiner and clients to meet the conditions for my certification. But the question that preoccupies me is what will *fulfill* me. A barely audible voice inside urges me to be patient and have faith.

* * *

Faith carries me through the next year. Without warning, I realize one day when I'm watching Chris rolling on the floor playing with his friend's two young children that I want to have kids. As I run my fingers through his strawberry blond hair in bed that night, I say, "The way you fawned over those kids today makes me want to take on the biggest science experiment of my life." I had always seen my reproductive system as an inconvenience—a liability in my arena. Now, I'm fascinated with the miracle.

A year later, Chris sits beaming in the chair beside my hospital bed. The nurse helps turn me and arrange the pillows to prop our newborn son against me. My nose hovers above our baby's head, taking in his scent. The nurse squishes baby Robin's face to my breast and I feel him latch on for the first time. Love blows my heart wide open. Chris brushes his tears away.

Just then one of our doctors waltzes in on his rounds. "Well, what was harder," he asks, "a twenty-four-hour labour followed by a Cesarean, or Everest?"

I am taken aback by this bizarre question. It was well intended, I'm sure, but I resent how that mountain has permeated my life, my identity—even here. Even now!

Marni comes to visit me and her new godson in the hospital the next day. A few minutes later, the nurse scoops Robin up and urges me to take my first walk while Marni can escort me. Every step wrenches my freshly sliced, gutted and stapled belly. With one hand I clutch the bag of jelly that was once my stomach to keep it from jiggling. And with the other, I grip a handrail as I shuffle to a sitting room at the end of the hallway.

"Are we there yet? This feels like my hardest climb ever." I start snivelling, "What's happening to me, Marni? What did they do with the woman we knew?" A flood of emotion presses in my throat. My confidence plummets, my world shrinks, I shrink.

She grips my bicep to support me and says, "You're a mother now."

"No kidding. How am I ever going to manage anything in this state beyond caring for Robin? I can't, is how. Marni, I can't be your friend anymore."

She laughs. "Oh honey, I'm here to stay—and to give you perspective. You're in shock after all you've been through, and under the influence of some drugs and heaps of hormones too, I imagine. Give yourself some time to recover before you make up your mind about what your life is going to be like and who you will or won't have room for. I think you'll be surprised."

Six weeks after Robin is born, Everest comes calling again when I am contracted to speak to a company based in Calgary. The theme of the talk is accomplishing more with less. I can relate. Twenty kilograms more of me, and much less brainpower. I pull on the only bottoms that fit, a pair of maternity pants, and I cover my top half with a dark blazer. Robin wails when I hand him to our nanny on my way out the door. I hover there, taking one last look at him, as she rocks him in her arms. Looking down at Robin, Ruth croons, "We'll be fine won't we, won't we. Yes, we will." This kind older British woman says this as much for me as for Robin. I step across the threshold and wonder how I will close the gap between now and speaking at the podium.

A senior partner in the law firm introduces me to a mostly male audience—all I see are starched white shirts and cinched ties—filling a smattering of chairs. Intimidating. A few people stand in the back close to the door, ready to bail.

A bloom of milk soaks my blouse as I step up to the podium. I congratulate myself on the choice of the loose dark blazer for this occasion. Blank faces stare back at me. I reach for help and Albi flashes through my thoughts. Some have judged him arrogant for his brash confidence, but he believed he was good at whatever he took on, and therefore he was remarkably effective. With his example in mind, I begin. "You might wonder—what does climbing Mount Everest have to do with you? Everything," I declare.

The audience asks a surprising number of questions afterward, including, of course, "Once you've climbed the highest mountain in the world, what's next?"

I hesitate, then say, "What's next is this," and I flash the last image I've held back uncertainly: a picture of a swaddled newborn Robin. "Everest was just training for this: the biggest adventure of my life."

Everyone leaps from their seats and claps. I keep the picture of Robin up on the screen, rejoicing inside for their endorsement of "what's next." For the first time, Everest *isn't* the darling of the show.

When our second darling, Daniel, arrives in February of '92, Chris is in increasing demand as a snow safety consultant, which takes him away most of the winter and mires him in reports and contract bids in the off-seasons. A dozen or more speakers' bureaus now represent me. They warn me to keep building my career or I will lose it, so I accept up to fifty engagements a year throughout North America. Nannies come and go, and we hire an office manager. I let go of guiding for the less time-consuming yet more stress-inducing work of speaking. The reality of what needs to happen, and all at once, in a woman's thirties if she wants to establish a family, a career and a secure future, rankles me. Stressed, hormonal and strapped for time does not make me a good wife or mother at times. Then just when I think I can't take on another commitment, a wave of inspiration transports me from feeling beleaguered to impassioned.

School is imminent for Robin, and I attend a public meeting with the school board to discuss upcoming budget cuts. When I listen to what is going to get cut, it sounds like the kids are going to come up short. I walk out with another mother whose child is Robin's age. Within minutes of talking, we hatch a dream to start our own school.

I lie awake in bed that night as that spark of a new dream lights me up. In the morning Marni laughs when I tell her about my concerns from the school meeting and the idea of starting a school. "There it is," she says, "a gift in unfamiliar packaging! That's what you call setbacks and obstacles in your presentations, isn't it?"

"It's an impossible dream, though. I'm not an educator and I don't know a thing about starting a school."

"Well, as Kevin would say, 'What's the worst thing that can happen by trying?'"

So I try, pouring my energy, with a like-minded group, into starting a school. The gift in unfamiliar packaging is a level of passion and engagement that I haven't experienced since I was gunning for Everest. Mountain Gate Community School opens in September of '96 with a first class of thirteen students, grades 1 through 3, in a single room. The school will expand to five classrooms, kindergarten through grade 6, by 1998. And I will remain in a leadership position until Robin graduates and moves into the public system. Ironically, Everest lends me the credibility to attract donors and raise funds for families who couldn't otherwise afford to pay for a private school. I have never worked harder. The pride I find in this thriving and vibrant community we have created means everything.

In a school that once seemed an impossible dream, it feels like we're changing the world kid by kid, family by family. And the biggest surprise: this gift comes in the giving, not the taking.

* * *

The humbling experiences of motherhood and the school shift my approach in my presentations from performing to giving. I feel invigorated as I integrate this new sense of empathy and connection into my scripts. I elbow Everest aside for a change, turning the mountain into the stage rather than the star. My shift in perspective becomes apparent when a booking takes me to Orlando to speak to a conference of five thousand nurses, the largest crowd I have addressed yet.

I take long, slow, deep breaths and chant my mantra, *believe and begin, believe and begin,* as the emcee introduces me. My title slide "Everest—the Impossible Dream" comes up on the screen behind her and on the six other eight-by-eight-metre screens along the sides of the stadium. I walk up a dozen or more stairs to the stage while Elvis Presley's "The Impossible Dream" booms through the speakers. I put this outrageous fanfare out of my mind to focus on what is important to me.

I feel the power of my intention as an improbable hush falls over this immense crowd. I focus on the nurses in the first few rows as I say, "To make the impossible possible on Everest, we had to raise our baseline from surviving to thriving. Thriving is not about working harder, carrying heavier loads or putting in longer days. Thriving starts with altering our perceptions. I have spent a disproportionate amount of time wishing: if only I had more of something, or better conditions—a myriad of if-onlys. All that does is take up energy and hold me back. Once we get over the if-onlys and commit, all form of resources and assistance become available. The trick is to recognize these gifts, wrapped in unfamiliar packaging. That takes an open mind."

As I close I say, "I'd like to answer the question I'm asked most often: Once you've climbed the highest mountain in the world, what's next?" I advance to the last slide of Daniel and Robin, four and seven years old, wearing climbing helmets and standing on either side of me holding onto my harness. "This is what's next," I say, "raising two sons. I realize this is considered an ordinary affair—one that society expects of us. But this is my next. And it is the most difficult yet most rewarding climb I've ever taken on!" Five thousand people stand in a wave of thunderous applause.

When I arrive home three days later, no one greets me at the door. I find the boys in the playroom engrossed in their Lego construction.

When Chris arrives home a few minutes later, he shouts out, "Hello this house!" The boys rush him squealing, "Daddy, Daddy!" They leap up into his arms.

"How're my boys?" Chris blows a raspberry fart into Daniel's bared tummy. Robin hangs off his other arm, tugging him into the playroom to show off their latest box fort.

If only he would kiss me. If only he was that happy to see me. Oddly, I am jealous of how he cherishes his boys more than me. It's as if I existed in his heart only long enough to bring forth a new male generation and now that that's done, he's done—with me. *Doesn't he know our love is what will hold our family together?* The truth is we're both so busy thriving in our work lives. All we have time for before one of us is gone again is who's paid the bill for what, how the latest nanny is working out, and what changes there have been in school and homework routines.

As I watch Chris with the boys, I think, *What the hell is going on with me? Is it the big fall from the adulation of thousands of strangers, to this—feeling like a stranger in my own home?* I feel selfish for wanting this love from Chris and I know it isn't right. I carry my own little war around inside: resentment versus shame and self-loathing. I castigate myself, thinking that I should be able to alter my perception, open my mind, see the gifts of this husband and two beautiful boys!

I cherish times when I lie flanked by Daniel and Robin at bedtime, reading aloud the adventures of Harry Potter. I love to voice the characters as Robin nestles in and his brother clings to me. I stroke Daniel's head and knead Robin's fingers as the boys drift off to sleep. I float in these sublime moments. I swell with pride in the wild times, such as the day we're at Marni's place and she gasps when she looks out the window to see Daniel trailing Robin across the peak of their garage roof. Of course, we stop them from trying to leap across to the neighbour's garage. But I know they are irrepressible and adventurous souls by now, not mine to own but to love and protect as best I can. These magnificent boys show me a capacity for deep, fierce love and tenderness in myself.

Chris's mom dies the following summer, then my dad in December and Chris's brother in January. The losses devastate Chris and me and further strain our relationship. We fly directly from my dad's memorial to Chris's brother's service in Toronto. As president of the school—keeper of the peace between teachers, children and parents—and motivational speaker, mother, and co-ordinator of nannies and office managers, I have no time to pause.

The respite I find in my boys and my work begins to crumble. And the slightest things begin to unhinge me: Robin refusing to do his homework, Daniel dropping a glass on the floor, a scrap between the two of them. I hate it when they fight. They are vicious. I shout at them, call them little shits, push them around and hate myself for it. My doctor urges me to try antidepressants, but I'm too proud and too afraid of the stigma attached to mental illness. *I'm not depressed! I know I can fight this. I know I am strong. These problems should be trifling compared to the mountains I've climbed.*

But no amount of strength, will or pride helps me now. I get worse. I am driving our boys and some other kids home from school, and their mother, Jo, meets us at the car. This Australian woman takes one look at my red-rimmed eyes and says, "Get out of the car. You're coming in for a cuppa."

While the kids play, Jo settles me at her table with a hot cup of tea and then says plainly, "So, what's going on?"

I trace the paisley pattern on the tablecloth with my fingers, look at my hands—anything but her—as I say, "I can't stop crying. I cry when I drop a plate on the floor. I cry at the dread of getting through another day. I feel out of control, Jo. I'm terrified by this outpouring of sadness."

She has watched me start and manage the school, the board of directors and my life, with will, strength and competence. When Jo, a nurse, midwife and proponent of natural remedies, declares, "You're depressed; you need drugs," I surrender.

The act of surrender is powerful. I reduce my commitments with the school and work. Within a few weeks I feel a side effect of the antidepressant when my fingers begin to tingle. Then soon after when I'm riding up a long hill on my bicycle, I feel a sudden rush of euphoria and clarity. My only guess is that the meds are combining with the exercise-induced endorphins and, voila, turbo power! I feel a fluttering sensation in my chest as if I've just pushed hard off the bottom of a murky pool and am rising upward. The cause behind the depression is biological. It's not all me.

I continue to see more light in my life. In November, I bow before Governor General Roméo LeBlanc at La Citadelle in Quebec City as I receive the Meritorious Service Medal of Canada. As he places the medal around my neck I register the irony. I bow too to the duality in my life: gift and curse. The constant movement and striving that have earned me this medal have also staved off the depression I've had most of my adult life. I would never have asked for this epiphany to come to me this way, but I trust that I'm still being guided to slow down and allow room for self-compassion. But it seems there is still more ground for this new state of being to take.

* * *

It's a balmy New Year's Day. I'm wheeling fast down a trail on my bike when my back tire slips on the snow as I go to jump over a log. My bike hits the log, comes to a hard stop and I soar over the handlebars. I hit the frozen ground headfirst, suffering a concussion and fracturing some facets in my cervical vertebrae. The accident pins me down with nausea and dizziness. The doctor tells me to avoid any fast movement and busy places.

Fortunately, it is off-season in the conference business. First, I pick up a papier-mâché project I've been working on with the kids at school. One day I conjure wings boned with coat-hanger wire; the next I sculpt claws and teeth out of a paper clay. Soon, long past when everyone in the house has gone to sleep, I'm listening to Handel's *Messiah* and, as if under a spell, rendering armatures for life-sized coyotes. Night after night, I cover the mishmash of rebar and aluminum foil tubes with paper pulp and sculpt it into muscle, hide and fur. From inspiration to reality, from garbage to spirit, these creatures take shape. This flurry of intense engagement is a refreshingly private affair of no importance to anyone but me. This creative process nourishes me.

Bookings made a year in advance have Everest dragging me back to the podium by early March. I wonder how I will manage on stage in this vulnerable state. Remarkably, I find myself speaking with stronger conviction and Everest sliding into the back seat. After my presentations, people come forward and say, "I can be honest with you now. A few of us were wondering why they brought in someone to talk about Everest—of all things for an insurance company! But oh, do I get it now! You've inspired me take on a whole new approach with my support staff." Others say, "It's like you were talking directly to me, like you were referring to my challenges alone." People come forward to confide their stories to me. And I listen with new ears to the similarities in their challenges and our narratives. My anxiety moves toward a sense of ease as my public and private persona inch closer to becoming one.

This state of surrender is deepening my connection with my audiences. But the opposite is happening with Chris and me. The contrast is becoming unbearable, and I realize this on Easter Sunday morning when I'm fulfilling my duty as parent-janitor of the week at the school. I'm scrubbing the tops of the children's desks, puzzling over the discussion Chris and I had about the logistics of childcare and our travel schedules before I left the house. As I lean in to work on a stubborn streak of ink, I realize that our arguing stopped some time ago and in its place is indifference. Somewhere in one of the many books I have read on the mysteries of human behaviour, it stated that the opposite of love is not hate but indifference. This premise thuds home as an unassailable truth and a feeling of calm resolve infuses me. I phone Chris and tell him I want to separate. He says flatly, "I've had enough too."

Although we dread telling the boys, we sit them on the couch. Kneeling before them with a hand on each of their knees, I say, "Mommy is going to move into another house, so now you'll have two houses." Nothing changes in ten-year-old, wise-beyond-his-years Robin. But there is no cajoling Daniel, who starts wailing—inconsolably. I sweep him up into my arms and hold him tight as he clutches my shirt and sobs into my chest. I thought I would cry too. But strangely I don't. I feel his despair yet I know this is what I must do. I trust my decision in the way I trust airline attendants when they tell adults to pull on their own oxygen masks before helping others. We must help ourselves before we can assist our children. There is no argument over custody, as I know the boys will need Chris even more than before. I hope he'll stay home more often now. And I don't utter an unkind word about him.

"So what do I call Chris now?" I ask my friend Genevieve during what we call our running dialogues on one of our regular trots along the mountain trails. "I can't get my head around the term 'ex-husband.' Surely there's got to be a more compassionate title for the father of our children."

"Well," she huffs, "I call mine my 'wasband.'" With no better option, I adopt the term on the spot.

After our run that day, I invite Genevieve in to see my new place. I hear my voice echo off the walls of the empty living room. "The worst part of separating is thinking about how I'm going to bear living apart from my kids in the same town."

"You're the one who says in your presentations that the anticipation is the worst stage of doing anything difficult."

"Yeah, and how many times do I have to learn this before I get it?"

"A mere nine times and nine different ways before it sticks," she says. "I don't know where the nine times comes from, but the point is: it's a cumulative process. One day, you get it and a voice inside you shouts, 'Aha!' And there you are: living your future, thriving in the present."

Her theory starts to prove itself when a couple of days after Marni and Steve's wedding in August, the newlyweds help me move into my house and make it a home. I ask myself, *How is it I'm so lucky to have friends who help me move on their honeymoon?* This extended family *is* my family. This support and sense of belonging helps me quit the meds. Hard as it is to be on my own with or without the boys, I begin to notice how satisfying it is to run my own little home and business with a comfort I couldn't have imagined a short time ago. As I settle in, the rest of my world does as well.

Chris and I finalize our divorce the next year. On a good day I trust that I am embracing my new life. On other days I am tested, as I am when I find an essay Daniel has written for a school project. I step back and wilt as I read it: "I knew happiness until I was eight, then it stopped when my parents got a divorce. I'll never be happy again." Of course I consider my responsibility for his despair, but I hold fast to faith in my decision. The length and degree of Daniel's suffering stretches beyond its due time, which prompts Chris and me to take him to talk to a psychologist. As any competent practitioner does, the doctor treats the whole of the problem by asking Chris and me several questions about our own history. He's confounded by how we speak so kindly of one another and asks why we split up.

Chris answers, "We buried my mother, my brother and Sharon's father, and then I buried myself in my work. I wasn't there for Sharon's mourning."

His admission astonishes me. Tears trickle down my cheeks as forgiveness opens my heart to let us both in. It dawns on me that my compassion is taking a slow turn toward a new and deeper love for Chris, who I've blamed for not being who I wanted him to be. Although we will remain divorced, a fierce loyalty begins that day for this friend and father of our children.

* * *

I soon cut back on my speaking. And I feel pulled to begin guiding again. Although I have been climbing consistently, guiding demands high standards in client care in the mountains. I ask Dwayne, Albi and fellow guides to coach me in bringing my skills up to current industry best practices. I'm surprised when old friends and colleagues welcome me back to this profession, and I feel like I'm coming home.

I am surprised at how much I have missed this craft of guiding people in how to move on rock, snow and ice; conserve their energy; and find their way and sometimes themselves in the mountains. By showing others, I remind myself that difficulty and discomfort are often a matter of perception, not necessarily reasons to stop what we are doing. And I love it best when my clients, and for that matter anyone other than a speakers' bureau, are not aware I have climbed Everest.

I like that Everest seems to be edging out of my life, yet it still manages to catch me off guard. At Chris's annual Boxing Day party, when I join the crowd in the kitchen, a hand clutches my arm. A woman I don't know exclaims, "Oh, you're the Everest Lady, aren't you! Come with me, I *must* introduce you to my family." Once she has us assembled, grandchildren and all, she says, "So! Tell us the Everest story."

I'm surprised to hear myself shout, "No!" I watch this woman's smile morph into a big O. "I'm sorry, I don't mean to be rude, but I'm here to visit friends I haven't seen for ages."

I excuse myself and head straight for Chris, who's at the sink. I wrap my arms around him from behind and whisper into his ear, "I just said no for the first time!"

He turns and hugs me. "Good for you!" he says and squeezes me tighter. He knows I mean that I have just stood up to my overbearing friend, Everest. From this point onward I'm more polite, yet firm about who's in charge.

Jane tells me one day that I'm more available.

"What do you mean?" I ask.

She replies, "You're kinder and gentler with yourself and it shows on the outside."

While out climbing another day, James tells me, "You're less intense."

I balk. "What does that mean?"

"You're more fun to be around."

I laugh.

"See," he says, "that's what I mean. You might've bitten me if I told you that in the past."

Laurie tells me I'm more confident. "You don't put yourself down so much anymore, Sharon. Don't worry, though, I know you're still in there."

I realize that twenty years on from *the* climb, it still comes up every day. Although it never ceases to amaze me, I am growing to accept that *the* mountain is a part of my life and here to stay. And I am content and grateful.

I realize my perspective on Everest has shifted dramatically as I stand amidst about a hundred students, aged ten to seventeen, in the gym of a small independent school. As I bring up pictures on the screen, the kids' hands shoot up, some pumping their arms with urgency. Everest is the platform for what feels like an intimate chat about life—mine *and* theirs.

A little boy asks me, "What's it like to be famous?"

"What does famous mean to all of you?" I ask back. After the kids shout out several definitions, I give my own slant: "Being famous can be lonely. Or it was. I've learned that it is most important to feel famous in the eyes of the people who matter most to me: my family and close friends. I don't recommend fame unless it happens because you're doing what you love to do."

"I want to be an astronaut cuz I love space science," says a little girl. "Just like Roberta Bondar!"

"Fair enough!" I say. I ask half a dozen other kids what they love to do. If they tell me what they want to be, I ask them again what they love to do. "Don't do something to become someone. Think of getting there another way. Love what you do, *then* become."

I know by now that the kids nearest to me, those whose hands pop up and who are most vocal about their passions, will be fine. I look for the ones who sit quietly with their hands tentatively wavering by their ears. I catch the eye of a teenaged girl whose hair hides half her face, and I nod. She asks, "Where did you find the confidence to climb Mount Everest?"

"Hmm, confidence. I struggled with that. Does anyone else?" I get a resounding agreement in reply. "I've learned that confidence has to come from the inside, in believing whatever you're doing is really important to you. Love what you do, practise and have people in your life who want you to succeed. We will all have moments of doubt and need to remind ourselves of this, won't we?"

"Yeah!" they all sing. And my heart sings as I rejoice over how at home I feel these days, on stage or off.

CHAPTER 22

Reunion

AT DAWN ON THIS day in October, my mind is already awake and churning over all that I hope the day may bring. Tonight the members of our Everest Light team will gather, some of whom I have not seen since we parted at Vancouver International Airport twenty years ago. The reunion was Dr. Bob's idea, and Jim suggested my house because of its big country kitchen. *What was I thinking when I agreed to host the event in the house that Everest bought me?* As I shrug into my housecoat I think, as I do often these days, about how I feel more grateful than guilty to own this home.

I spend the morning in the kitchen, pushing around tables and chairs, pulling out glasses and plates and preparing food. By early afternoon, I am rearranging furniture in the living room when the phone rings.

"Hi, it's Jane. How're you doing?"

"I'm looking forward to this event and oddly nervous," I tell her. I flop onto the couch, relieved to settle into a conversation *outside* my head. "My dad used to say, 'If you think you've evolved, spend time with your family.' Well, these guys feel that way to me, and the thought of stirring up stories of our expedition might be like pulling scabs off old wounds. I'm afraid I'll revert to my twenty-eight-year-old self again. I've worked hard to get here, Jane."

"What a way to be thinking about a reunion! Look at it this way, Sharon. Think of surprising yourself," she says. "Have you decided on a story?" Jane has suggested that everyone bring a story to tell.

"Nope. Oh, Jane—do you think everyone is just going to stand around with their hands in their pockets wondering what to say?"

"Hell, no! Not me, anyway. I've been waiting twenty years to do this! I've shipped the kids out and am leaving the lot behind. I'm coming early to help set up."

"When?"

"Should be outta here by three." She lives in Golden, two hours away.

Jane and I remained close until we started having children. Pregnant with her second child, she was confined to bed rest in a Calgary hospital for six months. By that time I had an infant and a toddler, was juggling a career in public speaking and battling chronic depression. Although she was an easy hour away, I didn't visit her once. *Why would she want to come early and help?*

My heart somersaults when the doorbell rings at four. I open the door a crack, prepared to shoo a solicitor away, and see Kevin standing on the front porch, beaming with his arms stretched wide. "Woodeee!" He envelops me. "Sorry, I couldn't wait, I thought you could use some help. That okay?"

Kevin is the last person I expect to see at my door—early. He should be one of the disappointed ones. After schlepping loads for two months on Everest and supporting Dwayne and me all the way to Camp Six, I expected he might have become bitter, even though when I asked him if he resented that effort, he said, "Woody, I wanted to be a part of the team, play a role in doing something great, and I'm proud of it." He'll joke, though, when people ask him about his role. "I tell them I carried lunch for the first North American woman to climb Mount Everest."

Kevin steps back to look at me. "You're looking gorgeous as ever."

"Ditto to you, handsome!" I say, holding myself back from running my fingers through his thick thatch of chocolate-brown hair.

"Yeah, check this out." He unzips his jacket and pats his belly. "Here's what I've got to show for twenty years of beer."

I pull him into the house. Kevin's head swivels. "Nice pad you've got here." I start prattling to fill nervous space as I think, *The work you did bought this house.* But I halt, reminding myself that it's an old story. I leave Kevin scrubbing potatoes while I go and shower.

At five, we greet Jane at the door. "Ha, another gorgeous woman!" says Kevin. "Don't worry, Woody, there's enough of me these days to love you both."

Jane brandishes a bottle of scotch and says, "Let's wet some glasses with a wee dram to ease our fretting selves, shall we?"

Kevin says, "Who, me? Fretting? I've been looking forward to this for months! But I'll have that scotch anyway."

While we work, we joke and laugh as the smell of roast beef wafts through the house. Outside, the temperature plummets and a storm blows in. By 6 p.m., a finger or two of scotch and a layer of new snow soften the edges. By 7 p.m., comers are streaming in, leaving a trail of coats, boots and bags that leads to the kitchen. Crammed back to back, people huddle in clusters to catch up. The counters, island and table are laden with casseroles, pots of soup, salads, bottles and bread.

The doorbell chimes one final time and as the chatter pauses, Dan says, "That's gotta be Skreslet! The guy's on Skreslet time again."

Of course he is late. He is always late. Cold air and snowflakes rush in behind Laurie as I greet him at the door. His big hands encase my ribs as he pulls me into the solid wall of his chest in a vice-like embrace. It feels so familiar. He held me like this twenty years ago when he met Dwayne and me on our return from the summit. His cold, wet face presses against mine as he plants a kiss on my cheek. I expel a breathy whisper into his ear: "I'm so glad you're here."

Everyone shows except for Chris Shank, who is in Afghanistan on a bird study. We are twelve team members, various partners, my two boys and our major cash sponsor—forty in total. Jane, Kevin and I bustle fetching glasses, opening bottles, collecting abandoned offerings and filling dishes with food. Jane sidles up mid-flurry and tilts her head toward the scene. "Can you believe this?" Being together again feels like we've never been apart.

After dinner, Dr. Bob steps up onto the fireplace sill, cups his hands into a loudspeaker and shouts over the chatter, "Now that

Skreslet is finally here, we can get started." He flashes a smile in Laurie's direction and proceeds to arrange us around the fireplace for the twenty-years-later picture. Once we are all in place, Kevin says, "Look at us! Holy shit, here we all are—and still looking good!"

We laugh, cameras click and flashbulbs pop.

After the photo, everyone pulls up chairs, upturns rounds of wood to perch on, leans into the wall or their partners and settles in. I panic in a sudden flush of deficit, and then spy Robin patting the place beside him on the couch. I wedge in beside him and my seventeen-year-old boy drapes his arm over my shoulder and pulls me in.

Last to arrive but first to speak, Laurie edges his way around the crowd to stand on the raised sill of the rock fireplace. Candlelight flickers across his face as I scan him for any sign of change. His straight hair now travels farther to sweep across the expanding landscape of his forehead. Although I have seen him often since Everest, on this occasion I compare the sight of him to the one of twenty years ago.

When conversations trail from murmurs to silence, he begins. "I don't know whether all of you know that I went back to Everest this spring with the British military to attempt the West Ridge—the same route we did twenty years ago. They had state-of-the-art equipment, a generous budget, twenty of the UK's best climbers, plus twenty or more Sherpa, and still they didn't succeed. They wanted to be sure I told you that what we did then was extraordinary, and still is. Not only did we make a first ascent of that route from Tibet, no one, I repeat, no one, has successfully climbed our route since and it's not for lack of trying. I hope you're proud of that."

Are we? The room falls quiet.

Jim clears his throat and steps up. "No one could have told me that I would be standing here twenty years later and feeling like it was one of the most important events of my life. By everybody showing up tonight"—he looks down to collect himself—"I think it's a sign that this trip means a lot to all of us. Yeah, I feel proud."

"Proud, or more likely stupid!" Kevin blurts. "We didn't know any better. It was way too windy up there. It was insane that day we climbed to Six! At one point, the fucking wind was so strong it picked a rock up off the face and hurled it at me. That rock came from below, not from above!"

Barry says, "Yeah, and that same day, I remember planting my pick in the snow and admiring the perfectly turned bamboo shaft of my new Chouinard ice axe. So there I was facing in, right? The next thing I knew I was on my back, facing out, looking at Tibet. Then another gust slammed me back hard into the face so I was looking at my ice axe again, as if I was a door swinging open and slamming shut." Barry slapped his hands together, "Bam! Just like that. Yep, we were either really tough or really stupid."

Kevin butts Barry's shoulder and says, "Stupid! Like I said before, we didn't know any better."

"Oh yeah." Barry grabs Kevin's arm and says, "So we'd decided to use oxygen that day for the first time, right? And 'Wally' here says, 'If I've gotta use this shit, I'm gonna *use* it!' And in classic all-or-nothing Doyle style, he cranks his regulator to full and runs out of O's halfway across the face. But he still makes it to Six!"

Everyone in the room is listening carefully. I realize that the partners and supporters are hearing these stories for the first time and, in a way, so are we. None of us had dared to recount the events then with such generous admission to hardship. The only way to go on was to normalize what would be unacceptable conditions at any other time.

I shiver with the thought and feel Robin pull me in, his hand kneading my shoulder. Earlier that day I had asked him and Daniel to stay long enough to meet the team and then they could go. Daniel has slipped out, and Robin could have by now. But he stays. I want to say to him, "See, aren't they amazing, wasn't that something? It really did happen!" A swell of pride takes me by surprise, and with a force that I have never felt before.

Barry's chest thrusts out and his shoulders angle back, defying decades of carrying heavy packs that threatened to shape them otherwise. His once-cropped, jet black wavy hair is now intermingled with grey and tied into a ponytail reaching halfway down his back. I have always envied his storytelling prowess. Blessed with a gravelly purr, he turns out one story after another, winning our rapt attention by including his "contribution to science." He says, "I was by myself at Camp Five one night feeling a little bored and found myself wondering if it was possible to ejaculate at 7,600 metres above sea level. The answer is: affirmative."

Kevin punches his arm. "What a stud, Blanchard!" Many people were surprised that Barry wasn't one of the summiteers and deemed him noble for giving his spot to me. This interpretation of events used to irk me because I thought, *Why not me! I deserve it as much as the next man!* But I was a woman, and women were sometimes expected to walk first through the doorway and sometimes not at all. On the other hand, I thought my stepping forward to claim a spot on the first team was selfish. Perhaps it surprised us all when I stepped up, and he aside. Thinking about it now, I believe he is indeed noble.

Jane steps forward, her face aglow with determination. "Woody! We were so bad and so good together! But damn! I always thought I should have been the climber and you, the cook. I'd give your skinny little back those massages when you came down from carrying up high. But the worst was on our way home from Everest when they'd ask me"—her voice lowers—"'Are you the woman?' Christ, that bugged me!" Yes, that bugged me too. It had separated me from us.

"Dan Griffith!" Jane's finger rounds on him. "What an asshole! You were sick and frustrated because you couldn't climb high and you took it out on me, didn't you? I've held onto my resentment for all these years—so many years. Tonight, I forgive you. And I'm genuinely happy for you for finally climbing Everest at fifty-seven years old, and for climbing the Seven Summits in world-record time. Congratulations." She exhales and the rest of the room does too.

All eyes are on Dan. Everyone has stopped, mid-pour, mid-breath. I watch Dan's head rise in an expression of surprise that I've never seen before. I expected that hint-of-a-sneer look that says, *Do you realize who you're talking to?* Has something softened that shell? Otherwise, all he has to show for the passage of time is some grey in his full head of thick, wavy hair and lines etched a little deeper into his face. He slowly looks up from the floor, proffers a gentle smile and tips his glass toward Jane.

As she takes a gulp from her glass, I want to jump in and credit Dan for the difference he made for me—for the team: the talk he gave me at Camp Two, the way he helped me understand that this was our climb and he wasn't giving up when I unravelled at Camp Five. But I am still gathering my thoughts when Jane turns to Albi.

"Albi Sole," she continues, "I've got something to say to you too." Albi has been leaning up against the wall, wedged into the overflow in the hall, and uncharacteristically quiet. He has shown up tonight in a button-down shirt and cravat with his thinning hair neatly combed back, looking every inch the devoted husband, father of three children and Mountain Programs Coordinator and Operations Manager at the University of Calgary. He uncrosses his arms then crosses them again, unable to predict whether Jane will bite him or stroke him.

She says, "You are one classy guy. You"—she looks up and then back at Albi—"you were the only one who had the courage to stand up for me when Dan was giving me such a hard time. No one talked to Dan like that. No one! I'll never forget that. Thank you."

Albi tips forward in a slight bow to Jane. He pulls at his shirt collar and cranes his neck to look at Jim. I brace myself. A few years after we returned from Everest, Albi wrote a letter in a climbing publication accusing Jim of manipulating the trip for his own fame and glory. It had cut Jim to the core. Albi says, "Jim, I really thought you were a scheming, controlling bastard for what you did to me. But I forgive you." I think, *What Jim did to him or what I did to him?* A few years before, Albi told me he'd thought I was his ticket to the summit. "I'm good with all that now," he'd said. But now I keep my eyes on him until he shoots me a wink.

"It's my turn to say something," says Dave, clearing his throat. "I was down at Camp Two and Dr. Bob had just diagnosed me with retinal hemorrhages. I knew then that I'd lost my chance for the summit. Worse, my wife hadn't been writing me so I had no idea how my son was doing. I was feeling lonely and sorry for myself. But one morning I crawled out of my tent and found all these balloons tied to it, and I remembered it was my birthday. Jane had baked me a cake at Camp Two! That was really special. You went above and beyond to look after all of us, Jane. Thank you."

I scan the crowd to see who else might speak. James and I live in the same town and have climbed together many times since the expedition. He rarely says a word about Everest and it's no surprise he doesn't tonight. He once told me he looked at Everest as just another trip. "Once you're finished," he said, "you unpack your bags—period—end of trip." I couldn't agree then, and I still don't.

I imagined, as recently as this morning, that for many of the members on the team, Everest left them with questions and regrets. Some, I had thought, still hadn't recovered from Everest '82, let alone Everest Light. Sure, you can unpack your bags, but how do you leave the effect of the mountain behind?

Everest came home with me. For years I believed I abandoned Dwayne on our descent from the summit. He said to me once, "How could you know how close I was to the edge when I didn't know myself?" His words didn't comfort me then. I was still blinded by the harsh glare of my own judgement.

The quiet ones are still the quiet ones. Dwayne, like James, has an enviable way of not dwelling on the past. He laughs when I ask him how Everest has impacted his life. "Why should my life change as the first man to accompany the first North American woman to climb Everest? I'm one among thousands who have climbed it by now." Modest and understated, he behaves as though nothing changed and has resumed his work as a mountain guide.

Meanwhile, I have tuned and turned our story into a motivational tale I tell in sixty minutes or less. After all this time, I wonder, is the story I tell still true? As I ask myself that question, I glance around the room and realization sets in. Truth is subjective.

Tonight, as if for the first time, I hear Kevin's reassuring words about his role on the expedition. His truth. And I hear Dwayne's too. He never judged me. My teammates have spoken with pride, as if they knew twenty years ago that they would be accounting for their actions now. Listening deeply to my teammates, who are honouring our climb and one another, I allow another possibility to rise.

Dan startles us all as if from a spell when he shouts, "Jesus! It's already eleven o'clock! We've gotta hit the road." People begin to stir, retrieve bags and dishes, and tug their partners toward the door. The evening is over and I haven't said anything yet. I'm reeling, still revising my outdated assumptions.

I'm standing in the hall as people press by and thank me when Jim bumps up against me. "Aren't you going to say anything, Woody? You being the big public speaker and all?" I flush with self-consciousness. "Come on." Jim prods me, not wanting me to miss out. "It's not too late."

"I need you to stand by me," I whisper.

He grasps my arm, pulls me back into the living room and says, "Listen up, everyone. Woody's got something to say."

I begin. "I've told the story of our climb to over a thousand audiences. I've talked about all of you. It's you who have made the story that so many want to hear. One that makes me proud to tell. It's a privilege to have been a part of this team. Thank you. I'm grateful."

I now know this is all I have to say—and every word I have spoken is true.

* * *

It has been more than ten years since the reunion. Today I accept that every teller may have a different story about our experience and every listener may hear a different message—none of which may match mine. I used to obsess over my scripts, revising and rewriting them to ensure the message I was conveying was true for *me*. And it's no wonder; the message had to shift, as I did through my life. Now I end my presentations with a blessing: "May we keep surprising ourselves."

I believe my Everest story is about the power of being wholehearted in whatever we choose to take on. I've learned it is our actions and our relationships that remain with us for a lifetime, and they are what matter most. Not the trophy. The trophy—the dream—is just there to capture our imagination. And when it is beyond our reach, then we rise—to our potential. Each time we do this we are transformed—from living a life confined by our limitations to living a life defined by our possibilities.

I am indebted to my climbing adventures, for they showed me the promise and joy in ascending. There have been other challenges since, many of them messy, not all of them fun. Yet they continue to help me evolve. To thrive, not just survive.

In the end, it is relationships that give value to survival. None of my accomplishments have any meaning without the remarkable people in my life.

It is because of them, and with them, I rise.

Acknowledgements

It has taken a community to write this book. Deep gratitude to Marni Virtue and Barbara Parker, dear friends, muses and coaches through it all. And many thanks to Tom Hopkins and mentor Charlotte Gill for their patience in the early stages of teaching me how to write.

I am grateful for the opportunities the Banff Centre and its benefactors provided, and the support of talented faculty members, including Charlotte Gill, Trevor Herriot, Marni Jackson and Tony Wittome. I am also grateful for the numerous participants in these programs who furthered my development as a writer.

On several occasions, I considered tossing this manuscript in the fire. A special thanks to those who read my manuscript and prevented its demise: Steven Ross Smith, writer in residence and former director of Literary Arts at the Banff Centre; Joanna Croston, director of the Banff Mountain Film & Book Festival; Tom Hornbein, author and first ascensionist of the West Ridge of Everest; and Mary Metz, senior editor at Mountaineers Books. I valued their encouragement.

Thank you, Anna Comfort O'Keeffe, managing editor at Douglas & McIntyre, for accepting my manuscript and choosing the right editors "to tighten things up and strengthen the narrative thread." And many thanks to my editors, Lucy Kenward and Brianna Cerkiewicz, in following through with Anna's promise!

I feel deep appreciation for my family and their support backstage. My husband, Garrett Brown, for his patience, understanding and careful eye on the pages. My mom, who gave me the confidence to accomplish anything I put my mind to. My late father, who fostered the concept that the value of a person is in their strength of character rather than in their education or status. And my boys, Robin and Daniel, who echoed back unconditional faith and ceaseless encouragement.

I extend my gratitude to all those who let me write in their homes while they were away. The solitude was invaluable in keeping my mind on task and my butt in the chair.

I have benefited from the feedback of many readers: Barbara Bay, Garrett Brown, Colleen Campbell, Steve DeKeijzer, Jim Elzinga, Jane Fearing, Caroline Marion, Cathy Ostlere, Geoff Powter, Karl Siegler, Albi Sole, Chris Stethem, Daniel Stethem, Robin Stethem, John Stevens, Marni Virtue, Ken Wylie, editor Erin Parker and the women in our Monday night writing group. And I feel blessed with many exceptional adventure partners and friends who have bolstered my resolve to share my story and stick with this ever-evolving craft of writing. You know who you are.

This story would not be worth telling without the exemplary efforts and actions of my Everest Light teammates: Barry Blanchard, James Blench, Dwayne Congdon, Kevin Doyle, Jim Elzinga, Jane Fearing, Dan Griffith, Bob Lee, Dave McNab, Chris Shank, Laurie Skreslet, and Albi Sole. Thank you.

In addition to family, friends, teammates and teachers, I am grateful for the powerful and formative influence that Outward Bound and the YMCA had on my development and orientation as a lifelong student and leader. May it ever be so.